THE
WARM BREATH
OF AN
ELECTRIC PIXIE

THE WARM BREATH OF AN ELECTRIC PIXIE

A US ROAD TRIP FUELLED BY TEA

JJ TOPPING

JJ Topping was born in Liverpool in 1966, a few days before England won the World Cup. His mother missed Geoff Hurst's famous "They think it's all over" goal because young JJ was crying in the next room. The third of six siblings, JJ spent his childhood below his parents' radar, enjoying the freedom to make the mistakes and learn the lessons that have been lost to subsequent generations. His nephews and nieces ply him with drink at every opportunity, whilst sitting at his feet in awed silence to hear his tall tales of teenage excess.

A 30-year career managing projects for a variety of global corporations hasn't taken away JJ's delight at seeing new places, meeting interesting people and discovering absurd bits of history. The Warm Breath of an Electric Pixie is his first effort at putting some of his American travel adventures on paper, largely to save his liver and his young relatives' drinks bills.

JJ is married to Áine Two and lives in West London, where he nurses his passions for Liverpool FC, Jaguars, birdwatching and beer. He really likes beer.

He has an ambition to learn where commas are supposed to go in sentences.

The Warm Breath of an Electric Pixie

Published by Nettlebron Limited
Registered office 109 Uxbridge Rd London W5 5TL England
First published by Nettlebron Limited 2017
Text Copyright © 2017 JJ Topping
Photographs Copyright © 2017 JJ Topping

The moral right of the author has been asserted in accordance with the Copyright, Designs and Patents Act 1998.

All rights reserved.

Without limiting the rights under copyright reserved above, no part of this publication may be reproduced, stored in or introduced into a retrieval system, or transmitted, in any form or by any means (electronic, mechanical, photocopying, recording or otherwise), without the prior written permission of both the copyright owner and the above publisher of this book.

ISBN: 978-1-9999010-0-4 (paperback)
978-1-9999010-1-1 (ebook)

Edited by Linell van Hoepen
threebluedragonflies@gmail.com

Cover and book design by Jane Dixon-Smith
www.jdsmith-design.com

www.jjtopping.co.uk

For Áine Two,

my travelling companion for life

INTRODUCTION

In the Lafayette Cemetery in the Garden District of New Orleans is the headstone of William Anderton of Earnscliffe, Blundellsands, near Liverpool, who died of yellow fever in 1878.

William was born in Liverpool, married Alice Prior and fathered eight children. Alice is buried in Toxteth Park Cemetery in Wavertree, South Liverpool, along with four of their offspring.

My parents lived in Wavertree when they were first married, and I was born there in 1966. William Anderton's gravestone caught my eye because I grew up in Great Crosby in North Liverpool, of which Blundellsands is a part. Earnscliffe was William's house, and I used to walk past it every day on my way to school.

Almost 140 years have passed since William died so many miles from his home and family, and we now live in an era of a prolonged global recession, wars in the Middle East, a refugee and immigration crisis in Europe, the resurgence of far-right politics, Trump, Putin, Brexit, and the prospect of nuclear war with North Korea: all of which provide the perfect backdrop for a middle-aged Scouser and his Irish wife to pack in their jobs, lock up the house and head to the USA for a road trip.

The journey we had originally planned was a straightforward three month drive from San Francisco on the West Coast to New York on the East Coast, via Key West in the extreme southeast corner. In 2005 we completed a similar road trip from Boston to Los Angeles, via Seattle, so we had a good idea of what it would entail. Flights and costs were researched, a new edition of our trusty guide book purchased, and our respective bosses informed of our plans. Then my sister announced that she was getting married in Cornwall, slap bang in the middle of the schedule. Naturally, that was not a family occasion to miss, so we re-jigged things to take a week's break from the road and return home to join in the festivities. The timing worked well and we were able to divide the journey into two six-week segments: San Francisco to Miami and Key West to New York.

In a family in which both parents are teachers, failing any O level is normally frowned upon. I failed my history O level twice, much to my mother's dismay. My excuse is that the curriculum was all kings and queens and dates of battles, none of which were interesting or brought the subject to life. Also, it was taught either by the "open your books at chapter 10 and read whilst I catch up with my marking" or "copy down what I'm writing in longhand on the board" methods of boring teenagers to death. We never touched on American history at all, even though the links between America and Liverpool, the main Atlantic seaport of the British Empire, must provide fantastic resources to an enthusiastic teacher. Sadly, to my late 1970s self, history lessons were an opportunity to catch up on my sleep or carve imaginary band logos into the desk lid.

For me, geography is a more interesting subject because it is physical. You look at pictures and draw diagrams and understand why mountains, rivers and towns are that shape. In America, rivers are indeed deep and mountains high; plains are great and lakes superior. Pints are smaller and portions in restaurants aren't as massive as some would have you believe, but you can't have everything, can you?

This road trip was very much an epiphany for me regarding the European history of America. I knew very little about it before the journey began, but now I've got a vague grasp of some of the key events and timelines, as well as some of its more absurd events. For example, in addition to the better known War of Independence and Civil War, Texas had a war over where to house its archives, and the British burned down the White House in 1814, during the War of 1812. In Memphis, Tennessee, a Civil War general escaped a Confederate raid in just his nightshirt, and had to pay a ransom for his captured uniform. Belfast Protestants rebelled against their Spanish overlords and created the short-lived Republic of West Florida. A town in South Carolina celebrates its history by flying the seven flags under which it has been governed over time. Add to these the Center of the World on the California/Arizona border, a German blues band, an Englishwoman whose forebears left their homeland in 1640, and the most glaring open goal miss in the history of Hollywood tie-ins, and you have a flavour of the America we encountered.

America is also fertile ground for one of my lifelong passions: birdwatching. I weighed myself down with binoculars, camera and iPhone app, and was on the lookout for anything feathered that was new and interesting.

To meet people when travelling in America we'd eat in bars, sitting "belly up to the bar". Ordering a couple of pints or a meal in an English or Irish accent more often than not catches the ear of the person on the next barstool, and you're away. If there isn't anyone to talk to there are always the ubiquitous television screens showing one or more of the three main American sports: football, basketball or baseball. Many American B&Bs provide breakfast at the kitchen table at a set time, creating another opportunity to meet and chat to fellow travellers.

I don't want to refer to my wife as "my wife" throughout this book so I will introduce her as Áine Two. Áine is Irish for Ann and is pronounced "Awn-ya". Áine One is her aunt, is also Irish, is also called Ann and is very much the original. Áine One lives in New Jersey and appears later in the book.

During our 2005 trip, Hurricane Katrina decimated New Orleans and its surrounding area, and George W. Bush's lack of response precipitated the beginning of the end of his domestic popularity as president. The 2017 trip was played out in parallel with Donald Trump's inauguration and the first two months of his presidency. History will tell how he will have performed as the 45th President of the United States.

This book reflects the journey we took, where we went, what we saw, who we met and what we learnt about America. It attempts to knit together a series of strange coincidences, starting with our friend William Anderton from Blundellsands, near Liverpool, and ending in a graveyard in

Annapolis. On the journey we drove along some astonishing roads, took in vast galleries of glorious scenery, visited a number of America's famed roadside attractions, and came across a few of its less well-known backwater towns. We ate many burgers, plates of ribs and bowls of Buffalo wings, and drank a great deal of beer, some mediocre and some brilliant.

Most of all, we rediscovered our love for America, its stunning geography, fascinating history and wonderful people.

CHAPTER 1
SAN FRANCISCO

Nob Hill in San Francisco was not named intentionally to generate schoolboy sniggering, although the puerile amongst us might get a kick out of reading its name. It stems from the prominent and wealthy businessmen who lived on the hill in the posh end of town who were considered local nobility, or "nobs", hence Nob Hill. Sitting on the peak of Nob Hill is the beautiful Grace Cathedral, with its main entrance graced by a reproduction of Ghiberti's "Gates of Paradise" from the Baptistery of Saint John in Florence. Another copy is in the Harris Museum and Art Gallery in Preston in Lancashire, which, coincidentally, is where my mother was born.

Our hotel in San Francisco was also at the top of Nob Hill, and required a climb up Powell Street from the underground station to reach it. Our bags were too big to fit on the already crowded cable car, so we decided we'd give it a go dragging them up the hill. They had wheels and it was only half a mile. How hard could it be? As with many of the hills in San Francisco, it began with a gentle slope and got steeper the higher we climbed. By the time we reached Bush Street and the French Quarter, we were wearing crampons and contemplating roping ourselves together for the particularly tricky overhanging kerbstones.

San Francisco's French Quarter is not one of its better-known neighbourhoods. Few people are aware that nestled three quarters of the way up Nob Hill, at the southern end of Chinatown, is an area with a peculiarly French feel. It houses the French Consulate and the French National Church of Notre Dame Des Victoires, and several cafés and restaurants bearing names like Café de la Presse and Le Central.

Our hotel was the Cornell Hotel de France, which combines themes of Joan of Arc with French art. Each floor is dedicated to the works of a particular artist, including sections of paintings copied by hand onto each bedroom door. Our floor was Henri Matisse, and others include Monet, Manet and Toulouse-Lautrec. That, however, isn't the best of it. There is a statue of the fully armoured Maid of Orleans in the foyer, and the basement restaurant celebrates her life and achievements. The restaurant has an extraordinary array of posters, artworks, suits of armour, implements of torture and even farm machinery hanging from every wall and beam. In addition, the room is done out to resemble the crypt of a gothic cathedral, with tromp l'oeil wallpaper painted to look like stone blocks. The excellent and very friendly members of staff are Vietnamese, which is perhaps not as unlikely as it might initially sound, and they serve breakfasts consisting of eggs any which way you liked.

Despite, or possibly because of, this eccentricity, the Cornell Hotel de France is a splendid place to stay.

The Parisian feel to the French Quarter is enhanced by its own bit of Pigalle. Two doors down from the hotel is the Nob Hill Theatre, with its sign in which its "nude male performers" proudly entice punters to "touch our junk". One can't help feeling they have missed the chance of a really good pun there. San Francisco does have a very liberal reputation so it is inevitable that one will encounter something like this during any visit, and in my mind the city is all the better for it. The presence of the theatre and its sign made me smile and remember the days when similar places were more evident in Soho, London's party district. I'm sure Áine Two and I would be most welcome in the theatre, although I doubt we are its target market.

Almost every city in the world has an Irish bar. Ireland has one beer of note and no empire to speak of, but has somehow managed to conquer the global pub trade. Its sons and daughters did build much of the world's transport infrastructure, and of course, they needed somewhere to relax amongst their own kind and remember home.

We don't always seek out Irish bars when travelling, but they do exist almost everywhere and it would be churlish of us not to support Áine Two's fellow Irish exiles. We found

The Irish Bank down a tiny side road in the French Quarter, and wandered in to check out the craic. The bartender was a young lad from Cork who had only been in America a few months but had settled in, got himself a job and was doing grand, thank you very much.

As we sat at the bar chatting and enjoying a local brew we overheard a couple next to us ask for a round of drinks with a very strange title. The bartender produced their order and they finished them in one go, accompanied by much a-whoopin' and a-hollerin', seemingly intent on getting beyond very drunk to plastered as quickly as possible. Quietly, we asked him if we had heard their order correctly. It was something new to him when he had arrived in the country too, but he confirmed that they had indeed ordered two "Irish Car Bombs". The recipe for an Irish Car Bomb is as gruesome as its name is tasteless: a measure of Jameson whiskey, topped by a measure of Baileys, served in a shot glass that is dropped into a half pint of Guinness. The whole shebang is downed in one – in order to stop the Baileys curdling, apparently. It's much like a Jägerbomb, but without the subtlety and finesse. I just hope the *Daily Mail* doesn't hear about it or there will be moral outrage in abundance.

Many in the UK have a mistaken belief that American cities are built for cars, not pedestrians. This is not always the case, and San Francisco is a perfect example of how the American city grew up around people. It boomed during the famous Gold Rush of 1849, and by 1890 it was a city of nearly 300,000 people. This was all long before cars were invented. After the infamous earthquake of 1906, San Francisco was rebuilt quickly and on its original street pattern, much like London after the Great Fire of 1666. Hence it was never built as a city for cars. Horses, carts and trams maybe, but cars were a much later consideration.

This makes San Francisco a very walkable city, as long as you can handle the hills. A stroll through the Financial District on a weekday shows the usual hustle and bustle of a major commercial centre. Blue suits and briefcases abound, working cheek by jowl with the less conventional skateboard-and-iPad brigade. Office blocks are not as tall or as imposing as those of New York or Chicago, but still bear the logos of some of the world's big corporations. The major coffee shop chains are all present and incorrect, along with one or two less familiar names like Peet's Coffee, a local institution founded in the 1960s. Lunchtime is a scramble for sandwiches and soda, and there are plenty of places to enjoy them al fresco.

As we wended our way around some of the side roads off Market Street, we had to pause for a few moments while a crane lifted a huge double-height section of prefabricated steel and glass into place on the first floor of a shopfront. We got chatting to the construction worker who was supervising the pedestrians and he told us how working at ground level was quite unusual for him. His normal workplace was 40 or more floors above ground, putting glass cladding on newly built tower blocks. When he found out we had travelled from London, his eyes lit up and he described several happy months he had spent working there on one of the City's newer glass towers. It made me proud that all the British lads he worked with were, in his eyes, completely bonkers, and that the Scousers were the maddest of all. He even knew how to pronounce "Scousers" with a hard middle "s", not "Scouzers" like some poor uneducated souls say, and he did a passable imitation of a proper Liverpool accent. He shook my hand warmly when he found out I was a "Mickey Mouser".

At the end of Market Street is the Ferry Building Marketplace, a dramatic brick-built ferry terminal that stretches along the eastern shoreline of the city, facing the bay. It was constructed in the late 1890s, closed in the 1950s and reopened in 2003, not only returning it to its original use as a ferry terminal, but also as a rather splendid food market.

The building is long and narrow, with a tall elegant clock tower that is reminiscent of the wedding cake design of St Bride's Church on Fleet Street in London. The Nave, as the market hall is rather appropriately known, runs the length of the building and has a double-height glass roof, allowing natural light in on the stalls housed in archways on either side. The items for sale are not cheap, but they are mostly locally produced and appear to be of good quality, giving things a prosperous, upmarket feel. There is also a Farmers' Market around the outside of the building on three days a week. If you are lucky enough to work close by, it must be a wonderful place to grab some lunch to eat facing the beautiful blue waters of the bay.

San Francisco did eventually pay homage to the car by building not only its two iconic bridges but also the Embarcadero Freeway, a double-decker motorway that used to run along the eastern shoreline between the port and the city. It was demolished after being irrevocably damaged in another earthquake in 1989, and its absence opens up the vista of the bay and the Ferry Building, reconnecting them both to the city. Walking along Market Street towards the eastern shore, you see the elegant Ferry Building rather than a hideous two-storey freeway.

San Francisco's public transport system is unique in that its cable and streetcar rolling stock are all vintage vehicles. I don't lay any claim to real transport geekery. I don't log train or bus numbers, or point at aeroplanes, but I do love a good, properly old piece of transport history. The Market Street Railway runs along the shoreline, past the Ferry Building Marketplace, and whilst we were there a splendid canary yellow streetcar emerged from the fog. It dropped a few passengers off at the Ferry Terminal stop, and as it rattled off into the distance, I stood in quiet awe, savouring every last glimpse, like a child saying goodbye to a beloved grandparent. It turns out that the streetcar is from Cincinnati and was built by the St Louis Car Co. in 1948.

The stroll along the Embarcadero northwest towards the famous Fisherman's Wharf is very pleasant, and weary feet can be rested by hailing one of the pedal rickshaws that ply their trade along the side of the road. The shore is lined with Art Deco wharf buildings in various states of disrepair, many used as car parks. Hopefully, over time these will be renovated for other uses, making the walk even more satisfying.

Fisherman's Wharf is a tourist trap of overpriced bars and restaurants, many plagued by pigeons and seagulls. It is quite the opposite of the classy Ferry Building Marketplace. We ate lunch in a chip shop where the birds wandered in and out at will, sat on the tables whilst customers were eating, and generally made a nuisance of themselves. The put-upon staff did their best to keep them out with water pistols and general shooing, but to little avail. Maybe a municipal bird of prey would help scare them off.

There were plenty of tourist shops on the wharf selling the usual T-shirts, fridge magnets and hats. One shop was called Treasure Ireland, and was painted to resemble a traditional Irish pub, including a tiny door for the leprechauns.

San Francisco is renowned for its fog, and by that I don't mean pollution related smog but proper, natural, airborne water vapour. It is caused by a combination of climatic conditions and the local physical geography, and can envelop the city and Bay Area at any time of the year.

On a particularly foggy January morning, we walked from our hotel north through Chinatown to Fisherman's Wharf, turning west along the shoreline towards the Golden Gate Bridge. As we strolled past the ziggurat-like former Ghirardelli chocolate factory and the Art Deco charm of the Maritime Museum, we looked back at the city as it emerged from the clearing fog. To the right the tallest buildings were peeking out above their misty shroud, and to the left we could make out the ghostly shapes of container ships and ferries moving around the bay, warning people of their presence with their booming fog horns. As we climbed around the headland at Black Point, we caught a glimpse of the very tips of the towers of the Golden Gate Bridge peering out through the top of the fog bank. One fog horn seemed to remain in a constant position, and I assumed that it belonged to a large ship waiting at anchor at the mouth of the bay. I only realised later that it belonged to the bridge itself, booming its warning to nearby ships that it was big, in the way and not moving anywhere.

It didn't take long for the bridge to emerge from the mist, and it did so in spectacular fashion. The fog bank began to subside from the top down, until the upper halves of the towers were visible. It then split in the middle, drawing back towards each shore, gradually revealing the lower halves of the towers. The bridge is a truly elegant piece of architecture that graces a magnificent landscape, and forms the backdrop for almost every view around the northern end of the city.

Our walk took us past the fabulous seafront properties lining Marina Boulevard towards Crissy Field, site of a former US Army airfield on the shore of the bay. Its backdrop of the Golden Gate Bridge and parkland, beaches, marshlands, walking and biking trails and plenty of opportunities for birdwatching make it a fabulous place to spend a sunny afternoon. The Warming Hut Café and Bookstore, run by the Golden Gate National Parks Conservancy organisation, made us enormous sandwiches, which we munched while looking out over the beautifully calm water.

In Crissy Field I managed to kick off my list of birds seen on this trip with, amongst others, a marbled godwit and the ominously named killdeer, which is nothing more dangerous than a gangly American version of ringed plover.

Fort Point sits on a rocky outcrop overlooking the Golden Gate entrance into San Francisco Bay, directly underneath the bridge. It was built before the American Civil War, with the brief to protect the entrance to the most important harbour on the burgeoning West Coast. How anyone would have spotted ships sneaking past through the dense fog is a mystery to me. Maybe that was why it never saw action and was decommissioned after World War II.

The closest Fort Point came to being attacked was when the Confederate Navy ship CSS *Shenandoah* was on a heading towards it in August 1865, intent on sacking San Francisco. En route the captain of the *Shenandoah*, Lieutenant Commander James Waddell, discovered that the Civil War had finished five months earlier, so he turned around and headed elsewhere. We'll meet Lieutenant Commander Waddell and the CSS *Shenandoah* again later.

Like many decommissioned American military sites, Fort Point is a National Park, and for a few dollars' entry fee you can wander around the well-preserved structure. One particularly pleasing view is from the northernmost corner of the fort, from where you can see directly along the Golden Gate channel and out to the Pacific Ocean.

A large print of an Ansel Adams photograph taken in 1932 hangs in our kitchen in London, showing San Francisco Bay looking north from Sea Cliff, through the gap that is now spanned by the Golden Gate Bridge. A headland juts out from the right of the photograph, almost to the centre, and on its end can clearly be seen Fort Point before the bridge was built over it. Had I realised that Sea Cliff was only half a mile further on from the bridge, I would have made the extra effort to get there. Such is life.

After our walk, we took a bus back to the city via Fisherman's Wharf. From there we wandered towards Washington Square and the Rogue Ales Public House which came highly recommended to us by a close friend. He had spent a few days in the city and enjoyed himself in the pub's warm embrace.

I have a long and very enjoyable relationship with American beer, and I have been able to observe at close hand the changes that have taken place in the marketplace over the last 20 years. Huge numbers of craft breweries have sprung up nationwide, displacing the staples of Bud, Bud Light, Coors, Pabst and Miller from bars across the country. Also, the strength of locally brewed beers, especially on the West Coast, has rocketed to 6% and above.

The beer menu on the wall of the Rogue Ales Public House showed that they had no beers on tap lower than that mark, so I asked the bartender if he had a 4 – 5% session beer available. "You need to put on your big pants to drink in my pub," he laughed. I shrugged my shoulders, hoisted my jeans over my ample girth, and bought a couple of 6% pints. The lady next to us was curious as to why we had ordered beer by ABV, so we explained to her that 6% was strong for a UK beer, and not what we would recommend for an early evening starter for ten.

She ordered herself another pint of whatever impressively strong ale she was drinking, and we settled in for a chat. She was an artist who lived on a boat on the other side of the bay, and regularly sailed across to visit the city for inspiration. She was enjoying a few quiet beers before an early night and a walk along the coastline in the morning.

As with most Californians we met, she was definitely not looking forward to the looming presidential inauguration, due to take place the following week. "The man's giving me nightmares," she said rather miserably.

The distinction between Republican and Democrat politics in America often appear blurred to someone from the UK. They can be described as centre-right and very-right, a bit like the difference between Tony Blair's New Labour and David Cameron's Tory Party. However, on the surface, President-elect Trump seems to have polarised opinion less on party lines and more on personality. According to our drinking companion, he has a Democrat past but aligned himself to the Republicans for the sake of expediency. Her fears were more around his attitude to women and immigrants, and what he might do to Obamacare. "He's going to force us backwards to when only the rich had medical cover," was how she put it. The term "sanctuary city" had been in the news in the lead up to the inauguration, and she explained that a sanctuary city was somewhere where the local authorities don't always comply with federal requirements when questioning or detaining illegal immigrants. It means that immigrants are safe from having their immigration status questioned if they are stopped by police, and have a reduced risk of being turned over to the federal authorities if they are arrested. It seems extraordinary to me that civic disobedience of federal edicts is not only needed in America, but is becoming widespread as fear of presidential policy begins to bite. It turns out the sanctuary cities are not a new thing, and the UK even has some, apparently.

We drank a couple of stupidly strong beers together and wandered back to the hotel, happily off kilter, and a little better educated about American politics.

A pint in the UK is 20 fl oz, whereas an American pint is only 16 fl oz. It does come as a bit of a shock when you are presented with something that makes your hand look huge, but you get used to it. The reduced size of the glass isn't enough to compensate for the increased strength of the contents.

The following day we got chatting to the owner of a different bar in the city and asked him about the increase in strength of beer. He agreed that it was getting silly. "It's an arms race," he said, and went on to explain that at the end of Prohibition beer was restricted to a maximum of 3.2% ABV, which may be an influence on modern breweries trying to gain notoriety by making the strongest beer on the market. He also agreed that by not brewing session beers, they are missing out on sales. I'll happily drink two pints of beer at 6 or 7%, but I'm more likely to drink four pints of beer at 4 or 5% for the same price. Sensibly, unlike the Rogue Ales Public house, he had a 5% IPA on tap, and we enjoyed several pints of it. And I didn't need my big pants to do so.

The American beer scene strikes me as being akin to the approach the British took to Indian food when it first became widely popular as an after-pub filler in the 1980s: we were drunk and wanted the hottest curry possible, and to hell with the taste. Vindaloos, tindaloos, phaals and other ring stingers were the norm, and we consumed them by the plate load. By the late 1990s it had all calmed down, and now we tend to view Indian food as an everyday option for a civilised evening out, with the desire to be burned alive from the inside residing only in a few diehards. Maybe the American beer market needs to mature a little and calm down to maximise its profits. In the modern social media vernacular: #justsaying.

The Irish have a particularly relaxed, inventive and very colourful attitude to language, with day-to-day conversations littered with "eejits", "fecks", "gobshites", and many more besides. A common expression to describe someone who is being particularly irritating or stupid is that they are "acting the bollix". In the window of a community centre on Powell Street was an advert for a "Bollywood-inspired dance-fitness program", and emblazoned across it in large letters was, "FREE **BOLLYX** CLASS". The queue of fecking eejits would be around the block if the classes were staged in Dublin.

Budgetary constraints meant that we were not able to splash out on expensive meals on our road trip. As it was, the post-Brexit referendum exchange rates made the trip 30% more expensive than when we had originally planned it. You could say that we sacrificed a culinary adventure for a cross-country pub crawl. Occasionally, a meal was outstanding enough to comment upon, although none stood out in San Francisco.

Like most major world cities, to do San Francisco justice requires at least a week of wandering the streets, taking in the architecture, geography, museums and galleries and enjoying the nightlife. It is a wonderful place to visit, with a relaxed atmosphere, reasonably reliable weather and charming, friendly and interesting people. However, said budgetary constraints meant that we had to pick up our hire car and move on.

CHAPTER 2
THE BLOCKAGE OF BIG SUR

Renting a car in America is a peculiar experience. Simultaneously, it illustrates all that is bad and good about American customer service.

Our car was booked months in advance and the hire company knew what we had reserved, the date and time of our arrival and where we would pick it up. Of course, when we turned up at the agreed place at the appointed hour, our car wasn't ready. Not only that, but there wasn't another of the same category due in later that day. That's the bad bit.

The good bit was how the staff reacted to this situation, presumably because it is an hourly occurrence. Elsewhere we might be required to wait until something more suitable becomes available. However, without the smallest quibble or additional dollar, we were given the next car off the line and it was better than the one we had requested. So instead of being given a humdrum, travelling-on-a-budget American Tiddly-pom or equivalent, we drove off in a swanky four-door Japanese Howsyourfather, with a vast boot and comfy seats.

Bearing in mind that we would have the car for six weeks and drop it off in Miami, it was a bit of a result for us.

Now that we are in the car and on the move it is a good time to introduce the third member of our travelling party. MacDuff is a small yellow and purple dog who we won at a funfair in Surfers Paradise on an Australian road trip in 1990. We placed him on the dashboard of our 1969 MkII Ford Cortina (two door, automatic, 1600 engine, no aircon, plastic seats – loved it!) from where he led us on, hence his name. He travelled back from Oz with us and has been living in the UK ever since, most recently on the windowsill of our bedroom. He was reinstated to his rightful position on the dashboard of our 2017 tour bus, and led us on again with pride.

In Macbeth, Macduff doesn't lead anyone on. The actual quote is, "Lay on, Macduff, and damned be him who first cries 'Hold! Enough!'" Obviously we couldn't really encourage our MacDuff to get stuck into every American who crossed his path or he'd have been locked up before we knew it. So onwards he led, peacefully and in all his yellow glory.

Our first stop was Santa Clara for Sunday lunch with an old college friend and his lovely wife and daughter. We ate at the excellent BJ's Restaurant and Brewhouse in nearby Cupertino, where we sampled four local beers on a paddle, all of which were splendid. Driving back from lunch we passed the vast circular Apple Campus, the new corporate HQ of Apple Inc.

During our stay in San Francisco we had failed to procure a critical piece of travel equipment: a selfie stick. We wandered in and out of all sorts of fine emporia, searching for a simple and inexpensive contraption to take photos of ourselves in interesting places. One shop in Chinatown wanted to charge us $20 for a basic example. Another shop wanted $25 for one that used Bluetooth technology to link the stick to the camera. Eventually, thanks to my friend's clever wife, we bought one for just $2.53 from Target in Santa Clara. Áine Two's nieces in Ireland watch junk American TV that seems to put Target on some sort of pedestal, and they were suitably impressed when they learnt that we had been shopping in one. Whilst in Target, we also bought another vital piece of road-trip equipment: a cool box. Most hotels and motels have fridges in their rooms, so we could chill things overnight, and the cool box kept them cold during the day too. A cold-ish beer once you have parked the car for the day is much more appetising than a warm one.

After lunch and our Target successes, we said our goodbyes and dropped down the coast through Monterey on California Route 1, for an overnight stop in the very pleasant Carmel-by-the-Sea.

Famously artistic and deeply conservative – Clint Eastwood was mayor back in the 1980s – Carmel is on the horns of a dilemma. How does a charming beachside community maintain the attraction for its residents, whilst maximising the income from the millions of tourists it draws every year with its siren song of loveliness? Venice in Italy has the same problem, but on a larger scale.

The tree-lined main street, Ocean Avenue, is made up of low-rise Hacienda-style shops, galleries and restaurants, most of which appear to be privately owned. The shopping centre just off Ocean Avenue is below ground, presumably to avoid it being visible above ground, and the residential back streets are quiet and as well-kept as you would expect. Incidentally, according to Carmel's municipal code you need a permit to wear shoes with heels higher than 2 inches or with a base of less than a square inch, to protect the city from lawsuits in case you trip over an irregular pavement.

At the bottom of Ocean Avenue is a small white sandy beach, surrounded by cypress-topped bluffs. One can only imagine what a tourist-infested hell it must be during the summer. Still, the residents of Carmel only have themselves to blame. If their town wasn't so lovely, people wouldn't come and spend lots of money to experience it.

We were there in January, and had the beach to ourselves for a peaceful early morning stroll. I even managed to increase my birdwatching tally with pelicans, willets and whimbrels, which sounds like a firm of Norfolk solicitors. "Would you like to see Young Mr Willets or Old Mr Whimbrels, sir?"

Golf isn't really my game, so I was completely unaware that we were quite so close to one of the sport's holy sites. The headland that makes up the northern end of the bay is occupied by the world famous Pebble Beach Golf Links. Tiger Woods won there at least once.

What I do know about Pebble Beach from one of my

other passions is that it hosts the world's poshest classic car event, the Pebble Beach Concours d'Elegance. Classic car owners from all over the world bring their exquisitely pampered, mint condition vehicles to be pored over and judged by the great and the good of the industry, and prizes are awarded for the best examples. A Pebble Beach Concours d'Elegance title can add many thousands of pounds to the value of a vehicle, and give the owner something with which to fund the grandkids through college. Not that he or she needs the money if they can afford to enter a car into the competition in the first place.

Some of the cars entered are works of automotive art, like the Al Capone-style 1932 Auburn Speedster that won a prize in 2016. Sadly, however, many are museum pieces that live, gleaming and undriven, in air-conditioned garages. They are wheeled out occasionally and trailered to what are little more than leather and chrome-polishing competitions. The cars must be able to be started and driven onto their show stands to prove that they work, but that's the extent to which many of them are used.

I am unashamedly jealous of the owners of such vehicles, but in my mind cars are there to be driven, not cosseted. They should be on the road doing the job they were designed for: moving people from A to B in style. I'd much rather use my rattly old 1970 Jaguar most weeks for the shopping, than have a beauty queen of a car that I would be too afraid to drive for fear of damage. The Jag is only locked away for security reasons, or when it has decided not to work.

Talking of Pebble Beach and classic cars, as we drove towards it from Cartmel, we were passed going the other way by a vast pre-WWII Hispano-Suiza motor car. It was two-tone burgundy over cream in colour, and had the archetypal running boards and side-mounted spare wheel of the period. It was instantly recognisable as an Hispano-Suiza, even going past at speed, by the unique flying-stork bonnet mascot. Luckily, I was in the passenger seat of our rental car at the time so we avoided a wobble as I craned my neck to see it disappear behind us into the distance.

Pebble Beach itself is on the Monterey Peninsula, between Carmel and Pacific Grove. A 17-mile toll road takes you around the peninsula, through cypress forests and along a delightful coastal route to some splendid beaches and picnic spots. What you lose by being amongst busloads of tourists, even in January, you gain from the views and, if you are prepared to trek a little way through the dunes, the peace and quiet. The 17-Mile Drive, as the toll road is officially known, is a very pleasant way to spend a couple of hours, especially if you are into seeing how the other 2% live.

On the southern shore of the peninsula, between the Cypress Point and Pebble Beach golf courses, is the Lone Cypress. This famous Monterey cypress tree sits precariously on a rocky outcrop, being bashed about by everything the Pacific Ocean can throw at it, kept upright by a number of wire tresses. It has survived, with some help from man, for over 200 years and has been incorporated in the logo of the Pebble Beach Company, which owns most commercial ventures in the area. Golf fans will be very familiar with its image.

We had discovered the previous day that our planned drive south along the almost mythical Big Sur coast road was blocked by a landslide. However, the road is so spectacular we decided we'd go as far south as we could, and then come back and take the inland route.

To understand the significance of this stretch of road you have to come to terms with its rarity, its beauty and how and why it was built.

The road between Carmel in the north and San Simeon

in the south is, at 76 miles, the longest stretch of undeveloped coastal road in the entire contiguous 48 states that make up mainland America. If the whole road was open, you could easily drive it in less than two hours.

There is no logistical reason for a road that hugs the coastline south of Carmel. Few people live there even now, and Interstate 101 travels north–south a few miles further inland, serving the area perfectly well. However, the coast road was built by convicts and men made unemployed by the Great Depression after President Franklin D. Roosevelt allocated funds to provide work for them as part of his New Deal. Unsurprisingly, it is also known as the Franklin D. Roosevelt Highway, and it is a monument to the hard work of men given little choice but to carry it out, and to Roosevelt's humanity and social conscience.

And boy, is it worth the drive.

The Santa Lucia Mountains plunge into the Pacific Ocean, and the road clings precariously to the cliff face for almost all of its 76 miles. It follows the contours of the land, sweeping in and out of inlets, over elegant bridges and around rugged headlands, in a long smooth twisting ribbon of driving joy. As we wallowed around corners in our flatulent, softly sprung, automatic, saloon rental car, I imagined myself in a Jaguar E Type, cruising majestically, changing down through the manual gearbox as we approached each corner, blipping the throttle to keep the revs up, the thrum of the 4.2L straight-six XK engine merging with Matt Monro singing "On Days Like These", as I relive the opening scenes of the original *The Italian Job* movie.

Sorry, I got a bit carried away there.

Unfortunately, unusually heavy winter rain, following hard on the heels of six years of drought in California, caused a number of major landslides in the Big Sur area. Some of the bridges had been damaged and parts of the road blocked, necessitating its prolonged closure.

The route south was open as far as Pfeiffer Big Sur State Park, itself closed to visitors. This meant we had the double pleasure of driving as far as there, stopping for a cup of tea, then turning around and doing it all again the other way. Such are the sacrifices one is required to make.

At Carmel, with Áine Two taking up driving duties, we eschewed the easy route to I-101 South via Salinas, and turned onto the Carmel Valley Road, or Monterey County Highway G16. Rivalling the coast road for glorious and challenging driving, it wends its way up into the mountains and through beautiful high pastoral valleys, past isolated ranches, small villages and sparkling rivers. The road eventually drops back down the east-facing slopes and into the flat Salinas Valley, joining the freeway at Greenfield.

Cambria sits at the southern end of the Franklin D. Roosevelt Highway, and was our target for the night. We had booked into the recently refurbished Bluebird Inn, a proper traditional American motel, arranged around a central carpark so that you can drive your car up to the door of your room. We have stayed in many such motels before and since, and the Bluebell Inn is a perfect example of what makes them such good value for money. Rooms are simply decorated, and contain the standard queen-sized bed, fridge, microwave, coffee machine, TV, internet access and bathroom. It is inexpensive, quiet, well presented, clean, comfortable, secure and convenient, provides free parking and the staff are helpful and friendly. You can't ask for much more for an overnight stop.

What most American motels don't do, and the Bluebell Inn is no exception, is serve an evening meal, which forced us to seek out a local bar for the American equivalent of a pie and a pint. It's another of those sacrifices that one just has to make.

We took an evening stroll around Cambria, enjoying the pleasant shops and galleries and wondering what the flock of huge birds were that was circling overhead. A quick check on my handy birdwatching App identified them as turkey vultures, and they, along with their easterly black vulture cousins, would be constant companions for the entire trip.

The Cambria Pub and Steakhouse looked like a good spot for dinner, so we wandered in and settled onto two barstools. Within a few moments of sitting down, I was chatting to an elderly couple to my left and Áine Two was talking to a couple on her right.

My companions were retired and lived fairly close by, but enjoyed coming to Cambria for short breaks in the sea air. Their lifestyle was the equivalent of living in happy retirement in Guildford and popping down to Christchurch via the South Downs National Park for a weekend by the sea. They were the proud keepers of a 1960 MGA Roadster that they had owned almost from new, and which they drove regularly. They showed me photos of it, like it was a favourite grandchild, and I must admit to reciprocating with pictures of The Jag. It was the sort of nerdy classic car conversation that normally has Áine Two rolling her eyes to Heaven. They couldn't have been more English if they drank tea and sang "Rule Britannia". Our new friends were deeply impressed that we had taken the Carmel Valley Road to reach Cambria. He told me, "It was axel deep in snow and ice until a few weeks ago, and is a bit of a challenge in the best of weather."

Áine Two's buddies lived an hour or so inland, had a one-year-old son, and were enjoying a few days away for the first time since he was born. They were a nice, normal, hard-working young couple in their early twenties; he worked as a mechanic in a local garage, and she was a stay-at-home mum. They were saving up for a deposit to buy a house but knew that it had to be inland, away from the coast, for it to be affordable.

Inevitably, the conversation between all six of us turned to Donald Trump and his impending inauguration. Both couples were terrified about what Trump was going to do, especially with Obamacare, which affects both old and young in equal measure and would leave all four of them without effective medical cover. They were in awe of our National Health Service, and were all confident that they would happily pay additional taxes to fund it for those that couldn't afford to do so themselves.

An American friend of mine who has recently retired once told me of her fears regarding old age. She was a senior manager in a global manufacturing organisation and had come to the end of a very successful 30-year career. Her final salary pension would see her and her husband through their retirement without any hardship. Her main worry, and the reason why she had worked her last three years, was that she needed to serve enough time to ensure that she had full medical cover once she had stopped working. As far as she was concerned, she'd be happy living in a trailer park in the Arizona desert, provided she had the medical cover so that she and her husband would receive proper care if and when they fell ill. Her greatest fear is falling into penury due to prolonged ill-health, and she has a great deal of sympathy with those who might be impacted if Obamacare were to be repealed, as Donald Trump promised during the election.

The younger couple also told us about the elephant seals and zebras that they had seen just north of Cambria. The following day we took their advice and headed north up the Franklin D. Roosevelt Highway to Ragged Point, which was as far as we were allowed before the road became impassable.

The elephant seals can be found north of Hearst San Simeon State Park, and they do make quite a sight. Their rookery at Piedras Blancas is well signposted, and there is a large car park to accommodate visitors. Friendly and informative volunteer guides, known as docents, provide information on the seals and how they live. There were hundreds of females and pups, organised into harems that are overseen by vast alpha males who spend their time either lounging around amongst the ladies or in the water roaring at each other. Any resemblance to British holidaymakers basking in the sunshine is purely coincidental.

Enjoying the ocean alongside the elephant seals was a sea otter, and we were privileged to watch him for a full ten minutes as he frolicked in the waves, diving for food and then lying on his back in the surf, munching away. For me, there is nothing more life affirming than watching an otter going about its daily business, and this chap seemed so full of fun and vigour. It really made my day.

We drove north as far as a café at Ragged Point, where we stopped for a cup of tea and a sandwich. This we shared with a Brewer's blackbird, another new species that would accompany us for much of our journey.

We had missed the zebras on our way up, but managed to spot them in a field on the landward side of the road on our way back down, just below William Randolph Hearst's mad castle. Hearst was the Rupert Murdoch of his day, building and running a media empire based on what we know today as tabloid journalism, and is well known for being the inspiration for Orson Welles' character Charles Foster Kane in his 1941 masterpiece *Citizen Kane*.

Hearst was unimaginably wealthy and spent some of his cash on a castle overlooking the Pacific Coast from a hilltop vantage point above San Simeon. It is now a National Historic Landmark and offers different tours that must be pre-booked over the internet. It was fully booked the day we were in town, so we were forced to give it a miss.

Hearst stocked his property with a menagerie of exotic

animals in what was the world's largest private zoo, and some of them survive today. The herd of zebras visible from the coast road are part of its legacy, and live wild on the estate. We saw them at reasonably close quarters grazing in a field about 100 yards from Highway 1.

Having had our fill of Big Sur's beauty and Hearst's eccentricities, we headed south for our next stop, the classic Californian beachside resort of Santa Barbara.

The journey took us through delightful rolling coastal landscape, and across enormous fields given over to production of fruit and vegetables. The area dedicated to agriculture looks vast, until you see its scale on a map in comparison with some of the larger valleys we encountered later in the trip. The drive was easy going and we arrived in Santa Barbara feeling very relaxed, as though the holiday bit of the trip had really started.

Santa Barbara is typical of the Californian adherence to Spanish architectural style, reflecting the area's colonial past. The original town was flattened by yet another of California's earthquakes, this time in 1925, and deliberately rebuilt in the Spanish vernacular that it maintains to this day. The beach end of the main street, State Street, was being reconstructed whilst we were there, and it was clear that the builders were not being allowed to stray from the town's architectural requirements.

Santa Barbara is on a network of 18th and 19th century Spanish missions, linked by El Camino Real, which stretched as far north as Sonoma, north of San Francisco. The missions were roughly a day's ride apart, reducing the risk of travellers having to spend the night in the hostile outdoor environment. The cities we know today as San Francisco, Los Angeles, San Diego and Santa Barbara all have Spanish names because they grew up from the original missions.

Until 1848, Mexico owned a huge swathe of the western half of modern-day America, which is why the Spanish influence on population, language, culture and architecture is so enormous in those areas, and why Santa Barbara is a typical Californian town.

It is on a south facing bay, with beautiful golden sands that are literally vacuumed clean overnight, so that the multitude of joggers, dog walkers, sunbathers, volleyball players and other residents have a pristine playground each morning. State Street runs at right angles to the beach and contains a good selection of inviting shops, bars and restaurants. It also seems to attract more than its fair share of hippies and drifters, keen on the relaxed vibe and open-air lifestyle. The ones we came across seemed a harmless bunch, occupying benches and doorways on State Street and busking or smoking dope.

Incidentally, cannabis was legalised in California in a public vote that was, hilariously, taken on the same day that the rest of the country elected President Donald Trump. Self-medication comes in various forms.

Dinner and a few beers in Santa Barbara were courtesy of a bar and restaurant in which the staff were old and the décor even older. We perched belly up to the bar as usual, discussing this and that with the bartender, until his attention was drawn by a young lady who slouched in and slumped onto a stool at the end of the counter. It was obvious that they had known each other for some time, as the greetings between them were disinterested nods. Almost immediately she launched into a teenage tirade about some injustice or other, and he listened patiently before wearily trying to calm her down and reason with her. It all looked like it was part of a daily routine between a young tearaway and her older confidant. Eventually, she sloped off somewhere else as he looked on sadly. He shrugged his shoulders and carried on as though he had seen it all a thousand times before. Someone with more imagination than me would be able to come up with an idea and a full screenplay based on the little vignette we had witnessed. After all, Hollywood is just down the road.

For breakfast the following morning we were recommended Farmer Boy, at the top end of State Street on the way out of town. It turned out to be a traditional diner with shiny chrome stools lining an equally shiny chrome bar, and booths along the opposite wall. There was even a fantastic neon sign above the bar ordering us to "EAT PIE".

American breakfasts are something to behold, and then eat with delight. The Farmer Boy Classic of two eggs (scrambled), home fries, crispy streaky bacon and white toast with a cup of English Breakfast tea was no exception.

Home fries are an excuse to have chips with your breakfast. They are not those deep-fried triangles of shredded potatoes called hash browns that we get in hotels in the UK, but cubes of parboiled potatoes that are shallow fried until golden brown. They sit seductively on your plate, alongside your eggs and bacon, tempting you with their luscious golden potatoiness. I, for one, can't resist them, and think that they are near the top of the list of most civilised things the Americans have ever done for us.

Unfortunately, after a lifetime of dietary abuse, my body decided a few years ago to become lactose intolerant. I have no idea what triggered it, but it now means that I cannot digest any products made from cow's milk. This excludes most brands of milk, cheese, cream, butter, yoghurt and ice cream from my diet. Tragically, pancakes, that most wonderful of American breakfasts, are lost to me. No longer can I delight in a pile of those milk-based wonders, heaped with sweet banana, contrasted with crispy, salty, streaky bacon and drowned in glorious smoky Canadian maple syrup. I am almost weeping as I write these words. Sometimes you have no control over the sacrifices you have to make.

Our hearty Farmer Boy breakfast was important, as it came before the toughest drive so far on our trip, north to south through Los Angeles. I've succumbed in the past to the glitz and razzamatazz of Las Vegas and the crowded buzz of New York, but am still unable to bring myself to visit LA. Its vast sprawl, lack of a discernible centre, Hollywood insincerity and general soullessness put it beyond the pale. Maybe one day I'll relent and give it a go, but our challenge for today was how to get through it and out the other side in one piece, or two at the most.

We stuck with our policy of keeping off the main routes wherever possible, and continued on Route 1 along the coast, passing through Malibu with its expensive-looking properties perched precariously between the highway and the beach. We stopped at Santa Monica for some lunch, and took the time to wander along the pier that forms the end point of Route 66, the legendary cross-country road that begins in Chicago. It provided space for a bewildering variety of buskers, from the Russian beatbox kid performing drum rhythms with just his voice, to the John Denver-lookalike country and western performer with his box of self-recorded CDs. Fishermen lined the end of the pier, and a pair of fearsome young LA gang members, sporting facial prison tattoos that made them look like circus clowns, took a Sunday afternoon stroll amongst the crowds with Mom and girlfriends. Lurid ice creams and candy floss were being consumed in bulk by children and adults alike. Seagulls were hoovering up the leftover fish and chips, abandoned by Japanese tourists who had had their fill of disappointing American misappropriations of British culinary classics.

After girding our loins in Santa Monica with a picnic on the beach, we launched ourselves onto I-405 South. As it was mid-afternoon on a weekday, we faced traffic that was merely hideous, as opposed to gridlocked. There is no road in the UK that comes close to the size, complexity or sheer terror of driving through LA. The M25 around London, M60 around Manchester and the M6 past Birmingham are country roads compared to the I-405. Even the A303 past Stonehenge on an August Bank Holiday is a doddle in comparison. At one point the freeway had nine lanes going each way, with slip roads leaving and entering it from both the inside and outside lanes. On top of this, undertaking is legal on American roads so you have cars passing you on both sides. And you're on the wrong side of the road, in the wrong side of the car.

I drove and Áine Two navigated, and we stuck resolutely to the middle lane, 20 yards or so behind a big truck that was chugging along and not changing lanes much. Trucks would rumble up behind us before deftly slipping past as though we were a minor inconvenience. Cars swirled round us like an automotive dream sequence, but we ploughed on regardless, with knuckles white and buttocks clenched. Our tactics seemed to work and we emerged unscathed at our destination, having covered 56 miles in a little under three hours. I haven't concentrated so much whilst driving since the day I passed my test, on a Tuesday lunchtime in a traffic jam in Croydon.

Laguna Beach, just southeast of LA, was our stop for the night, and it turned out to be a particularly pleasant surprise. We were both expecting a downmarket holiday resort with high-rise hotels and a wretched sea front, but we couldn't have been more wrong. Laguna Beach is a swanky, upmarket part of the LA conurbation, with very pleasant shops and restaurants and a seafront of greensward and promenade that is ideal for joggers and dog walkers (Situation Vacant – the Reverend Spooner need not apply).

Our hotel was the Crescent Bay Inn, conveniently situated on the main road into town, and perched on top of a cliff. Once we'd checked in and shifted bags from car to room we decided on some fresh air to shake off the terrors of LA traffic. At the bottom of the cliff, through an exclusive little housing estate, was Crescent Bay itself, a gorgeous little cove that would make a Cornish fishing village proud. We sat quietly for an hour, revelling in the calmness and trying to decide whether the grey wading bird was something new or another bloody willet.

The following morning we had more of those home fries-laden breakfasts that set us up for the drive into San Diego for a weekend of fun, frolics and presidential inauguration. Interestingly, whilst we were eating, there were a couple on the veranda of the restaurant having a beer with their breakfast. This is apparently a thing with Americans on holiday, and we saw it many times throughout the trip.

After our hearty but alcohol-free breakfast we set off for San Diego, stopping on the way to visit one of the missions on El Camino Real. Mission San Juan Capistrano is about 15 miles southeast of Laguna Beach, up in the hills. It is very badly signposted and we ended up pulling into an empty car park, occupied only by two police vehicles. The officers were in the process of moving along a couple of early drinkers, who may or may not have been bothering the trickle of tourists. I asked one officer, in my politest English accent, if he knew where the mission was. He looked me in the eye as though trying to work out whether I was taking the piss, before indicating a tall church spire through a gap in the trees. "It's the tall pointed building through there, sir," he replied wearily. I'm not sure what makes for a worse start to his day: herding homeless drunks, or acting as a tour guide for useless divvies.

You enter the mission through a gateway and gift shop and step into a peaceful, manicured garden surrounded by single-storey monastic buildings. The main building, the Great Stone Church, fell down during an earthquake in 1812 and killed at least 40 people attending mass, and its ruins stand testament to its former grandeur and dodgy build quality. A small museum depicts life on the mission in its heyday and afterwards, when it was the home of a wealthy caballero. The black-chinned hummingbird we saw in the garden was like an oversized, iridescent green beetle, hovering in front of the early spring flowers to feast on their nectar.

The mission is well worth a detour off the main road into the hills to get a feel of Californian life before surfing and the Beach Boys came along.

Buying petrol in America on a UK credit card is a bit of a palaver. In most cases, petrol stations require you to either pay at the pump, or pay for your petrol in advance at the till. The former requires you to enter the 5-digit US zip code of the card holder's home address, which we don't have. To use the latter option you have to have a good idea of how much is required to fill the tank, or overpay and trust the garage to reimburse your credit card with the difference.

After a while, we got very good at estimating how much petrol we needed but, as having a full tank is a good insurance policy when driving long distances across empty countryside, we eventually resorted to the pay-and-trust method. To be fair to all the many petrol stations we used, we did not encounter one instance where the difference wasn't repaid in full.

CHAPTER 3
SAN DIEGO AND A NEW PRESIDENT

Despite the best efforts of Margaret Thatcher and Tony Blair, we don't do presidential inaugurations in the UK. The nearest we have are royal coronations, but they only happen once or twice in a lifetime, not every four years. When a new British Prime Minister is elected they move into No. 10 Downing Street the next day, without much more fanfare than a wave at the cameras and a bland "Thank you for electing me" speech.

American presidential elections take place every four years, on the first Tuesday after the first Monday in November, and the president is inaugurated into office for his or her four-year stretch on the following January 20th.

We arrived in San Diego on January 19th and checked ourselves into the Comfort Inn on the edge of the Gaslamp Quarter. Despite being a hotel rather than a motel, it did have a car park so, for a fee, we were able to park up safely for the weekend. This turned out to be important, as the road outside the hotel had some rather eccentric parking restrictions. Due to nightly street-sweeping schedules, you are not allowed to park at the kerb overnight on the west side of the road on Monday, Wednesday and Friday or on the east side on Tuesday and Thursday. As you can imagine, this causes much confusion amongst visitors, and a number of guests turning up to stay during the week are left fending for themselves once the hotel car park is fully booked. Having said that, San Diego is undoubtedly a clean city, so the car-parking and street-sweeping palaver seems worth the bother. Áine Two had the foresight and good sense to book us into the hotel car park in advance, so we had a reserved space.

We had heard much from other people about how San Diego is a lovely, relaxed city that better represents the laid-back, liberal Californian vibe than big, busy San Francisco. Although it is a big place in its own right, it does seem to be on a more human scale than its fellow saint up the coast. There are many miles of splendid beaches all along its ocean shoreline that are used all year round by locals and tourists alike, catering for the surf dudes of popular imagery.

San Diego Bay is a huge deepwater harbour and, since the turn of the last century, it has been the major US naval base on the West Coast. Its position made it the obvious choice as the home of the Pacific Fleet during WWII. One of San Diego's major tourist attractions and a very entertaining and informative way to spend an afternoon is the USS *Midway*, a vast, decommissioned aircraft carrier permanently moored in the harbour. Today it is a museum where visitors can wander around the flight deck amongst a variety of retired military aircraft and hear entertaining tales of derring-do from equally retired veterans. Worryingly, I found myself nodding approvingly at some of their "back in my day" and "political correctness gone mad" sentiments.

A nice freebie attraction nearby is the walk along the harbourfront from the USS *Midway* southeast, past the pleasant Seaport Village of tourist shops and cafés, to the Embarcadero Marina parks. They are not much more than large grassy banks but we found them full of people enjoying the evening sunshine, flying kites or having picnics. The walk took us past the San Diego Convention Center, where we cut inland and came across a large sporting edifice called Petco Park. It turns out to be the home of the San Diego Padres baseball team, and is named after the team's main sponsor, the San Diego-based pet foods supplier Petco. The recent spate of newly built football stadiums across Britain has caused a few raised eyebrows as a result of clubs selling naming rights, but I don't recall any being named after a pet food company. Maybe Everton's proposed new stadium on the River Mersey will be called the Kitekat Bowl or the Purina Arena.

Also in the city centre, not far from the seafront, is the Santa Fe Railroad Depot. Built in 1915 in the ubiquitous Hacienda style, it still serves as the city's main railway station. The interior is particularly lovely, with original benches, tiles and signage, and provides a cool and calm refuge from the city bustle outside. Oddly for such an important transport hub, it was deathly quiet when we wandered in. Nobody hustled or bustled around the room and there were no queues at the ticket offices. Maybe the quiet times in San Diego really are quiet.

The trains in and out of the Santa Fe Railroad Depot clack and clang their way through the city on lines that run parallel with and a few blocks in from the harbour front. In places the lines are unfenced and cars and pedestrians are trusted to cross them sensibly and safely, when the traffic lights allow. The trains themselves are enormous, lumbering, noisy creatures, some with double decker commuter carriages being pulled by great honking Amtrak engines. One day I may let Áine Two persuade me to undertake an American Railroad Trip, just for the craic.

Whilst wandering along the harbour, you can't miss the aeroplanes that swoop low over the northern suburbs on their approach to the nearby San Diego International Airport. They are obliged to fly only a few hundred feet above the rooftops when coming in to land, which must make life hell for those unfortunate enough to live under the flight path. I found myself standing on the harbour wall pointing at aeroplanes.

On the edge of the San Diego city centre is Balboa Park, developed for the 1915 trade exhibition celebrating the opening of the Panama Canal, and now a series of small but excellent museums and art galleries. You can get a day pass that gets you into several of them, which easily fills a very rainy afternoon.

How's this for being conditioned to living in London and using public transport wherever possible? We had a car in a reserved parking space at the back of our hotel in Downtown, but walked three blocks in the pouring rain and took a bus three miles to the park, half of which is given over to vast acres of free parking spaces.

The San Diego Automotive Museum is one of the selection of excellent museums we visited in Balboa Park. It houses a small but impressive collection of cars from America and around the world, including a very lovely white Jaguar XK120. One of the other exhibits was a British-made Norton 750 Commando motorcycle which bore a sticker for the Ace Café London. This is a venerable 1930s roadside café, similar to those seen in period American films but situated on the old North Circular Road in West London. It became a bikers' hangout in the 1950s and was the base from which daring young motorcyclists would attempt to reach 100 mph, thus achieving the revered status of a Ton-Up Boy. It was closed for a period of time from the late 1960s, and was even a carpet showroom for a while, before it was bought by an enterprising former Metropolitan Police motorcycle cop and reopened in all its former glory in 1997.

I take The Jag there occasionally for classic car evenings as it is a 10-minute drive from our house.

Something struck me as we wandered between the Balboa Park museums in the rain. Balboa is a Spanish name, so how come Sylvester Stallone, that great Italian stallion, chose it as the surname for his eponymous Rocky character? Rocky even speaks Italian to his coach in the film.

One of the features of many American cities is the party district, where bars and restaurants are gathered together to create a strip along which revellers can enjoy the nightlife.

San Diego's Gaslamp Quarter consists of 16 square blocks of bars and restaurants, many in historic buildings. It is situated right next to Downtown and gets its name from the original gas lamps that line the streets.

On Thursday night, it was relatively quiet and civilised. Friday was more lively with after-workers and Saturday was party central. Benidorm could learn a few things from the San Diegans when it comes to being loud, proud and more than a bit drunk.

On the edge of the Gaslamp Quarter is a splendid brewpub called The Beer Co. A few examples remain in the UK of the trend of 20 years ago for giving pubs and bars names that combined sometimes unlikely bedfellows. Slug and Lettuce and Rat and Parrot were two such chains. They were soulless corporate barns that sold ice cold lager to reduce the risk of the average drinker actually tasting it. Americans like to give their bars simple, descriptive names to avoid confusing their customers. The Beer Co. is about as simple and descriptive as you can get. It is also a very fine establishment, with a huge selection of locally brewed craft beers (and not a Bud Light or Coors in sight), an excellent food menu (the prawn and pasta dish was just what the doctor ordered), barstools galore and the obligatory televisions showing wall-to-wall sport.

Watching sport in America is an oddly distracted experience. Nobody seems to sit and concentrate on what is taking place in front of them. At a live event, there is a constant stream of people leaving their seats and returning, clutching beers and vast trays of food. Many people go to the bars and foodhalls more than once during a game. In bars, sport is on television constantly, but only as a distraction for when drinkers have run out of things to fiddle with on their mobile phones. We had a great time propping up bars across America, trying to fathom out sports we didn't understand.

American Football is rugby league with forward passing, and four tackles rather than six. Baseball has been described as cricket on cocaine and, like cricket, rarely produces an exciting finish. Basketball flows back and forth for 39 minutes, and then slows to a snail's pace and extends the final minute almost to infinity. For all three, the commentary might as well be in a foreign language to the bewildered Englishman. And I love it all.

After our meal in The Beer Co. we stopped off in an Irish pub on Fifth Avenue called The Field. It claims to be an authentic Irish pub that was shipped piece by piece from somewhere in Ireland, although all the paper and digital blurb isn't specific about exactly where it originated.

We parked ourselves at the bar and were happily enjoying the very good live band who were doing reasonable justice to the Irish songs they were playing. A young lady joined us at the bar and we were soon chatting away. For the sake of this story, her name was Kate and she was from Donegal in the northwest corner of Ireland.

After a few beers, Kate began to open up about her life in America. She'd arrived several years earlier on a Donnelly Visa – won in the annual lottery where qualifying applicants are picked supposedly at random and have a visa to allow them to live and work in America bestowed upon them – but had been unable to settle anywhere, moving from place to place, and from failed relationship to failed relationship. She'd washed up in San Diego the previous summer and landed herself a job on the reception desk of a local hotel. Apparently, Americans just love her accent and can't get enough of her Irish charm.

It became increasingly apparent with every beer that she was a deeply troubled young lady, with an unhealthy line in cynicism and spite. Previous boyfriends were "bastards" and "arseholes", "fucking Mexicans" were everywhere and the barman who ignored her – he was in the process of serving someone else – was a "dickhead". These unpleasantries were interspersed between bursts of very funny and entertaining conversation, as though she could flit from Father Ted to Father Jack and back again in the blink of an eye.

She told us that her current boyfriend was a Canadian trucker whose regular journeys took him from Vancouver to San Diego every week, with a two-day stop with her before he turned around and returned home. She was in the bar waiting for him to arrive after his most recent southbound trip, and sure enough, just as she mentioned him he strolled in and was greeted with squeals, hugs and tears, much to his embarrassment. We made noises about making ourselves scarce so that they could enjoy some time together but he insisted that we stay and join them, perhaps to help him subdue his wild Irish colleen.

We staggered back to the hotel having had a splendid and slightly scary evening.

You can't visit San Diego without sampling either the Mexican or local seafood. We did both, in the cheap and cheerful Mariscos El Pulpo, and the slightly more upmarket Fish Market respectively, enjoying both meals enormously. In the former our places at the bar included a selection of proper chilli sauces, each designed to cause maximum discomfort to the unwary diner. I arranged ours into a little line so that I could compare the labels, only to find the chap next to me peering over my shoulder. He was expecting me to perform a feat of tongue-blistering bravery, or stupidity, and grumbled his disappointment when all I did was take a photograph.

"Oh man, I was hoping you were gonna go for it with the chilli sauces."

"After you," I replied with a smile.

"Nah. They're way too hot for me!" I wonder what the Mexican is for "Billy Big-Pants".

On our second evening in San Diego, after a wander around the Gaslamp Quarter and a couple of pints in an Irish bar, we plumped for a Thai restaurant for something to eat. During dinner we encountered local behaviour that, to me, was as baffling as it was boorish and selfish. We were seated in the middle of the restaurant, next to a long table obviously set out for a large group who duly began to arrive as we were reading our menus.

One member of the group – we shall call him Mr Gobshite – took charge of the proceedings. He organised where people should sit, settling himself next to the Birthday Girl, whose big day the group were celebrating. After ordering the staff around and complaining loudly about the lack of music, he placed his mobile phone in the middle of the table and began streaming songs through it. I have absolutely no problem with music in restaurants, as long as it is in the background and not being fed through inadequate, tinny little speakers, like overheard and impossible-to-ignore headphones on public transport. We made it clear with a few very British harrumphs and dirty looks, that we were not happy with the music, and eventually they got the message and turned it down. However, Mr Gobshite immediately stormed to the back of the restaurant and accosted a member of staff, moving him out of sight of the main room, presumably to berate him. Within a few moments of Mr Gobshite's return to his table, that poor, mortified member of staff approached us and asked if we would mind moving tables to somewhere quieter, dangling a 15% discount off the bill as an incentive. We did so reluctantly, obviously to the embarrassment of some of Mr Gobshite's friends, and enjoyed a lovely meal without the incessant "TssTssTss" of his tinny streamed muzak. We did have a minor pyrrhic victory when we left, as he'd stopped playing his music. Maybe somebody in the group had pointed out what a twerp he was being, or maybe his phone had simply lost the will to live and committed silicon suicide.

America spends billions of dollars emulating what they consider to be the best Irish pubs: all dark wood, green bunting, cheery bar staff and badly poured Guinness. They tend to also include either a live band playing dreadful country rock music, or a loud backing track of traditional diddly-Irishness. What they don't seem to realise is that the soundtrack for the very best pubs across Ireland is one of conversation, with a quiet undercurrent of racing commentary from the telly. It is rare that you'll get piped music. Occasionally you'll get a band in the corner, but they will more than likely be providing low volume entertainment for the tourists, not overpowering noise to drown out the conversation. I'd love to see Mr Gobshite walk into a pub on the High Street in Galway and ask for a customer to be moved so he could set up his mobile-phone disco for his pals. He'd be out on his arse before he could say, "My great-grandmother came from Cork, you know."

I'll probably see his face again one day being inaugurated as the 50th President of the United States, elected on a ticket of Fuckwittery For All.

Which leads us nicely on to the following morning and Donald Trump's official inauguration as the 45th President of the United States.

The event was taking place at midday Eastern Time, which made it 9 am on the West Coast, and it was on all five televisions in the breakfast room of the hotel. Conversation was a low murmur as the packed room watched the proceedings. Nobody expressed any sort of opinion out loud, and the atmosphere was so downbeat and depressed it was like attending the Queen's funeral.

Light relief was provided by a Japanese tourist having breakfast, dressed in a red suit with green Christmas trees all over it. Nobody knew why, or wanted to ask him.

California chose to support Hillary Clinton by a massive 62% to 32% of the popular vote, so it came as no surprise that Trump's inauguration was met with resignation and despair in San Diego.

Equally unsurprising was the strength of feeling on display in the city during the Womens' March the following day. Tens of thousands of people, both men and women, took part, many wearing pink knitted hats as a symbol of protest and kinship. Whilst the atmosphere was friendly, on display were banners expressing genuine anger and disgust, protesting against what the marchers saw as the president's aggressive misogyny and racist rhetoric. The march may ultimately prove futile, but it gave people an opportunity to express their opinions about their new commander-in-chief and let off some steam built up over a rancorous and acrimonious election. We shall see.

Talking of the Queen's funeral, the January 23rd 2017 edition of *Star* magazine was on sale in many local supermarkets. Founded by Rupert Murdoch, and now run from the same stable as that other bastion of journalistic integrity, *National Enquirer*, *Star* publishes complete twaddle in the guise of celebrity news and gossip.

The front cover of the January 23rd 2017 edition, I kid you not, had four banner headlines: "Palace Bombshell! William & Kate King & Queen!", "Dying Queen Elizabeth Steps Down!", "Why Charles is giving up throne" and "$500 million royal coronation will be 'event of the century'". These are all lies that will be believed by gullible news junkies across the country, many of whom will also be old enough to vote.

It is impossible to leave the Californian coast without passing comment on something that seems to blight its cities and larger towns. Homelessness is a problem everywhere, and has been on the increase since the global financial collapse of 2008. In both San Francisco and San Diego, and to a lesser extent in Santa Barbara, we encountered large numbers of rough sleepers, many of them with obvious mental health problems. In a hotel restaurant in Louisiana later in the trip, we overheard a middle-aged local man discussing the politics and economy of California with the couple sitting at the next table. By its nature the conversation couldn't be held quietly, and he seemed so strident in his views that few would bother to challenge him. He stated as hard fact that every homeless person in California gets $37,000 a year in benefits from the government. I am in no position to gainsay him, but I certainly saw no evidence whatsoever of homeless people in San Diego or San Francisco carrying that sort of cash around with them. Indeed, if the US banking system is anything like the one in the UK, no address equals no bank account.

Maybe the warmer weather and legalised cannabis attract more homeless drifters to California than other states, but that is no excuse for the numbers of people in obvious mental and physical distress sleeping in the open air.

Rant over. Time to leave lovely San Diego and turn left along the Mexican border.

CHAPTER 4
BIG SKIES AND BORDERS

The United Kingdom is small and overpopulated. California, Arizona, New Mexico and Texas collectively have a similar population, but are over six times its size.

If you live in London and want some open roads for a bit of roof-down, elbow-out-of-the-window motoring, your nearest option is northern France. Otherwise you're in for a five hour schlep to North Yorkshire or west Wales or five hours more to the Scottish Highlands. Everything in between is traffic, queues, road works, speed cameras, rain and misery. There is very little pleasure to be gained from everyday driving in the UK. I drive from west London to Liverpool every other Saturday during the football season, and the 420-mile round trip normally takes me seven or eight hours. Sticking to the correct speed limits, the whole journey should take not more than six hours. Add that to another home defeat to Crystal Bloody Palace, and I wonder why I bother.

Once you leave San Diego and turn east, especially if you stay off the I-8 freeway and take the old US-80 highway along the Mexican border, you are in for seemingly endless days of some of the most pleasurable driving in the world. In the past, we have driven together from Perth to Sydney in Australia, and from Chicago to the Oregon coast across the Great Plains and over the Rockies. However, for sheer driving pleasure, neither of these can touch the journey from Southern California to Louisiana.

There is one very simple rule about being a foreigner driving in America, and following it will save you a great deal of pain, suffering and expense. Under all normal circumstances, and despite what other drivers may be doing around you, do not exceed the speed limit.

On a drive along a country road in Upstate New York in 2005, I was stupid enough to be caught speeding one Saturday afternoon. There are four things I remember about the copper who stopped me. He came out of nowhere, he was armed and I could see in the wing mirror that his hand was hovering over his gun as he approached me, he had the most unbelievably piercing blue eyes I have ever seen, and he didn't want the hassle of doing the paperwork involved in issuing a ticket to a foreign driver. So he handed me the spurious excuse and let me go with a ticking off, "You have kilometres in Europe so you must have confused them for our miles. Go ahead, sir. Please drive carefully and enjoy the rest of your holiday."

Here's the scariest bit. I have heard since that, as I was driving on a foreign licence, if he had chosen to give me a ticket he would have had to put me in front of a judge to have the penalty ratified. I was stopped on a Saturday and the courts were closed, which meant I would have had to spend two nights in a cell before I could go in front of the judge on the Monday morning.

I'm too young and good looking to spend time in an American prison.

So, despite the apparent emptiness of the roads, resist the temptation to put your foot down. Relax, stick your elbow out of the window and take in the scenery. I assure you that it is worth savouring every moment.

San Diego is not only the start of El Camino Real but also the terminus of the Old Spanish Trail, a trunk route that starts in St. Augustine on the Florida coast and wends its way west through most of the major cities that lie close to America's southern border. The OST is based on a cross-country network of 18th century Spanish missions, and can be viewed as the southern equivalent of the legendary Route 66 that connects Chicago with Los Angeles.

It doesn't take long to get beyond the San Diego suburbs and reach the open roads that wend their way through valley after valley of scrub farmland. Low hills or flat open land border the road on both sides, showing no apparent evidence of active farming, other than a fence preventing any livestock from wandering into the traffic. We couldn't see any cattle, and can only assume that they were hiding to avoid being typecast in a thousand iPhone holiday videos.

The road meanders south through this beautiful landscape

towards Tecate and the Mexican border. Whilst the new president seems intent on building walls and implementing various travel bans, we decided not to venture into Mexico, and stayed north of the line. It's a shame, because Tecate is reputed to be a pleasant enough spot: the home of cheap dentistry and pharmaceuticals, and the brewery that started the trend for sticking a slice of lime in the top of the bottle.

During the drive along the Mexican border, we began to notice the presence of a number of white SUVs and vans with a prominent green stripe across the back. It took a little while to work out that they were US Border Patrol vehicles working in the area. Several miles outside Tecate, we came across a border checkpoint where traffic was slowed down by uniformed, gun-toting, intimidating-sunglasses-wearing officers, who were pulling aside likely sorts for a grilling. As we didn't fit the demographic of people trying to bunk over the Mexican border, we were waved through, but I wouldn't fancy being given a full going-over by those chaps.

As we pootled along happily, the countryside around us turned into an alien landscape of harsh, hilly, rocky desert. When the original pioneers created the dusty tracks that would eventually become proper roads across this desert, they found their way through the landscape using ancient native paths, skill, luck and trial and error. Evidence of the original routes – and how they have been reused or abandoned – can be seen from the fantastically bonkers Desert View Tower, just off I-8 northeast of Jacumba. Originally built in 1925 by an enterprising businessman to advertise his nearby bar, the tower is one of the few remaining original roadside attractions in the area. Today it is run by a friendly and welcoming gent and his dogs. The base of the tower is a small shop and museum, and for a few dollars you can climb the tower itself to take in its astonishing views of the surrounding area. Most days in the Southern California desert are clear, and we could see for hundreds of miles north towards the Vallecito Mountains.

In the rocky grounds of the tower are the products of a bored chap called Merle Ratcliff who, unemployed during the Great Depression of the 1930s, carved a series of crude human and animal figures out of rocks that happened to be lying around. Some he painted to highlight facial and other features. There is a short trail that requires you to clamber around the rocks to see the carvings, which is well worth the effort for the surprises around each corner.

On the short drive off the freeway up to the tower, we passed an old battered silver Streamline caravan parked next to what appeared to be a scrapyard. What caught my eye were two flying saucers on the backs of trailers. I discounted them as being the result of an overactive imagination and too much beer the previous night, and carried on up to the tower without stopping. However, on the return journey down the hill my initial impressions were proved to be correct. Sure enough, the caravan was the home of Coyote's Flying Saucer Retrievals and Repairs Service, and two of his most recent finds were indeed sitting on the backs of trailers nearby.

As we stopped to take photographs, Coyote himself wandered over from his caravan. He was a short, stocky individual sporting a straggly beard and dressed in a battered jumper, threadbare shorts and boots. His outfit was topped off by a knitted beanie hat and a pair of alien sunglasses with "PEACE" and "LOVE" scrawled across them.

He introduced himself and asked us about MacDuff and where we got him from. When we mentioned Australia he began to ask about various UFO sightings in the country. We told him we were from England and he corrected his course seamlessly, enquiring about sightings in somewhere called "Sheff Field". I denied all knowledge and suggested a government cover-up, which left him happily chuntering about conspiracy theories. Before we drove on, he very generously gave us a key ring of a fluorescent little green man which now hangs from MacDuff's collar as a special adornment and travelling companion.

Charmingly eccentric doesn't do justice to either the Desert View Tower or Coyote's Flying Saucer Retrievals and Repairs Service, and neither is untypical of the weird and wonderful things on view in this part of the world.

As an aside, we looked up UFO sightings in Sheffield. Sure enough, in December 2016 the *Mirror* newspaper's website reported footage from the University of Sheffield that shows a mysterious flickering light soaring slowly over the city. By definition it is a UFO because it is flying and unidentified. However, my guess is that it was either a drone or one of those annoying candle-powered lanterns that people bring back from Thailand and that set haystacks and houses alight. Either way, what was far more interesting to me was the peregrine falcon lurking to the right of the footage, but that has no bearing on this tale.

Moving on from the tower, the landscape changed once again as we entered the astonishingly fertile Coachella Valley, heading for our overnight stop at El Centro. At the northern end of the same valley, a famous music festival takes place at a polo club near Palm Springs, set up for its privileged middle-class audience.

We were in the more southerly end of the Coachella Valley, where Mexican immigrants perform back-breaking manual labour in an area of arable farmland the size of Yorkshire. They ensure that California gets its fresh fruit and veg on its market stalls and supermarket shelves every day. One wonders how much more the music festival attendees would have to pay for their five-a-day if the Mexican border was closed to all but the anointed few, and the cheap immigrant workforce was to disappear. A cynic might suggest that, as California doesn't vote Republican, a rise in the local cost of living for the wealthy middle classes would have no impact on the current presidency.

The infamous San Andreas Fault carves its way across the Coachella Valley, and we heard a story of someone who was planning to buy a new multimillion-dollar house in California that was perched on the edge of an attractive, steep-sided ravine. They employed a surveyor to make sure that the house wasn't going to fall in, and he spent some time wandering around checking things out. His advice at the end of his survey was not to buy the property, and he took them on a short trek into the ravine to demonstrate his findings. He pointed out a half boulder in the wall of the gorge just below the house they were intending to buy, and a similar half boulder on the opposite wall of the gorge, a few hundred feet downstream. In his opinion, they were two halves of the same boulder that had been rent asunder by an earthquake sometime in the past, and that they were standing inside the San Andreas Fault itself. They didn't buy the new multimillion-dollar house built on the edge of the world's most notorious geological rift, but someone else probably did. The story is obviously hearsay and may be apocryphal, but it's amusing nonetheless.

We stayed overnight in El Centro, a service town for the local agricultural industry and the birthplace of Cher.

Between El Centro and the Colorado River to the east lie the stunning Algodones Dunes. In the middle of a stretch of sand-and-scrub desert, sand dunes rise 200 feet or more above the valley floor, stretching 45 miles north to south and 6 miles west to east. They are proper sand dunes, just like you would find next to beaches in the UK, but about four times higher. A huge car park off the freeway provides an overnight campground and primitive toilet facilities for the thousands of off-road driving enthusiasts who are allowed to blast around in their dune buggies. This would be frowned upon in the UK for causing ecological damage and unnecessary erosion. In Southern California, it's not that the locals don't care about the environment, but the area of dunes is so vast that any possible damage is compensated for by the likelihood of a replacement being readily available nearby. Any wind erosion of sand being churned up by buggies will simply move that sand to the next dune, and tracks are covered over within a day or two. Also, driving is restricted to certain parts that add up to a tiny percentage of the total area covered by the dunes, and the visitors bring spending power into what is otherwise an economically depressed area.

We clambered up a big dune and looked across the car park and freeway to the vast sandy wastes beyond. They are a truly astonishing sight, as are the massive campervans in which the off-road enthusiasts live whilst they are enjoying their pastime. Some pull trailers containing their dune buggies; others have a special compartment at the back of the van itself that holds their vehicles. Big doors swing open and ramps descend to allow the buggies to be rolled out onto the sand. Safety checks are carried out meticulously, outfits with matching colours are donned, helmets and seat belts buckled up, and off each one blasts for a couple of hours of harmless hooning around. I looked on with more than a hint of jealousy, before getting back into our rented repmobile and sloping quietly away.

A little further along the road is an astonishing piece of Edwardian-era engineering. When the early cross-country roads were being built, the sands of the Algodones Dunes proved impassable. In 1915, after winning a race from San

Diego to Phoenix by taking a shortcut across the dunes, the self-styled "Colonel" Ed Fletcher began building a road by laying wooden planks on top of the sand. The Plank Road was a huge success, despite the costly effort to keep it from being subsumed by the desert like the victim of an elongated Dr Who monster. It took such a heavy battering from traffic that it was completely re-laid a year after it opened, and it only lasted another ten years before it was superseded by the new Highway 80.

A reconstructed stretch of the Old Plank Road can be found, fenced off and looking a little neglected, just off I-8 a few miles on from the Algodones Dunes car park. Standing at the end of the section, it is astonishing to think that a mere seven years after Henry Ford started making his Model T, motor cars were being driven across deserts on a wooden road that would have shaken them and their passengers to pieces. Most modern cars wouldn't survive that sort of treatment.

A few yards from the Old Plank Road was something a little more ominous. When we parked our car to view the planks, we walked past a US Border Patrol SUV and van, both with blacked-out windows and the latter with a CCTV camera on a telescopic aerial. The camera followed our movements going both to and from the Plank Road, swivelling on its mount to keep us in sight. We were definitely being watched this time, regardless of whether we fitted anyone's dodgy demographics, and the reason became obvious as we crested the next dune.

President Trump came to power partly on the back of a promise to build a wall between America and Mexico. It will come as a surprise to many that such a wall already exists, and there it was, right in front of us. It is not continuous and in some cases not very high, but it is there and has been since the early 1990s. A story in the press whilst we were travelling reported how a couple of enterprising Mexican drug smugglers had welded a *Game Of Thrones*-style medieval catapult to their side of the fence, and were firing consignments of drugs over it to their waiting conspirators. That is just the sort of inventiveness that would help Make America Great Again.

Our next stopping-off point is one of the oddest things we came across in a land where odd is often the norm. It makes Coyote's Flying Saucer Retrievals and Repairs Service seem like a humdrum, everyday business proposition.

Many road signs in America indicate the city limits of an upcoming metropolis, informing you at the same time of its population, and Felicity (pop. 4) is no exception. What Felicity's road sign doesn't tell you is that it is officially the Center of the World. The town's founder, parachuting pioneer Jacques-André Istel, penned a series of books about a dragon that lived in the centre of the world. To drum up publicity for his creation, he somehow managed to persuade two of the world's greatest military powers to agree, and certify, that Felicity was indeed the centre of the world.

For a few dollars, visitors get to wander around the site after viewing a video about how and why it was set up. For a few dollars more, they can also clamber inside the specially erected pyramid, and stand on the actual point that has been officially designated, by France, China and Imperial County no less, as the Center of the World.

Once you exit the pyramid and walk about a bit, it begins to get really strange. On entry a few signs are visible that seem to indicate that an additional attraction is the History of Granite, and the video did go on about it, but I was confused by then and had stopped paying attention. I'm sure the History of Granite is a bit of fun for a geologist, but not your average travelling punter. However, once outside it becomes apparent that it isn't the History OF Granite, but History IN Granite. Laid out symmetrically around the compound are a number of long, low, triangular walls, faced with slabs of granite onto which have been etched tableaux depicting scenes from history. One line shows the history of California; another, the history of Arizona; a third the history of the United States. You can also read about the history of mankind, the French Foreign Legion, France's early attempts at flight and the Parachuting Hall of Fame (unfinished). It is possible to reserve a slab of granite to depict your own family history, although all those currently on site have been reserved. One such slab showed the descendents of two families who had moved from Sussex to New England in the 1700s and had married once they got to America.

The pièce de resistance of this mind-boggling display is a chapel atop a man-made hill, overlooking the whole scene. It is non-denominational and can be booked for bar mitzvahs, weddings and wakes.

The gift shop was staffed by a lovely, earnest young lady who managed to relate the story of Felicity to us with a straight face. We decided that we had earned an "I've stood at the Center of the World" certificate each, and she asked Áine Two for our full names. "I'm Ann Burke," Áine Two replied, spelling out her surname, "and my husband is James Topping." When we received our certificates, Áine Two's was made out to "Ann Burke", and mine was made out to "James Topping Burke". This was presumably on the assumption that we Brits are no different from some Americans, and tell everyone our middle names. I'm surprised she didn't ask me if I was James Topping Burke Jr or James Topping Burke III. Technically, I really am James Topping III, but I'm British so I'm naturally discreet about these things.

We left clutching our incorrectly named certificates and carried on our journey, just a little more bewildered than when we started.

Another oddity about Felicity, as if it isn't already off the scale, is that it is in the wrong time zone for its state. California is in the Pacific Time Zone, an hour later than Arizona, which is in the Mountain Time Zone. The change is supposed to take place when you cross the border, but Felicity has taken it upon itself to be in the Mountain Time Zone even though it is 3 miles inside California. I've come to the conclusion with Felicity that the best policy is simply not to ask why; just accept that it is eccentric and move on.

We'd managed to squeeze the dunes, the Plank Road, Felicity and crossing a time zone into the morning, so by the time we did cross the border into Arizona and hit the desert town of Yuma, we were late for lunch and starving. As we were just passing through, we didn't stop at any of the town's attractions. However, it is home to one of the original Spanish missions, and a desert prison built by convicts in the late 1800s and known as the Hell Hole of Arizona because of the scorching and unrelenting desert heat.

Most of the obvious options for lunch were already shut up for the day, so we had little choice but to go for the elderly, eccentric and excellent Lutes Casino. Sitting on Main Street and sporting a windowless, rough-and-ready looking frontage, it wasn't the most prepossessing dining option we'd come across. However, it all changes when you step inside. A large U-shaped bar faces into a vast room hung with all sorts of paraphernalia, from film posters to bikes, footballs and even cricket bats. Most of the tables were occupied by happy, noisy people and we managed to grab a spot in the corner, not far from the kitchen.

Lunch for me was a chilli burger that was a portent of the delights to come as we headed towards New Mexico. The burger was excellent and the chilli sauce wasn't your normal splodge of bland brown mush tasting of beans and a tiny bit of spice. It was a proper chilli and bean stew, made with real chillies and delivering just the right amount of heat and depth to be memorable. Little did I know that I was in for something even more special in a few days' time.

Lutes Casino also runs its very own Gretna Green Wedding Chapel, where eloping lovebirds have been getting married on the QT since the 1930s. Back in the day it was even popular with Hollywood stars who wanted to avoid publicity. Loretta Young, Errol Flynn and Jean Harlow are just some of the celebrities who got hitched here.

Between Yuma and our overnight stop was another eccentric roadside attraction. Dateland is a town that grew up around a date farm and a WWII USAF airfield. The airfield is now closed, but the date farm continues to thrive, and a roadside shop sells its products in all their forms. Anything that it is possible to make out of dates is made and sold to passing travellers, including date shakes: milkshakes made from dates. Without going into graphic details, that isn't a concoction that should be passing my lips. So discretion became the better part of valour, and we got back on the road.

Our bed for the night was in a place called Gila Bend, pronounced "Heela", as in America's only venomous lizard, the Gila monster and the very pretty Gila woodpecker, both of which can be found locally.

Gila Bend was founded near a bend in the Gila River, and has seen better days. Only every fourth or fifth building was open for business. The gaps between them were occupied by derelict shops, or open spaces that looked like post-war

Liverpool bomb sites. It felt like we were driving through a deserted movie set, and I half expected to see Marty McFly and Doc Brown howl past in a flaming DeLorean sports car, arriving back in time from the 21st century to reverse the town's decline.

Gila Bend's one saving grace is the Best Western Space Age Lodge. Based on the normal model for a motel with a diner, reception and cars parked outside rooms, its eccentricities lie in its design. The exterior is covered in curved steel blinds that, from the road, make the exterior look like a rocket lying on its side. The roof of Reception is a flying saucer that has been stuck incongruously on one end. Inside Reception is a domed roof with paintings of space shuttles and satellites over a background of alien planets and moons.

The rooms themselves are normal, if deliberately 1950s décor can be described as such, and each door displays its room number inside a little flying saucer.

The attached diner was busy with pensioners and served a very hearty breakfast, if a little slowly. The middle-aged lady who tended to our needs moved around the restaurant at the pace of a somnolent glacier, and displayed a degree of disinterest that bordered on disdain. I guess recruitment options for employers and employees alike are a little restricted in a desert town in the middle of Arizona. Again, the décor in the diner is space related, with moonscape murals and astronaut memorabilia. There is also a little gift shop selling fridge magnets and other bits and pieces.

Apparently, the Space Age Lodge was even more bonkers in the 1950s and 1960s, but suffered a fire that destroyed many of its original adornments and some of its original charm. The cover for the water pump on the outdoor, roadside swimming pool used to be one of three mocked-up satellites that lived on the roof of the lodge. They were removed after the fire and this one is the only survivor.

Down the road, the star of Gila Bend's dereliction is the remains of the Benson Motel, with its battered signpost, fading paintwork and shuttered windows. Something about a knife and a shower, the whole scene backed by screeching music, sprang to mind as we drove past.

Gila Bend is one of the towns in the Arizona desert that migrants aim for as they make the dangerous and often fatal journey from Mexico. After paying a fortune to be spirited across the border and then abandoned in the scorching heat, with little water and several days' walking still to do, Gila Bend must give the exhausted desperados the feeling that the great American Dream is still very far away.

Gila Bend welcomed the railroad in the 1870s, and it was from the road heading east that we counted 150 freight carriages on an eastbound train.

By this point we were travelling through a landscape of vast, flat desert valleys, with vegetation changing from sand to scrub to cactus as we passed between each one. They appeared to be a set of dried-up lake beds, each surrounded by a range of mountains acting as the rim to contain the water, and connected by the road passing across them. Some might find such flat, arid repetition boring, but I find it exhilarating. You can see for 30 miles in front of you and 30 miles behind on a dead straight road containing no other traffic, you are in no hurry, the weather is fine and the views are awesome. "Riding along in my automobile, my baby beside me at the wheel…", indeed.

On the approach to Tucson, Arizona we drove for two hours through countryside populated by a few ranches and millions of the tall saguaro cactus that you see in the Westerns. We arrived at the Saguaro National Park that is, in turn, populated by a few park rangers and millions of the tall saguaro cactus that you see in the Westerns. We went for a short trek during which we saw some spectacular views, a rock wren, and millions more of the tall saguaro cactus that you see in the Westerns. You really wouldn't want a cactus phobia around here.

Also evident as we approached Tucson, Arizona were the cattle ranches in which animals are fattened up for the table. They stand out because they involve little fresh grass, and give off a stench that insinuates itself into passing cars. Apparently, it is no longer profitable for some cattle farmers to fatten their animals for market themselves, so they sell them early to someone who can do it more cost effectively. This involves swapping the animals' wide open ranges for a modest and very muddy enclosure, into which they are packed with numerous others, and fed industrial quantities of food. Once they reach their optimum weight they are shipped off to the slaughterhouse and onwards to our tables. The sight of these filthy compounds is as far away from the romantic image of cowboys driving huge herds across open grasslands as it is possible to be.

Tucson, Arizona is one of those American towns where it is obligatory to attach the state to the place name. Austin, Texas and Little Rock, Arkansas are other examples. Lennon and McCartney wrote in 1969 about Jojo leaving his home in Tucson, Arizona for some California grass. I've no idea whether he got back to where he once belonged.

Like Gila Bend, Tucson is a railroad town, and its overnight soundtrack is that of trains sounding their two-tone horns and ringing their bells to warn others of their presence as they move through the town in the dark.

We stayed in a lovely B&B called the Big Blue House Inn, in the University District. It was just that: a big blue clapboard house built at the turn of the last century, and surrounded by a classic American veranda. It says a lot about

America, and the basic honesty of its people, that millions of homes all over the country have verandas on which are kept all sorts of furniture and family possessions, and we didn't hear a single tale of any of them being stolen.

We had a suite at the back of the house that had a small kitchenette and Netflix on the TV. It made for a lovely, comfortable and private change from the string of motels we'd been staying in since we left San Francisco.

Like many towns and cities worldwide, Tucson, Arizona sells itself as a culinary centre, with some justification. There are a number of award-winning restaurants grouped in districts around the city, and several times during our first conversation with her, the landlady of the B&B plugged Historic Fourth Avenue as somewhere we MUST visit. As it was on the way to Downtown from the B&B, we strolled along it to see what the fuss was about. Granted, it was early on a Tuesday evening, but all we saw were some trendy-looking student cafés slotted in between a comic strip of tattoo parlours. Tattoos were once a symbol of machismo, and were procured by sailors on voyages to exotic places, in many cases out of boredom. Every Tom, Dick and Harriet under the age of 30 in Tucson must be as hard as nails and bored shitless, based on the evidence of our short visit.

Maybe we were in the wrong demographic for somewhere as trendy as Historic Fourth Avenue, but I honestly couldn't see the attraction of the area. Neither hipster coffee nor body art are my thing, I'm afraid.

However, Tucson redeems itself with the excellent East Congress Street, next to the modern Downtown area. It is similar to Historic Fourth Avenue in that the buildings are old, low rise and brick built. The difference is that the bars and restaurants are attractive, and there are no tattoo parlours in evidence. We had an excellent dinner propping the bar up in HUB, where the presence of chillies in most things on the menu became more noticeable. The bar staff were all tattooed to within an inch of their lives, and we overheard a fabulously geeky conversation between two of them as they discussed which superhero was their favourite. "Superman's got all the powers, but Batman's way darker and more interesting." "Yeah, but Superman's a force for good. Batman's just a thug with a rubber fetish."

Also on East Congress Street, at the junction with North Toole Avenue, is the Hotel Congress, famous for being the place where John Dillinger and his gang were captured in 1934. The hotel has a splendid lobby with many original features, a very popular bar and restaurant, and a daily happy hour with discounted and delicious martini cocktails. It also puts on live music, and we heard a wonderfully raucous heavy metal band giving it their all as we strolled past late in the evening. Opposite the hotel was the excellent-looking Rialto Theatre that also puts on live music, and even had some vaguely recognisable names booked for forthcoming gigs.

Tucson also has an excellent Barrio Histórico, made up of Hispanic buildings that formed part of the original military fort, interspersed with some splendid late Victorian-era mansions. It is well worth a wander around to get a feel for the old city.

Over breakfast at the B&B the following morning we met two couples who were in Tucson for different reasons. The first were an older couple who were passing through on their own road trip from Idaho to Texas, via the California coast and the Mexican border. We had begun to notice as we went further east that the average age of those travelling alongside us was increasing, and these nice people were a good example. They were retired and reasonably well off, and had travelled from the cold north to see the warmer bits of their country during winter, when it wasn't quite so blisteringly hot.

Like many from the northern states, they weren't Trump supporters, and expressed their concerns about his attitudes to immigration.

"Is immigration a particular problem in the northern farming states?" we asked.

"No, sir, definitely not," our breakfast companions answered emphatically, explaining that, "Farming is a seasonal job market, supported by a seasonal migrant workforce. Migrants move in and out of the state as and when the farmers need them. It's about 50/50 American citizens and illegal immigrants who come to Idaho during the harvest season."

I haven't found any numbers to back this theory up, but I've no reason to doubt the words of two decent Idaho residents. At the time, Idaho had not changed its approach to policing immigrants in anticipation of any edicts from the new president and, according to the press, was not planning to do so. Our new friends' concerns were around the impact on the local farming industry if immigration were curtailed. It appears that some of the fears about Donald Trump's proposed approach to immigration are very similar to those expressed by many in the UK about the possible impact of Brexit. We shall see. They were also very worried about any potential repeal of Obamacare.

Incidentally, the governor of Idaho goes by the fantastic name of Butch Otter. I wonder if his second in command is Aide-de-Camp Coyote.

It is very interesting to travel through a country that is going through the same sort of existential angst as the UK, at the same time. Brexit has divided British voters almost down the middle, with the metropolitan areas – with a few notable exceptions – voting to remain in Europe, and rural areas voting to leave. The Brexit referendum campaign was characterised by two sides shouting at each other, with little or no backup from facts or data. The winning side have publicly acknowledged that what swung it was a spectacularly blatant but brilliantly executed lie about the amount of money that will be saved each week by exiting the EU. Interestingly, the debate rages on, regardless of the referendum result, with many people hoping that the country will somehow be able to reverse the result.

The US election was an equally difficult choice between two divisive candidates, and the result was very similar to the Brexit referendum. Donald Trump won the Electoral College but lost the popular vote, with results showing that the heavily cosmopolitan northeastern states and California voted as expected for Hillary Clinton, and the deep South and rural Midwest voted for Donald Trump. Again, the campaign was about personalities not policies, and time has shown that President Trump has so far failed to make any of his main electoral promises stick. At the time of writing, repeal of Obamacare has failed, his travel ban on people from certain mainly Muslim nations has been challenged in the courts and his Mexican wall has so far failed to materialise. Again, similar to the UK, many people in America have continued to protest against the election result, and many doubt its legitimacy, with accusations of Russian interference being investigated. President Trump's proposed visit to the UK has been postponed indefinitely, allegedly due to his fears that he won't get the sort of welcome he might expect from his country's closest ally.

There were two mornings in 2016 when I woke up and my first words were, "Oh, shit!", and neither of them were to do with excess alcohol.

The second couple we met over breakfast were middle-aged ladies, in Tucson for the oldest and biggest gem show in America. It came as a bit of a surprise to us that it was taking place, as we hadn't seen a single poster, flyer or advertisement anywhere for it. It turns out to be an annual winter event in locations right across the city, where busloads of traders and collectors meet to buy and sell semi-precious stones and associated paraphernalia.

One of the ladies was an IT consultant who had taken early retirement to set herself up in business in a shop in Sonoma, California. Her partner had an interest in "sacred geometry" and they were attending the gem show to stock up on goodies to sell. So far on day one they had already half filled their van, and were heading back for more on day two. Needless to say, they weren't Trump supporters either.

I asked, "What is it was about him that you don't like?" The IT lady shivered and growled, "Everything".

I've looked up "sacred geometry", and I'm afraid I remain none the wiser.

The daily litany of "no dairy please" that preceded every breakfast paid off that morning, when the excellent landlady came up unbidden with a pile of pancakes made from coconut milk. They were accompanied by crispy rashers of streaky bacon and I drowned them in gloriously smoky maple syrup. I was happier than the happiest person on National Happy Day in Happyland.

The landlady drove a British-built Mini Cooper S that was parked in her driveway. She loved its size and how it whizzed about the place, but hated the build quality. She also found the cost of repairs and customer service she received from the local BMW garage very un-American. Sadly, she was reluctantly planning to buy American next time around. She expressed no political opinions, perhaps wisely.

One of the local tourist attractions is Colossal Cave, on the Old Spanish Trail southeast of the city. Used historically as a shelter by local Native Americans and as a hideout by outlaws during the Wild West days, it now runs excellent guided tours starting from its equally excellent gift shop. It is part of a park in which we had a picnic and saw a dusky flycatcher, another of those small, unimpressive grey birds that got me all excited because I will never get to see one in the wild in the UK.

The lady giving the guided tour told a tale of how working for the Civilian Conservation Corps during the Great Depression of the 1930s helped many young men in unexpected ways. The CCC was set up by President Franklin D. Roosevelt to provide paid work for unemployed men and women around the country, and it involved many being shipped to unfamiliar places to take up their jobs. Working parties were formed of young men, overseen by foremen and often had local women doing the cooking and housekeeping. The story goes that a large number of young men were brought south to Tucson from the Dust Bowl, where crops had failed for several years. They were housed in camps, given work and three square meals a day, and many actually put on weight. Most would have returned home with reusable skills acquired through education and training, plus bodies bulked up by hard work and a relatively healthy diet.

We only plan a few days in advance on our road trips so that we have a degree of flexibility if we are recommended or come across something interesting. The "sacred geometry" lady suggested our next stop should be Bisbee, which she couldn't recommend highly enough. She used to live there as a child, when her father had a job as an actor recreating Wild West scenes in nearby Tombstone, the town famous for the O.K. Corral and Boothill Graveyard. We booked ourselves into a likely-looking B&B in Bisbee, and set off for Tombstone and its gunfights.

Tombstone was a lawless silver town, with a short and bloody history. It was founded in 1879 but by 1886, after catastrophic mining disasters and fires, it was left to rot by most of its inhabitants.

Today, Tombstone has been recreated as a Wild West town, with a dusty main street, wooden boardwalks and authentic saloons and gift shops. It is populated largely by actors playing roles in various gunfighting tableaux, including the infamous Gunfight at the O.K. Corral, in which the Earp brothers and Doc Holliday fought a gang of local cowboys. For more than a few dollars, you can join the other tourists in a specially built stage set inside the original O.K. Corral to watch the story of the shootout being told through the eyes of Doc Holliday. It is splendidly loud and overacted cowboy-style entertainment, in which the good guys win and the bad guys get shot.

Also around Tombstone are stagecoach rides, a local museum detailing life in a Wild West town, the Bird Cage Theatre and the office of the local newspaper, *The Tombstone Epitaph*. The story of the man who established the *Epitaph*, one John Philip Clum, is far more interesting than that of the local gunfight, but the latter is what the town is known for so that's what gets prominence. Clum was an Indian agent in Arizona, managed to capture notorious Apache leader Geronimo without a single shot being fired, was Tombstone's first mayor and a friend of the Earps and later became Postal Inspector for Alaska, where he would traverse the vast territory on muleback to inspect existing post offices and open new ones.

The Boothill Graveyard, on a hill half a mile or so outside Tombstone, contains the graves of some of the colourful former residents of the town. It is still consecrated ground and should be treated with respect, but some of the grave inscriptions are very entertaining. The best of them is, "Here lies George Johnson, hanged by mistake 1882. He was right, we was wrong, but we strung him up and now he's gone."

Whereas Tombstone was a silver town, Bisbee was a copper town. Founded in 1880 to support the Copper Queen Mine, Bisbee prospered, especially during both World Wars when demand for copper was huge. By the 1950s copper mining was no longer profitable, and the mine closed in 1975. Since then the town has relied on tourism to keep it going, with the vast open-cast copper mine the main attraction.

Bisbee has an unspoilt charm about it. The town centre seems to have remained unchanged since it was built. A lovely 1930s department store has been converted to house a number of local businesses, and the town's main hostelry, the Copper Queen Hotel, maintains its original Wild West feel. It's supposedly haunted by an alluring young woman who whispers in the ears of male guests and sometimes treats them to a striptease. We didn't stay, so I can't comment on the veracity of these claims.

A string of interesting antiques shops and restaurants line the main road up the hill towards the School House Inn B&B, where we were staying for the night. As its name suggests, it is a former school that has been closed since the 1930s and was converted into tourist accommodation in the late 1980s. The owner was very welcoming and talkative, and the building is full of school related items. We stayed in the Music Room, with its big comfortable bed and clunky old plumbing.

That evening we went for dinner in town and ended up in Table Ten, in the aforementioned converted department store. We shared the corner of the bar with a couple who were local farmers out celebrating their wedding anniversary. They were fifth or sixth generation Bisbee people who could trace their families back to when the town was founded, and ran a modest livestock farm outside of town that produced beef, pork, chickens and lamb. "Modest" in their terms probably means half of Somerset. They used us as a bit of a sounding board for a business idea they were looking to pursue. Copper miners were imported into the area from Cornwall way back when, and they brought the recipe for Cornish pasties with them. Our friends had been brought up eating pasties, and wanted to start producing them to sell at local markets. They were interested to find out what we knew of the Cornish pasty, and whether there was anything we could tell them about its history. What we told them backed up their knowledge, and they were delighted that we were familiar with what they were thinking. They were a lovely couple and I genuinely hope their business idea takes off. It would be nice to see a bit of Cornwall doing well again in Arizona. Maybe the recent success of the remake of *Poldark* will help, although I'm not sure the producers give the humble pasty the prominence it so richly deserves.

Previous American road trips have uncovered New Belgium Brewery's Fat Tire Ale, Deschutes' Mirror Pond Pale Ale and Dogfish Head Brewery's 60 Minute IPA, all of which are now nationally and internationally renowned. Not that we had anything to do with their respective rises to fame. The big discovery on this road trip was available at the bar of Table Ten. Old Bisbee Copper City Ale, from the Old Bisbee Brewing Company is, ironically, amber not copper coloured. At 5% ABV, it is an excellent session beer. Being hidden away in the Arizona desert may not help in any campaign for world domination, but, like our pasty-making friends, I hope it prospers.

If I remember rightly, my dinner wasn't a pasty but another excellent burger. I must say that the quality of beef burgers in America has risen at roughly the same pace and over the same timescales as that of American beer. At no point on the trip did we have a burger of disappointing, fast-food restaurant standard. But then, we didn't eat in any fast-food restaurants.

The following morning over breakfast, we met two new couples whose plans mirrored those of our eating companions from Tucson, Arizona almost exactly. One couple from Phoenix, who were roughly our age, were off on a road trip, and the other, a young couple from Albuquerque, New Mexico, were heading to Tucson, Arizona for the gem show.

We talked about the notion of the great American road trip, and what it means to Americans. The Phoenix couple were of the opinion that it was all about the sense of freedom and adventure that driving through such a vast country gives you. "We're pretty local. We've only driven into the next state," said Mr Phoenix, "but it feels like we're on a big adventure. The landscape has changed, the people have changed, even the food has changed. It's much more Mexican down here closer to the border, and we could be in a different country." They had two months available, were not cash constrained and were pootling around parts of their own country that they had never seen before, recreating their own family history.

"My great-grandparents travelled across country in the early 1900s from the East Coast, when there was nothing here," he continued. "It was a classic settlers' tale. They had nothing and had no reason to stay where they were, so they upped sticks and moved on to try and find something better. Eventually they ended up settling in a small town which was in those days still outside Phoenix. I guess the roadtrip is all about trying to recreate their journey in some way, to get a sense of what they went through." He was quite happy to admit that they were travelling in comparative luxury, but it meant a lot to him to at least do something similar to what his family had done.

The Albuquerque couple said they weren't old enough to have the same sort of hankerings, but they were sure that after a lifetime of work, they'd want to do the same thing.

Our next destination was the imaginatively named New Mexico silver-mining town of Silver City. On the way we passed through a town called Douglas, where we turned off the main road via the Business Loop just to see if there was anything of interest in the town. The top end of Main Street was as dead as a doornail, with nobody moving and only a few businesses open. However, further along the street there seemed to be a flurry of activity centred on a nondescript building. A queue had built up of people of all ages pushing and pulling shopping trolleys of differing sizes. They were shuffling slowly into the building as others were leaving, their carts filled with groceries. It took me a few moments to realise that we were looking at a food bank.

At the end of the street we came to a T-junction formed by a whacking great steel construction slicing across the road at right angles. It took me another few moments to realise that we were facing the border fence separating America from Mexico. We did a swift U-turn, and got back on the highway to Silver City.

Many of the towns we passed though on the trip to date have survived the demise of their original purpose, some better than others. At one end of the spectrum, Gila Bend is the best example of a town that appears not to have reinvented itself. At the other, Tombstone and Bisbee have embraced tourism to prosper, albeit in different ways. All of them have main streets that contain empty shops and former restaurants, where people have tried to run businesses during times when the town did not have the critical mass of residents and visitors to enable them to flourish. When the northeast of England suffered the catastrophic collapse of the coal-mining industry in the 1980s, it struggled for a number of years before embracing car manufacturing and call centres which, along with booming local universities, have resurrected the area's working culture.

Sadly, it appears that great swathes of the Southwest of America, particularly in the desert regions along the Mexican border, do not have those options. Apart from the agriculture in the Coachella Valley, the only evidence of current industry and employment we saw in this part of the country were tourism, livestock farming and the military.

Silver City suffers from this phenomenon, and has more than its fair share of empty shops and business premises. It is a pleasant, modest, grid-pattern town built, as its name suggests, on silver mining after a strike in 1870. The silver soon ran out, and the town is now heavily reliant for income on a copper mine situated 15 miles away. Silver City sits in classic "Indian Country", and has a history of a proper Wild West town. It is reputed to be the place where Billy the Kid was first arrested, and the town's museum proudly displays details of his various aliases and his mother's grave in the town cemetery.

Silver City's grid-pattern layout, which is much the same as that of almost every town and city in the country, gave it a degree of notoriety in 1895. The original design placed the main street along a natural watercourse, with the side streets running at 90 degrees to it. These channelled water into it, and during periods of heavy rain the main street would flood, turning the road into a river and damaging local businesses. The powers that be ignored the problem for a number of years, until the night of July 21st 1895, when heavy rain caused a flood that washed the entire street away, leaving a 55 ft deep channel in its stead.

The town's vacillation turned to pragmatism, and they simply shifted the main street one block over, renaming the channel "The Big Ditch" and leaving it to become a small river. It remains today as a monument to bad town planning and civic stupidity.

We stayed at the once magnificent Palace Hotel, where the parking was at the very high and waterproof kerb outside the front door, the lady on reception was lovely, the rooms were very comfortable and the breakfast was dreadful.

During a wander around a local antiques shop, we were stopped in our tracks by the sound of the saccharine song "Galway Bay" that featured in the John Wayne and Maureen O'Hara film *The Quiet Man*. Áine Two went to university in Galway, and her home-town train station is mentioned in the film.

Outside the antiques shop was a pick-up truck parked at the kerb with a dog sitting on its roof. It looked at us expectantly as we walked past, and was still there waiting patiently for its owner to return when we came back again an hour later.

Dinner and a few too many beers were had in the excellent Little Toad Creek Brewery & Distillery, seemingly the centre of the community. A lady called Tiffany Christopher was on stage, playing some great music, and what seemed like the town's entire population, including grandparents and toddlers, were eating, drinking and dancing away happily. It was a Friday night so the place was full, and halfway through the evening a local romantic young fool got down on one knee and proposed to his girlfriend, in front of everyone. He had dressed up for the occasion in his best American football shirt, and had smuggled a single red rose in under it. Thankfully, she said yes, and we all gave them a big round of applause and ordered another beer. A wander through the bar later found the happy couple with their noses buried in their mobile phones, presumably posting their good news on whatever social media site is de rigueur for their age group.

We had stationed ourselves at the bar and fell into conversation with a couple in their early thirties. She was a professional photographer and he was a lecturer in photography at a local college. She was lovely but very intense and earnest and he seemed to spend his time tip-toeing around her more robust statements. She was very open about her mental health and told us the story of how she had served in the US Army in the 1990s, and had seen active service in Somalia as part of the UN peace-keeping task force in 1993. She had been quite badly injured there and was eventually given an honourable discharge from the army on medical grounds. She returned home to Silver City and took up a photography course where, as fate would have it, she met and fell in love with the lecturer. It was impossible not to feel for a young woman who had fled a dead-end future in New Mexico to serve her country, only to return permanently damaged, both physically and mentally. I did wonder whether she might have met her husband anyway, without having to go through all of her traumas beforehand. He obviously adored her and was clearly willing to accommodate her more intense moods.

As we chatted to the photographers, a voice from the end of the bar chipped in. "What's a Scouser doing in Silver City?" it asked.

"What's a Monkey Hanger doing here too?" I replied.

"Noooo! Don't call me that around here!" came the anguished response, but it was too late. All the nearby locals had pricked up their ears and were hanging on any further talk for an explanation.

"What did you call him a Monkey Hanger for?" asked the lady photographer. I had no choice but to regale them, with more than a little glee, with the tale of how a Napoleonic war ship had reputedly been washed up on the shore near Hartlepool, on the northeast coast of England. The crew had abandoned ship and left their mascot behind: a monkey dressed in full uniform. The locals had never seen a Frenchman before and, believing the monkey to be the enemy, had hanged the poor creature. Hence, people from Hartlepool are known as Monkey Hangers, and have a very distinctive accent which identifies them as such all over the world.

The mascot of the local football team, Hartlepool United, is called H'Angus the Monkey, for several years really a chap called Stuart Drummond in a costume. Stuart stood for mayor of Hartlepool in his H'Angus costume in 2002 and was successfully elected to the post. Since then he stood as himself twice more, in 2005 and 2009, becoming the first mayor in Britain to have been elected for a third successive term.

So, not only did the town of Hartlepool hang a monkey by mistake, but they deliberately elected one as mayor not once, but three times.

Our monkey-hanging friend at the end of the bar took his medicine in good spirit and we exchanged rounds of drinks and a long chat. It turns out that he was the manager of a branch of ASDA supermarket near Hartlepool when the company was taken over by American giant Walmart in 1999. He was fed up where he was so he successfully applied for a job in a Walmart store in Nebraska, since when he has done very well, moving around where the company needs him. He is loving his life in America.

Following on from the pleasures of Old Bisbee Copper City Ale, it felt like we were beginning to hit our beer discovery stride, and the Little Toad Creek Brewery & Distillery helped by serving up some excellent beers, all brewed on the premises. The bar itself was draped with a number of local, state and national flags, including those of England, Ireland, Scotland and Wales and, bizarrely, a Burnley F.C. scarf. Nobody knew why it was there. Presumably it was presented by a passing Burnley fan one day.

A number of people had recommended that we go and see the Gila Cliff Dwellings, in the mountains above Silver City. The dwellings are caves with man-made walled entrances created by pre-Columbian Native Americans, and are protected by a National Park. We had heard that the road was a bit iffy because of recent snow, but we set off in our ill-equipped rental car to see if we could make the journey. The depth of fairly fresh snow either side of the road, and the presence of ice on it, made it obvious quite quickly that we were on a fool's errand and were putting ourselves in unnecessary peril. So we turned around and headed back down the mountain to the splendidly silly town of Truth or Consequences.

Truth or Consequences was a radio and TV game show that became a bastion of American entertainment for over 40 years. In it, contestants deliberately failed to answer a question correctly, leading to a stunt of some sort that usually ended with a tear-jerking family reunion.

For the show's tenth anniversary in 1950, and to promote its move from radio to television, its makers ran a competition to rename a town somewhere in the country after the show, and committed to holding an annual fiesta there.

Hot Springs, New Mexico, at the time a fading spa town, won the competition and was renamed Truth or Consequences in 1950. To be fair to the show's host, Ralph

Edwards, he stuck to his commitment to the town and attended the fiesta every year for the next 50 years, and it still takes place annually. Sadly, the modern-day town of Truth or Consequences has few redeeming features. There is the visitor centre for Virgin Galactic's Spaceport America, which was closed for refurbishment when we turned up, and the rather special Veterans Memorial Park, which incorporates an excellent military museum and a replica of the Vietnam Veterans Memorial Wall in Washington, D.C.

The drive from Truth or Consequences took us south through Hatch, the epicentre of world chilli (or chile) growing. Hatch chillies are prized throughout America and can be found in most Mexican meals. I'm a huge fan of curries and a good bean chilli or chilli con carne, but have always shied away from putting real chilli peppers in meals. A rather uncomfortable experience with a chicken jalfrezi in an Indian restaurant in the UK left chilli-related scars that have lasted for years.

However, chillies are considered to be just another vegetable by many Mexicans, and are included in most meals, not to add heat but to add flavour. Hatch is famous for producing all sorts of varieties of chillies, the most abundant of which is the large green, relatively mild variety of chilli pepper known as jalapeño. They are sold either raw or in jars, sliced and preserved in vinegar. Jalapeños are added to almost every meal, including breakfast, and we had omelettes or scrambled eggs with them in on a number of occasions.

Hatch is on the banks of the Rio Grande, and the road snakes south along the river through miles and miles of fields of chilli plants, like miniature vines, interspersed with the occasional stand of pecan nut trees. As we drove past field after field of little green wonders, I began to anticipate a proper chilli-related dinner that night.

Our next stop was in Las Cruces, and we were booked into the wonderful Lundeen Inn of the Arts, where we were made extremely welcome by Mrs Lundeen and her daughter. As I was unpacking a few things in the room, Áine Two went downstairs in search of a cup of tea, and didn't return for nearly an hour. During that time she had a hugely entertaining conversation with Mrs Lundeen, whose opening gambit was that she was English. Áine Two assumed that meant she was maybe second or third generation English, but she was wrong by several generations. Mrs Lundeen's Englishness came from one Barnabas Horton, who emigrated from Moseley, near Birmingham, to Long Island, New York in 1640. She felt so connected to her Englishness that she even had a little solar-powered model of the Queen that waved maniacally after being left out in the sun. That reminds me, I did promise to look out for a matching corgi for her when I got home.

As its name suggests, the Lundeen Inn of The Arts doubles as an art gallery, and its main room is packed to the rafters with paintings and sculptures from nationally and internationally renowned artists.

That evening we wandered around the downtown area of Las Cruces, looking for a likely spot for dinner. We failed to find anything, so we decamped to the small satellite village of Mesilla, a couple of miles down the road. Mesilla is a preserved Hispanic village that refused to participate in the railway boom that created its larger neighbour. Its town square contains a bandstand which celebrates the end of the Mexican–American War in 1848, and when Mesilla joined the USA in 1853. Mesilla claims to be the setting for one of Billy the Kid's murder trials, and there is a gift shop in the town named in his dubious honour.

The square is a bit of a bugger to find but it is worth the effort. It is picturesque, with a lovely brick-built church at one end, and shops and restaurants around the other three sides.

On the square is a wonderful restaurant called the Double Eagle, in which I was introduced to the full glory of the jalapeño chilli. We ate in the charmingly over-the-top covered courtyard amongst colonial architecture and potted palm trees. Lots of potted palm trees. The building also houses a fantastically ornate à la carte restaurant, with vast chandeliers and some extraordinary artwork, and is reputedly haunted by the ghosts of two murdered young lovers. Áine Two used going to the loo as an excuse to have a good nose around.

I ordered a burger accompanied by a stuffed jalapeño, only to be told by the waitress that the chilli contained cheese. She suggested I go for the unstuffed version, and what came out was superb. A large jalapeño pepper had been topped, split open down its length, de-seeded and then roasted until just soft. It was draped over a huge, succulent, cooked-just-as-I-like-it beef burger, with no other adornments, and it was a complete revelation. The depth of flavour of the chilli was like nothing I've ever tasted. The combination of delicious chilli and brilliant burger was a spicy, beefy tribute to the plant and animal from which they came, the farmers who produced them, and the chef who cooked them. I normally wolf food down but, obliged to do such a simple culinary delight justice, I took my time with every bite.

After dinner, I found in a shop on the square a chilli recipe book that contained many variations on the themes of meat or bean chillies. Since then I have sought out good jalapeños, but nothing has quite matched the legend that is the Burger of Mesilla.

Breakfast the following morning included a long conversation with a couple of retired architects from San

Francisco who were on holiday in the area. It turns out that Mr Lundeen, unfortunately absent due to illness, is also a retired architect who lectured at the local university. Our Californian friends were very disappointed not to be able to meet him. Nope, they were not Trump voters either, quietly suppressing their disappointment and rage at their country's apparent stupidity at electing him.

They knew London very well, and were deeply impressed with the sense of architectural adventure that the City had shown in recent years with buildings like The Shard, The Gherkin and The Walkie-Talkie. They also loved the irreverent way in which London names its iconic buildings. We told them that the Gherkin was officially called 30 St Mary Axe, after the medieval road on which it was situated, and that it was originally nicknamed the "Erotic Gherkin" because of its phallic shape. This caused mock shock and schoolboy sniggering in equal measure.

After recovering from the shock of discovering that the English were a childishly puerile bunch, Mrs Lundeen strongly recommended that we go and see the White Sands, and insisted that we take a pair of large plastic tea trays that she lent us. We would understand when we got there, she said mysteriously.

The White Sands National Monument is an astonishing 275-square-mile desert of white gypsum sand dunes, situated in the bed of a dried-up lake called the Tularosa Basin, in the Chihuahuan Desert of southern New Mexico. The National Monument is, in turn, a subset of the even more astonishing 3,200-square-mile White Sands Missile Range, infamous for being where the very first atom bomb was tested in 1945.

On the drive to White Sands, we had another encounter with the US Border Patrol, and this time we were stopped. Damn you, California licence plates! The armed officer in the scary shades wandered over and asked, "Where are you from, folks?" "England and Ireland," I replied as his eyes lit up. He asked us for our passports which were, of course, back at the B&B in Las Cruces. He settled for our driver's licences and took them away to be checked out. We were asked to park to one side and wait until the white smoke appeared over the little hut. We could see our man reading our details and typing them laboriously, forefinger by forefinger, into a laptop set up beside the road. He then went into the little hut for a chat with his sidekick. After five nervous minutes, Officer Two, also armed and also wearing dark glasses, wandered over. He looked me up and down and handed back our licences with a smile, a "Have a nice day, sir. Ma'am," and a polite salute.

The checkpoint was a good 50 miles from the Mexican border, but made sense when you realise it was also 50 miles or so from a significant military installation.

The drive to White Sands also took us over a mountain pass that afforded views for many miles across the southern end of the missile range. Thankfully, the atom bomb was tested at the northern end. As we drove up the very flat valley floor we eventually caught sight of the astonishingly beautiful White Sands. We turned off the main road and stopped off in the visitor's centre to pick up a map and pay our entry fee. After driving the mile or so into the middle of the dunes along a white sand road, rolled flat like driven-over snow, we selected one of the car parks. We stayed as far away as possible from the family who had drawn their three huge pickup trucks into a circle, presumably to protect their barbeque from surprise attacks. They were blasting out Mumford & Sons' current hit, just in case any of the other visitors to the silent desert wilderness had forgotten to bring their own musical accompaniment.

Much bigger than the Algodones Dunes in Southern

California, the White Sands seem to stretch for ever. They are made of incredibly fine, bright white gypsum crystals, washed down from the surrounding mountains into the lake, and then crystallised when the water evaporated.

Stories abound of people getting horribly lost in the dunes and the park ranger in the visitor's centre hands out warning leaflets, so we didn't stray too far from civilization. However, we did go far enough to get the sense of being completely alone in a desert.

I was particularly keen to see two birds that I would never get close to again: a horned lark and a roadrunner, of Wile E. Coyote fame. We saw much evidence of their tracks in the sand, but nothing of the birds that had left them.

After a picnic lunch watching a nearby family having a whale of a time bobsledding down the dunes, it became obvious to us what Mrs Lundeen's plastic tea trays were for. We dug them out of the car and had a fantastic half hour scrambling up the dunes and sliding down them again. I am very proud of our collective efforts, although I don't think either the Great Britain or Ireland Winter Olympics teams need be troubled by us.

After a day in the dunes I remembered why I'm not really a beach person. Every pocket, turn-up and seemingly inaccessible crevice was full of white sand that leaked out at the most inappropriate moments. Even the car was treated to a white undercoat. I'm glad I didn't have to explain that to the guy whose job would be to wash it off at Miami Airport in a few weeks' time.

On the way back to Las Cruces, we stopped at a viewing point at the top of the mountain pass to take a final look back across the valley, and that's when I saw it. No more than 50 feet away, standing quite still on the other side of the road, camouflaged against the brown rocks and brown bushes, was a roadrunner. I looked up cautiously, just to check there were no anvils or giant rocks falling towards us. Meep! Meep!

Back in Las Cruces that evening, we returned to Mesilla for dinner and found a local brewery called the Spotted Dog, situated in a low-rise roadside diner on the forecourt of a petrol station. We crunched our way across the floor to a table on which sat a small galvanised bucket full of unshelled peanuts, apparently provided free by the brewers. The crunching was because guests were encouraged to discard their empty shells on the floor. A couple of excellent beers and some deliciously spicy chicken wings later, and we were a happy pair of travellers.

The beer was quite strong and most of the clientele were students, so the proprietors restricted them to a maximum of four pints each. Cultural acceptance of drink driving across America meant that some people did indeed only have four pints of strong beer, and then hopped into the driving seats of their enormous pickup trucks and headed off home.

In the car park of the Spotted Dog Brewery, we came across a large, noisy member of the blackbird family called a great-tailed grackle. It was to become another constant companion on the trip.

In Las Cruces we also found our first self-confessed Trump supporter. I will afford the person the dignity of anonymity, but her reasoning for voting for Trump was, "I like the way his children have been brought up."

CHAPTER 5
TEA FOR TEXAS

The late, great country and western singer Jimmie Rodgers had a huge hit in the late 1920s with "T for Texas". Many people in Texas, like all other states in America, can't make a decent cup of tea to save their lives.

Maybe everyone stopped drinking tea after the Bostonians decided to chuck a boat load into their harbour in 1773, but most Americans simply have no idea what to do. I take my tea black, so I'm not talking about the "does the milk go in the cup first" debate either. The problem is far more fundamental than that.

As any fule kno, tea needs boiling water, and almost all American residential and commercial premises DON'T HAVE A KETTLE! Most homes and hotel rooms have coffee machines: either the simple ones that percolate hot water through a coffee bag, or the more sophisticated contraptions that force it through an expensive proprietary pod. The incorrect assumption made by many is that you can simply remove the coffee bag or pod and percolate water through the machine into a cup, drop a teabag in and Bob's your uncle. Unless the machine has been taken apart, scrubbed to within an inch of its life, and then flushed with mineral water drawn from the artesian wells of Upper Patagonia, all that method gets you is a cup of tea that tastes of coffee.

Most hotel rooms do have a microwave, but that doesn't boil water; it merely nukes it until it's quite hot and has formed a nice layer of scum on top. Plus, a microwave has no place in the tea-making process.

In bars and restaurants across the land, when you ask for a cup of tea, you are invariably handed a cup of hot water and a tea bag still in its individual paper wrapper. The water will have come from the hot (not boiling) water tap on the coffee machine behind the bar, and will have cooled further in its journey to you, before the teabag has even been immersed.

Across the South, the drink of choice is iced tea, which to any self-respecting British or Irish tea drinker is an abomination on a par with the Devil himself, or the World Series of Baseball.

To combat this apparent lack of tea-related capability, a seasoned tea-drinking traveller in America must find alternative means of obtaining a decent brew. Hence, our luggage contained a half-litre travel kettle, along with two mugs and a packet of Tetley tea bags. Small kettles such as ours are not available in America, and the main problem with my little life-saving device is that it runs on British 240 V electricity. American electricity is a weak and feeble 110 V, so the kettle takes about a week to reach boiling point. There are glib fools in this world who say patience is a virtue, and that good things come to those who wait. They've obviously never waited for a 240 V kettle to boil on a 110 V circuit.

A secondary issue is that for some reason the kettle doesn't like chlorinated tap water. According to the problem pages on the right internet sites, it reacts badly with the plastic components of the kettle and makes the tea taste rubbish. However, it works just fine with unchlorinated spring water. The tap water in America is perfectly drinkable, but we had to lug bottles of the natural stuff from shop to car to hotel room every day.

Each morning in our kettle-free hotel room, I would get up before Áine Two, carefully measure out a mug full of spring water, and then wait patiently whilst the mighty kettle struggled to come to the boil, powered only by the warm breath of an electric pixie. Only then could I make a proper brew and enjoy the best drink of the day.

Ironically, whilst all this tea-making palaver was going on, Áine Two was smugly drinking coffee, lovingly prepared by muggins here using tap water percolated through whatever machine was available in the room. Her biggest problem was whether there were enough bags, pods or sachets available to keep her sufficiently caffeined up for the day. A policy of hoovering up spares and raiding unattended hotel housekeeping trolleys kept her in emergency supplies.

Such was our daily, pre-breakfast ritual, and our last morning in Las Cruces, New Mexico was no different.

When we talked to people about our plans for driving across Texas, the general consensus was that there's nothing to see and we should get across as quickly as possible, probably on I-20 through Fort Worth and Dallas. Ever the contrarians, we took a different route, the first leg of which involved another of those epic open drives through scenery that takes one's breath away.

Many people in the UK live under the misapprehension that American motorways have a 55 mph speed limit. Actually, most of them are 70 mph, with the big boys in Texas going up to 80 mph. The other thing that a lot of people don't realise is that trucks, the big 18-wheeler *Smokey and the Bandit* jobbies, are not constrained to a lower limit than cars, like they are in the UK. This means that if you're doing something akin to the speed limit, which you are well advised to do in Texas more than anywhere else, you will probably be overtaken by some or all of the trucks on the road with you.

You may be driving at 83 mph through a vast tract of nothingness on a dead straight road, with no traffic as far as you can see ahead of you and behind you, when in your rear-view mirror you see the cab of great big truck through the shimmering heat haze. Slowly and inexorably, it gets closer and closer, like a scene from the Steven Spielberg film *Duel*, the unseen driver stalking you as he powers his huge vehicle to within a few feet of your rear bumper. Then, without breaking stride, he pulls into the outside lane, and with a cheerful PAAAARP on his horn, rumbles past you doing at least 90 mph, with his gleaming hubcaps only inches away, reflecting the terror in your face.

Some of the oddest sights available from the open roads of Texas are the occasional battered RVs, seemingly dumped in a clearing in the middle of nowhere. Most of them appear to be occupied, with an awning attached to the side and a beaten-up pick-up truck parked nearby. Some have satellite dishes attached to the roof; others have dogs lying around in the shade. Goodness knows who occupies them. It may be a mix of agricultural workers, alien watchers like our friend Coyote, or just people who have dropped out of society and wish to live the simple life. Fair play to them is what I say.

Once we had circumnavigated El Paso, it took us an entire day of driving through the vast emptiness of western Texas before we reached our overnight stop, a place called Junction which was just that: a junction on the freeway. The most notable sights on the way to Junction were a mountain that looked suspiciously like the flat-topped Ingleborough Hill in North Yorkshire, and the occasional nodding donkey pumping crude oil out of the ground.

In Junction, we stayed in the perfectly serviceable Legends Inn, part of the Americas Best Value Inns chain. It was run by a nice young couple from India, who must be wondering how they ended up in such a God-forsaken backwater. Hopefully, after a bit of hard work, their fortunes will take an upturn and they'll get a busier motel in a more prosperous town. The aroma of proper curry coming from their kitchen made me feel homesick.

We had dinner in Junction in a proper local Mexican family restaurant, appropriately called La Familia. We were served by the matriarch who bustled around the room like a mother hen. The food was good quality Mexican, laced with just the right amount of chillies, and the beer was bottled and had a slice of lime in the top. We selected La Familia largely because it was the only eatery in town with a full car park, which is normally a good indicator of popularity. It turns out that there was a meeting of the town's great and good taking place in a side room, and when it broke up it turned into a throng of happy Texan farmers and business people, greeting each other and discussing local things. Everyone wore cowboy boots, jeans and their best check shirt, and one or two even had big cowboy hats on. We sat quietly in a corner and enjoyed the spectacle.

At the next table were three locals in their early twenties. They appeared to be a couple and his sidekick from work, and they had a very young baby in a pushchair next to the table. Feeding time came around for the little one and the mother sorted herself out to breastfeed him. I looked away, not out of distaste at such a public display of family normality, but to give her some privacy. When I glanced back, the mother had draped a large bib around her neck and the nipper was tucking in in private underneath. I exist in a world that rarely includes babies, so I'd never seen such a simple and elegant way of avoiding the faux outrage that blights feeding mothers in coffee shops and restaurants across the UK. If they were introduced here, the *Daily Mail* would have one less thing to report on quiet news days.

After our night in Junction, we aimed for Austin, Texas via San Antonio and the site of that most celebrated of American battles, the Alamo.

To comprehend the reverence in which most Americans hold the Alamo, it is important to understand the context of the battle.

Texas fell out with the Mexican government and declared itself a republic in 1836. Mexican President Santa Anna put an army together to take it back.

The Alamo was actually the mission of San Antonio de Bexar, a church within a walled compound that housed clergy, a small garrison of 100 troops and approximately 300 civilians, including women and children. Reinforcements took that number up to approximately 550, led by Lieutenant Colonel William B. Travis. He was accompanied by Jim Bowie, of Bowie knife fame, and Davy Crockett, the King of the Wild Frontier.

They held out heroically against Santa Anna's 1,500 troops for 14 days, before eventually succumbing to his overwhelming force. The Texan troops were slaughtered where they stood, and the meagre few who did surrender were executed without mercy or ceremony.

America commemorates its heroic military defeats, such as the Alamo and General Custer's Last Stand, in the same way that the British do the Charge of the Light Brigade and Dunkirk.

A sarcophagus sits in the foyer of the nearby San Fernando Cathedral containing the remains of those killed in the Alamo, including the three great American heroes, Travis, Bowie and Crockett. Rather disturbingly, shortly after the battle, the remains were exhumed from their original burial places and put on public display for a whole year.

As an historic footnote, an embassy was set up in London to represent the Texas Republic during its brief period of independence between 1836 and 1846. A plaque commemorating it can be found in an alley called Pickering Place, just off St James's Street.

The remaining parts of the Alamo, including the church and much of the grounds, have pride of place in the centre of San Antonio and are the city's main tourist attraction. It is free to get in and it takes a couple of hours to do it justice, especially if you include the small museum and the extensive gift shop.

Our stop in San Antonio was only brief, but we did have a pleasant stroll through the centre of the city, including a look inside the San Fernando Cathedral and a wander past the magnificent Spanish Governor's Palace. A plaque in the city's main square lists the names of 15 families who were brought from the Canary Islands in the early 1700s to help populate San Antonio. It must be quite a badge of honour in the city for anyone who can trace their ancestry directly back to those original settlers.

In the centre of San Antonio, opposite the Alamo, is Pat O'Brien's Bar. Next to the door is an important-looking plaque that tells the reader of the pub's links with its alma mater, a legendary Irish pub of the same name in the middle of New Orleans. We took note, as we were heading that way in a few days' time.

After three weeks on the road, we pushed the boat out a bit in Austin, Texas, and booked ourselves into an apartment hotel called The Guild, on the edge of Downtown.

Our third-floor apartment had two double bedrooms, a large kitchen/diner opening onto the living room and a balcony overlooking the road below. Importantly, it also had a washing machine and dryer. We both brought two weeks' worth of clothes with us and hotels and motels with laundry facilities were few and far between, so we grabbed clothes-washing opportunities as they came.

The apartment also afforded us the chance for a bit of much-missed domesticity, and after a raid on a local supermarket I had the pleasure of cooking a student-style spaghetti Bolognese, which we scoffed, along with a couple of decent bottles of red.

For most of the first evening we were the audience for a cacophonous performance in the trees outside our window. It turns out that we were in the midst of a huge roost of thousands of great-tailed grackles that made an absolute racket until around sundown. After that they settled down for the night, with just the occasional squawk, as one of the orchestra tuned up for the following day's performance.

Austin, Texas has a similar reputation to San Diego's for being a relaxed bohemian city and, like San Diego, it also has a street dedicated to eating, drinking and entertainment. East Sixth Street has bars and restaurants liberally distributed along both sides. We were there for a relatively quiet Wednesday night but even then, some of the emptier bars were blasting out loud music, scaring away the after-work crowd who seemed to want a few beers and a chat. The fullest bars were the ones with the more moderate volume, and I can't believe that the bar owners and restaurateurs have missed that connection.

The happy hour is a nationwide American institution that many places in the UK have tried and failed to copy. From 4 pm to 7 pm on weekdays, a selection of drinks and food items from the menu are reduced in price to tempt the office worker to stop in for the proverbial pie and a pint on their way home. Bars are normally full and at their best during this period, and it is definitely the right time for a traveller to get value for money when out and about.

Why, therefore, if you are offering the same deals as other bars in the area, would you choose to blast music at your customers when they are eating their dinner with some work pals? It seems to make no sense whatsoever.

Incidentally, I believe that the reason why happy hour has never taken off in the UK is because we Brits are happy to stop for a pint anyway, regardless of the price. All the pubs in the City of London are rammed between 5 pm and 8 pm every weekday, and generally close around 9 pm when the last stragglers have gone home. They often remain closed all weekend. In cities like Liverpool, Manchester and Newcastle, people's commutes are generally shorter, and many office workers go home for their tea, before returning to the city centre if they're meeting friends. Hence pubs stay open later on week nights and don't really need a happy hour. The notion of a happy hour in a pub in Yorkshire just doesn't bear thinking about.

A sign on the door of one of the bars on East Sixth Street gave us some food for thought. It read something along the lines of, "No guns allowed on the premises, regardless of whether you have a license to carry a concealed weapon, or a license to carry a weapon openly. Guns are not allowed on the premises." Once we had seen this sign, we began to see them at the entrance to every bar and restaurant we passed.

The highlight of Austin, and its finest feature, is Lady Bird Lake. The Colorado River flows through the centre of the city and was dammed in 1960, creating a ribbon lake as a cooling pond for a nearby power station. By the 1970s, the surrounds of the lake had been neglected, to the point that they were a civic embarrassment and an eyesore. The local authorities decided it needed fixing, and roped in former President Lyndon Baines Johnson's wife, Lady Bird Johnson, to head up the efforts.

She put her heart and soul into the project, and today the lake is the centrepiece of the city's civic life. It is surrounded by walking, jogging and cycling routes, and has parks and sport fields on the south bank. People use the lake to swim, row, sail, paddle board and fish and it is a superb place for birdwatchers. We saw buffleheads on Lady Bird Lake. I like buffleheads.

In another musical reference, the late, great blues guitarist Stevie Ray Vaughan is commemorated with a life-sized statue on the shores of Lady Bird Lake. Stevie Ray was from Texas, and was tragically killed in a helicopter crash in 1990 whilst touring with Eric Clapton. It is his guitar-playing you can hear on David Bowie's hit "Let's Dance", and I was lucky enough to see him perform live in London in 1989.

One innovation that I think would work well in parks in the UK is the field on the lake shore set aside for letting dogs run free. Dog walkers are required to keep their animals on leads in all other parts of the lake's surrounds, but can let them go once they are within the clearly defined area. It seems a very social area for both dogs and their owners, and protects the rest of the public, who may not be fans of dogs, from being bothered by them. The good thing is that the civic-minded population of Austin stuck to the dog-walking rules. I'm not sure that would always be the case in the UK.

Austin is the state capital and a stroll up Congress Avenue toward Capitol Hill leads to an interesting piece of the city's history. Halfway along the avenue is a statue depicting a lady in flowing dress firing a canon. She is Angelina Eberly and her role in the story of the Texas Archive War adds another layer to the republic's already colourful past.

In 1839 the president of the Republic of Texas, the curiously named Mirabeau B. Lamar, persuaded the republic's Congress to name Austin as its new capital. The republic's archives, which had been spread around different insecure sites, were gathered together and deposited in the General Land Office on Austin's main thoroughfare.

Austin was vulnerable to attack from local Comanches, and Lamar's predecessor, Sam Houston, led a group of concerned politicians and citizens who wanted the state archive to be moved to the other city in the republic, the one that just happened to be named after him. Congress told him to stop being silly, and the archives stayed where they were.

Sam was elected president for the second time in December 1841, and declared Houston the republic's capital. His political manoeuvres to get the archives shifted to a new home there failed, so he quietly asked a couple of his pals to get on with the task of reclaiming the archives from Austin.

A group of about 20 men crept into Austin under the cover of night, and began loading the archive documents from their refuge onto three ox carts. Angelina Eberly, a local landlady, spotted them and fired off the handily placed and already loaded town canon at the General Land Office. She didn't cause much damage but the explosion alerted the city to the goings-on.

The raiding party legged it, as much as they could with three ox carts full of documents on muddy and rutted roads. They were chased down by a posse who nicked the archive back without a shot being fired, and returned it to its rightful place.

After an investigation by parliament, Houston got his wrist slapped and Austin was reaffirmed as the republic's capital. Such was the story of the Texas Archive War and how Angelina Eberly saved the day.

At the top of Congress Avenue, Capitol Hill is an impressive site. The State Capitol building sits in a lovely park that is open to the public, and when we were there it was full of parties of school kids on educational trips. On the steps of the building itself was a peaceful protest by a group of 30 or 40 people, making speeches about the disproportionate number of ethnic-minority people on remand in the state's prisons. The protesters were being watched by a handful of armed but apparently relaxed police officers.

As with many civic parks, the gardens around the State Capitol building are dotted with statues celebrating the great, good and dead of the state. These included the heroes from the Alamo and the legendary Texas Rangers. The monument that stood out for me was one to Confederate soldiers who had lost their lives in the Civil War.

So far on our travels through the Southwestern states we had seen little evidence of the Civil War, and this was the first time we'd come across anything that gave it more than a passing mention. My poor grasp of American history meant that I had no real understanding of Texas' role in the conflict, so seeing a memorial to Confederate dead was a bit of a surprise. Our travels further east, into the real Deep South, would reveal much greater detail about the causes, impact and ongoing legacy of the Civil War.

After our wander around Capitol Hill, we took a stroll through some delightful suburbs to a place where urban art, or graffiti if you want to call it that, is given a free rein. In the west end of Austin is a hill with a castle on top, called Castle Hill. A failed 1980s property development left the scars of unfinished footings and concrete walls at the base of Castle Hill, and these have been adopted by local graffiti artists as a place to practise their art. The city turns a blind eye to it, presumably on the basis that it keeps them from scrawling all over the rest of it, and occasionally whitewashes the walls to give the artists a new blank canvas with which to work.

Whilst we were watching a couple try to spray a not-very-good likeness of a cobra onto the walls, we got chatting to a family from Toronto. The husband is an IT consultant who travels around the US for his work. Over time he discovered that he could get his work done in less than half the time that his employers allowed, so he would sometimes fly his family down with him to visit interesting places. He pays for their flights and the company pays for the hotel room in which they all stay. That's not a bad gig if you can get it. "How America elected Trump is completely beyond me," he said. "The whole of Canada would be laughing its socks off if it wasn't scared to death of some of the things he might do."

Whilst I like the idea of a contained, safe environment for local street artists to practise their skills, the standard on display on the walls of Castle Hill was pretty low. Banksy it ain't.

On the walk back from Castle Hill we came across a Whole Foods Market, which is not a remarkable thing in itself, especially as the company's head office is in Austin. We wandered in to buy some dinner, and I was very impressed by what I saw. The store had a wine and craft beer bar, where the non-shopper could be parked whilst the responsible adult goes about his or her business. I was sorely tempted to throw a strop just to engineer a seat at the bar, but decided not to, partly on the basis that the look on Áine Two's face suggested she was going to beat me to it.

At the checkout, the bright and sparkly youth behind the till complemented me on my Led Zeppelin T-shirt, and didn't even make reference to them being his dad's favourite band. I liked him a lot.

As mentioned, Austin has its downtown strip of bars and restaurants on East Sixth Street. It also has a more bohemian alternative across the river on South Congress Avenue, where some very nice-looking establishments are dotted amongst the trendy clothes and antiques shops. It made for a lovely afternoon's wander and if we'd had more time in the city, I'm sure we would have spent an evening sampling a few local beers.

As it was, time had run out on us, and the next day we completed our traverse of the vastness of Texas and crossed the border into Lake Charles, Louisiana.

CHAPTER 6
LOU-EASY-ANN

Southern rockers Lynyrd Skynyrd covered Jimmie Rodgers' "T for Texas" on their 1976 live album *One More from the Road*, in my ever-so-humble opinion one of the finest live albums ever recorded, and one that is currently driving me nuts by being played in the wrong order on my iPod. They also covered "I Got the Same Old Blues" and "Call Me the

Breeze" by the late, great J.J. Cale. He wrote a beautiful song called "Lou-Easy-Ann" which contains the line "I hear you calling back to me", and I can understand why.

Louisiana is the western gateway to the Deep South, with its legendary Southern belles and Southern gentlemen and equally legendary Southern hospitality. It also has jazz and blues music, Creole and Cajun food, and an unavoidable history of cotton, slavery, segregation, lynching, civil rights and, casting a shadow over all of these, the Civil War. Bearing in mind my lack of even a basic understanding of much of American history, travelling through the Deep South was shaping up to be a real education for me.

To get to Lake Charles, our entry point for all of this future knowledge, we were obliged to drive through Houston, Texas (another double-barrelled city) via its complex set of concentric ring roads.

The inner ring road, known as The Loop, is a complete circle with a 10-mile diameter around the city centre. This is entirely surrounded by the Sam Houston Tollway, another complete circle a further 5 miles out of the city. Currently under construction is the vast Grand Parkway which, when finished, will form a third, 170-mile-long, outer ring road. The work carried out on the Grand Parkway to date has been to the west of the city, so those were the first road works we hit.

For what seemed like an eternity we crawled through heavy Houston traffic, past miles of building-works upgrading existing roads to accommodate the Grand Parkway. As we reached the main interchange we drove under vast, half-built flyovers that started and ended in mid-air, and past unfinished slip roads currently going nowhere in particular. Once we were through the Grand Parkway disruption, we hit more turmoil as we came across the upgrades to the Sam Houston Tollway, required to allow for increased traffic coming from the Grand Parkway. Again, we got through these, only to hit the bedlam that was the southern section of The Loop. To add to all of these fun and games, the Super Bowl was scheduled to take place in Houston two days later, and people were arriving in town to get warmed up in ways only Americans can. Imagine the North Circular Road around London, on a Friday night, in winter, with screaming kids and a grouchy husband. Actually, it wasn't that bad, but you get the general idea.

Having survived the ravages of Houston's ever-changing ring roads, we headed east and came across Crosby, Texas, where we turned off the road to explore, and promptly got lost. As with many such American towns, Crosby is a linear settlement principally made up of shops, restaurants and agriculture-related businesses. Its primary purpose appears to be to service the surrounding farming industry and nearby rail yards. We drove for several miles through pleasant-looking farmland until the signs for Crosby-based firms and churches ran out, at which point we realised that we'd probably missed our turning, and were in the next town north. After a bit of random redirecting on my part, we ended up on truck-laden backroads skirting the busy rail yards, until we eventually rejoined our intended route to Lake Charles. Similar to Crosby in Texas, Great Crosby in Liverpool has a Sacred Heart Catholic High School, where my education in navigation was as bad as my education in history.

Actually, we didn't go into Lake Charles, but stayed in one of two casinos situated on the banks of the wonderfully named Contraband Bayou, a canalised river that leads to the Gulf of Mexico.

In casinos in America, the money surrendered by gamblers subsidises the price of the accommodation. This makes it possible to get a very nice room for a very reasonable price. If you are able to resist the ever-present temptation to gamble, an overnight stop in a casino can be excellent value for money. Lake Charles' L'Auberge Casino Resort is a few miles out of town, but had everything we needed. There is a selection of restaurants and bars, and it's a pleasant stroll to its sister casino a couple of hundred yards downstream.

We wandered through the casino on a Friday evening to see what was going on. We passed the massed ranks of fruit machines, a few being used but most of them unattended. Some of the players were operating four or five machines at a time, spreading themselves thinly, or not, as the case may be. Each had a different system for reserving the machines and keeping them ticking over. What was interesting was that during our ten-minute stroll through this hall of homage to Lady Luck, we didn't hear a single clunking payout from the fruit machines. Disappointingly, it turns out that it's all done on an internal cash card that is preloaded by the gambler, and reloaded with any winnings by the fruit machine. I was hoping to relive my childhood visits to Southport, by wasting a pound's worth of two-pence pieces on one of those machines that pushes coins forwards until they reach a critical mass and collapse down the chute with a satisfying clatter. Can I have a go next time please, Dad?

In the middle of the room were the card, craps and roulette tables, all with a minimum bet of $25. How quickly can one go through $100 or even $1,000 without receiving a penny in return? Despite my grumpy judgmentalism, people seemed to be having a fabulous time, congratulating each other with whoops and high fives when someone's luck produced a win.

Chatting to a few of the punters afterwards, it appears that many of them save up for a few weeks or even months, and take a regular trip to the casino as part of their social calendar. They play the tables until they're bored or the cash has gone, and then blow their reserves in the bar. The general consensus is that as long as you only lose what you can afford, then nobody is hurt, and who's to say that that is wrong?

Happy hour in the bar involved half-priced drinks served at double the volume. So, for the price of a 16 oz pint you were presented with a full 32 oz glass. The beer was Yuengling, made by America's oldest brewery. All I can do is quote my wise father's punch line from a very old and long-forgotten joke, which he wheels out to describe any rank beer: "The horse is very unwell."

One feature of the bar worth remarking upon was the massive Stars and Stripes, made from painted chains, hanging from the ceiling. It must have taken someone a lot of effort to colour each link in turn and put them together in the right order. For someone like me, who prefers things in straight lines, seeing something constructed with such precision and order was very pleasing, and brought a smile to my face.

Before settling onto our barstools, we took a walk along the shore of the bayou for a bit of fresh air. On the way back we saw an extraordinary natural phenomenon that left me flabbergasted. We spotted a vast flock of what we took to be starlings, snaking its way south towards the sea in a long, slender stream. They kept coming and coming, and it took more than ten minutes for them all to pass, no more than 20 feet overhead. The following morning I sat and looked down on them from our 12th floor bedroom window, as they took a similar time to fly back upriver, presumably to their daytime feeding grounds. There must have been many hundreds of thousands of the birds, and it was a wonderful sight with which to start the day.

THE WARM BREATH OF AN ELECTRIC PIXIE

The journey from Lake Charles to New Orleans took us on bridges crossing mile after mile of bayous: slow-moving lowland waterways full of mostly cypress trees and, undoubtedly, alligators, snakes and mosquitoes by the million.

I was particularly looking forward to visiting New Orleans, and on the way encountered a word that was to become very familiar: antebellum.

Antebellum has nothing to do with elderly female relatives, small cheeses or cast-off members from the Addams Family who ended up on the clipping room floor. It means pre-war, and, as we're in the Deep South, specifically relates to the American Civil War. So, it's anything built before 1861. I had to look it up.

The towns and cities in the South are justifiably proud of their antebellum homes, and promote them at every opportunity. On our way to New Orleans we stopped off at a wonderful antebellum house called Oak Alley, the finest of Louisiana's River Road string of former plantations. It sits next to the levee for the Mississippi River, a few miles west of the city, and is a perfectly preserved example of its type. Its story is one of sugar, slavery, exploitation, family strife, bankruptcy and the tragedy of infant mortality, and is told against the backdrop of a glorious late Georgian colonial mansion, and an alley of southern live oaks that predates the house by about 100 years.

Southern live oaks are peculiar to the southeastern corner of America and appear almost everywhere, draped in mysterious shrouds of Spanish moss. They have short trunks and branches that extend horizontally for some distance, often to the point where they need propping up. If properly trained, their crowns join those of the trees opposite and they create a beautiful, shaded, tree-lined avenue. The 300-year-old southern live oaks at Oak Alley do just that, leading away from the house towards the Mississippi River, through the picket gate at the end of the garden.

Oak Alley was a sugar plantation worked by slaves, and the site is now a museum showing a sanitised version of how they and their masters lived and worked. The plantation was owned and run by Jacques Roman and his wife Celina. They had five children, two of whom died in infancy. When Jacques died in 1848, Celina started managing the plantation but nearly bankrupted it through her lack of experience and her heavy spending.

In 1859 the Romans' son Henri stepped in to try and save the estate. After the Civil War and the end of slavery laid waste to the regional economy, the plantation struggled even more and Henri sold up to pay off his mounting debts.

One remarkable member of the slave workforce at Oak Alley was Antoine, a gardener who revolutionised pecan nut growing. He successfully grafted different strains of pecan nut tree, until he came up with one that produced nuts that could be cracked by hand. Antoine made no money from his work, and lived his life out as a slave at the plantation. Upon Jacques Roman's death Antoine was listed in the estate's inventory as being worth $1,000.

Oak Alley's antebellum house was built in 1839 and is a stunning example of its type. It has many features of a Georgian house as we know them in the UK, with fan lights above the doors, small square window panes, high ceilings and wide doorways for equally wide dresses. It also has two beautiful verandas, on the ground and first floors, that reach around all four sides of the house. The views afforded down the oak alley itself when the main doors upstairs are opened onto the veranda are glorious.

The guided tour of the house gives the impression that life for the Roman family was one of wealth and opulence. It certainly was relative to that of the slaves they put to work to make them wealthy. However, life must have been very uncomfortable for men and women required to dress daily in the ludicrously impractical outfits of the day. One can only imagine the discomfort a Southern gentlewoman would have suffered wearing a corset in 40-degree heat and stifling humidity. Oak Alley's dining room even has a large fan above the table, manually operated by a slave in a role imported from British Colonial India, the punkah wallah.

Despite its beautiful setting and fantastic house, Oak Alley has a sombre atmosphere. One can only imagine how much more impressive it would be as an educational facility if the slavery aspect of its past wasn't played down quite so much.

New Orleans is famous, perhaps notorious, for many things, most recently for the nightmare of Hurricane Katrina. In August 2005, the category 5 hurricane caused devastating flooding and wind damage across the region. We were in the country at the time, travelling across the north, and watched our TV screens in horror as the long-predicted storm tore into the south coast. History shows that most of New Orleans' population was successfully evacuated, that those who couldn't or wouldn't leave were left homeless and helpless, and that the response from the authorities, from president downwards throughout the chain of command, was woefully inadequate. The fact that it wasn't until six days after the hurricane struck that President George W. Bush got off his pampered backside and flew down south to offer his support, is a direct contributor to the opprobrium in which he is held by many today.

Driving into New Orleans today, there is no visible evidence of the devastation and destruction wrought by Hurricane Katrina. That is not to say that the city has entirely recovered and that signs of damage do not exist, just that it has been cleared up around the tourist routes in and out of town. The city's population has been falling at an average of around 6% a decade since 1960. Between 2000 and 2010 it fell a staggering 29%, and it is not unreasonable to suggest that Hurricane Katrina caused roughly a quarter of the city's population to leave.

One of my pet hates is the abbreviations and acronyms given to areas of cities by their residents, or, more accurately, by the local estate agents. New York is the main offender with SoHo (South of Houston), NoHo (North of Houston), Nolita (North of Little Italy), Tribeca (Triangle Below Canal Street) and the admittedly brilliant Dumbo (Down Under the Manhattan Bridge Overpass).

New Orleans has a crappy acronym for the whole city, NOLA, which sounds like a dyslexic version of a Kinks song. It stands for New Orleans, LA (Louisiana), and can be seen throughout the city. It took me until just before we left NOLA to get over it and stop grumbling as I walked around the place.

Having said all of that, New Orleans is an uncompromisingly and unremittingly fantastic place to visit.

We stayed at the lovely Creole Gardens Guesthouse and Inn a few blocks from the Warehouse District, between the swanky Garden District and party central, the French Quarter. It is an antebellum townhouse with additional rooms in the plot behind, and had proper New Orleans jazz quietly plinky-plonking away in the background throughout the day.

The hotel wasn't fully booked, and the kindly and chatty manager took pity on two weary travellers and upgraded us to his best room, up on the first floor. Over breakfast we chatted to a local musician who, we think, was helping out at the hotel. He may have been a guest hanging around talking to all and sundry; it was difficult to say. Either way, he was studying medieval music and was putting on a performance in the city that evening. He surprised us by saying that he knew Canvey Island very well, and had spent a lot of time there working with Wilko Johnson. Wilko has the distinction of playing guitar in two of the finest rock and roll bands England has ever produced: Dr. Feelgood and Ian Dury's band, The Blockheads. Wilko was also the mute executioner, Ser Ilyn Payne, in the first two series of *Game of Thrones*: the one who looked like the bald eagle character from *The Muppets*. If you don't know Wilko's music or who the Muppets are, you are probably too young to be watching *Game of Thrones*.

We also came across a chap on our travels around the city who had been in London during the summer of 2011. He had been living with a wealthy Arab lady in an apartment on the Edgware Road, although he was unspecific about how he made his living. He told a story about how he was on the Seven Sisters Road in Tottenham when riots broke out over the death in police custody of a local man. Cars were being burned and shops looted, but he was very impressed with the way the local Turkish community managed to protect their businesses by simply standing in the doorways looking tough. I've walked the length of the Seven Sisters Road a few times on my way to and from football matches at White Hart Lane, and I can picture exactly what he described in my mind's eye. They serve great food in that part of London, but you wouldn't mess with them.

New Orleans' Warehouse District is the arty part of town, with numerous refurbished buildings converted into galleries and apartments. It has a very youthful, moneyed feel to it, and has some interesting-looking hotels, bars and restaurants for those with the cash to spare. Its main feature, and one of the standout attractions in the whole city, is the National World War II Museum.

America has a reputation for believing it won the war all by itself, and taken at face value, this museum does little to dispel that view. However, if you recognise that the museum's story of the war starts from the points in time when America joined the two arenas in which it was involved, you begin to see it differently.

The museum's two major permanent displays cover the War in the Pacific and the War in Europe, and start with Pearl Harbor and D-Day respectively. On entry we were allocated a pair of "dog tags", which were actually electronic keycards identifying real people who served in World War II, and we followed their stories throughout the war. At any given point in the war timeline we could scan the tags into machines dotted around the museum and see where these people were and what they were doing then.

My war hero was Sergeant Joe Diamond, from Camden, New Jersey. Joe joined up after Pearl Harbor and trained as a combat medic, seeing active service in Belgium and Germany. He survived the war and had a successful career as an insurance broker in New York, despite his struggles with post-traumatic stress disorder.

Áine Two's was Benjamin O. Davis Jr., the fourth African American ever to graduate from West Point. Benjamin flew with distinction for the famous Tuskegee Airmen in North Africa and Sicily, was awarded both the Silver Star and the Distinguished Flying Cross, and went on to command the 332nd Fighter Group. After the war, Davis saw out his military career, retiring as a Lieutenant General and moving into politics. His rank was upgraded to Four Star General by President Bill Clinton in 1998. Incidentally, his father, Benjamin O. Davis Sr., was the first African American general in the American military.

Both of the museum's major displays brilliantly depict America's role in the conflicts, and make for a very interesting and educational afternoon. The third display, encountered on entry, was possibly the most interesting and relevant to today's political environment. It was entitled, "State of Deception: The Power of Nazi Propaganda", and showed how weasel words were used to whip up hatred for the Jews and support for the Nazi Party in the lead up to the war. One particular poster summed up how propaganda works, and was eerily similar to some of what we have seen in both America and Europe in recent elections and referenda.

The Garden District is full of huge, fabulously well-preserved antebellum mansions, and is a favourite place for locals and tourists alike to wander around and gawp, admire and covet. Also in the Garden District is the Lafayette Cemetery, on the corner of Prytania Street and Washington Avenue, where we found the grave of William Anderton of Earnscliffe, Blundellsands, near Liverpool.

The graves in the cemetery are built above ground as stone mausoleums, to avoid bodies being washed away when the area floods. This makes the place look more like a miniature housing estate than a garden of rest. The cemetery gives the curious wanderer a fantastic insight into the history of the city, with surnames hinting at the nationalities that populated the place, and when the great waves of arrivals and deaths took place. William Anderton was a visiting merchant but his son, Edward Webster Anderton, who is also buried in the same plot, had by the time of his death emigrated from Liverpool and was living and working in Philadelphia. The Anderton family was married into the Burke family via another émigré sibling, and it is the Burkes who appear to have recently replaced the gravestone. Burke is one of Áine Two's family names from the west of Ireland.

I was one of the lucky 40,000 or so fans of Liverpool F.C. who travelled to Istanbul on May 25th 2005 to watch their miraculous comeback in the UEFA Champions League Final. After being completely outplayed for the first half hour and slumping to 3–0 down at half time, the Mighty Reds came back to draw the game 3–3, with three goals in 6 second-half minutes, and to eventually win the trophy for the fifth time in a penalty shootout. Yes, as Max Boyce would say, I was there.

It was in the Garden District, in a bar imaginatively named Tacos and Beer, that we witnessed another one of the greatest sporting resurrections of all time. The New England Patriots, one of the top NFL teams for a number of years, came to the end of the third quarter of the Super Bowl 28–3 down to the unfancied Atlanta Falcons, and the result seemed a foregone conclusion. Then came an astonishing series of plays in which the Patriots scored an amazing 25 unanswered points to draw level at 28–28 in the very last moment of normal time. In overtime, the inevitable happened and Tom Brady led the Patriots to their fifth, and his own fourth, Super Bowl victory. History will show that the game ended 34–28 to the Patriots, in the first Super Bowl to go into overtime, but that doesn't do justice to the excitement it generated.

And we watched it in an almost empty bar, amongst a largely disinterested bunch of Sunday-afternoon drinkers. The New Orleans Saints' biggest rivals are the Atlanta Falcons, so there was little local enthusiasm for them, and the Patriots are hated by most NFL fans except their own, so the lack of interest was understandable. To put it in English football terms, it would be like being in a Liverpool pub watching Chelsea play Man United in an FA Cup final.

The bartender was a Patriots fan, and was sporting a T-shirt emblazoned with their logo, but that was about as far as the enthusiasm went. Couples were arriving for a lunch of Tacos and Beer, but leaving when they realised that the bar was full of TV screens showing the game. A gent joined us at the bar at half time looking suitably depressed. He was a local Saints fan who didn't know whether to laugh or cry, and who had wandered into the bar to drown his sorrows. He had a bit of an epiphany by the end of the match, when he realised that he hated the Patriots more than he disliked the Falcons, so at least something good came out of it for him. He very generously bought us a round of drinks, possibly so that we would not leave him to drown his sorrows alone. This led to us buying a return round, and things getting a little out of hand for a quiet Sunday afternoon.

In trying to select a suitable venue to watch the Super Bowl, we had tested out an Irish bar around the corner from our B&B. The bartender was very friendly, if a little stern. She told us how the main historic districts of the city suffered mostly wind damage during Hurricane Katrina, substantial though it was, largely because they were built above sea level. It was some of the poorer districts, built below sea level, that bore the brunt of both wind and flood damage when the levees broke. She was living in the 9th Ward at the time and lost everything, but rather than leave like many of her neighbours, she relocated elsewhere in the city and carried on. "I love New Orleans and wouldn't live anywhere else."

We moved on from the Irish pub, partly because it was nearly empty and partly because a load of Canadians in the back bar were insisting on all the TVs showing curling rather than the build-up to the Super Bowl. Is curling the sport where they combine street sweeping with bowls on ice, or is it a hairdressing competition?

I've run out of things to say about New Orleans that don't involve the French Quarter and, specifically, Bourbon Street, so maybe it's time to address the elephant in the city.

Canal Street is New Orleans' main shopping district, and it separates the Warehouse District from the French Quarter. Bourbon Street leads directly off it at right angles. First impressions of Bourbon Street, even when it is just warming up on a Friday afternoon, are that you are walking through the gates of Hell itself. If they were in Bourbon Street, Ghiberti's Gates of Paradise would be melted down and exchanged for beer and bad things. It is long and narrow and lined with clubs, bars and tourist gift shops, many boasting live bands and "huge ass beers". It is legal to drink openly in the street in New Orleans, as long as the beverage is in a plastic container. Much of the huge ass-ness comes in the form of novelty drinking vessels shaped variously as hand grenades, yards of ale, AK47s and three-pint bottles of beer. The sight of the best of American youth parading their drunken selves is something to behold.

It is a complete myth that American youngsters are somehow worse at holding their drink than their British counterparts. They are louder and more boisterous perhaps, but their politeness and respect for authority is normally so well ingrained that they apologise when they ricochet off you, and still call you "Sir" if you have a quiet word. Many drunk Brits of that age sing football songs, fight and vomit. At least that's what the *Daily Mail* would have you believe.

Almost all of the bars along Bourbon Street have balconies occupied by drinkers who will throw a string of beads down to any girl prepared to flash her assets for cheap reward. We spent a very happy hour on one such balcony, chatting to a married couple of guys from Fort Lauderdale who were in the city for their first wedding anniversary. One was originally from a farming town north of Dublin who divorced his wife, came out, grew a big moustache and decamped (or upcamped rather) to Florida. We watched together as a group of drunken locals next to us successfully cajoled several girls to display their wares for a string of worthless baubles. You can buy huge bags full of strings of beads for about $20 from the local shops, and many go armed with them in the hope of a successful day. It is funny to watch, especially over a few beers, and bearing in mind what goes on in Liverpool most weekends, I shouldn't be too snotty about it. "I haven't seen so many boobs in 30 years," one of our drinking companions commented.

We chatted at length about being gay in modern-day America, and how it had been a battle to have gay marriages legalised in each state. Rory, the American, had retired to Florida for the relaxed lifestyle and warm weather. He met John, the Irishman, when he came over to Orlando for a holiday, and they carried out a transatlantic relationship until John's papers came through. They now live in a very safe and comfortable gated community in the outskirts of Orlando, where they are left alone to live their lives as they please. Apparently, the Dublin contingent caused a sensation by drinking the town dry when they came over for the wedding.

The subject of Donald Trump did come up, resulting in some unprintable comments that equate, in British terms, to two raised fingers and a very loud raspberry.

The music in the bars on Bourbon Street is very good quality, especially if you visit some of the proper New Orleans jazz bars. These are less like the ultra-serious Beat Generation jazz fans that John Thomson lampooned on *The Fast Show* ("Nice!"), and more of the lust-for-life swinging jazz that Louis Armstrong delivered so spectacularly. There is a park on the edge of the city centre dedicated to Satchmo that contains a wonderful statue of the great man, and a concert theatre that seems to have seen better days.

All of the bars play the music at the right volume, at the right times of day and for the right reasons. Mr Gobshite and Austin, Texas take note.

I must admit at this point to being an ageing heavy-rock fan. My T-shirt collection for the trip contained such masterpieces as two Lynyrd Skynyrd shirts, two AC/DC shirts, a Led Zeppelin shirt and two rather splendid Hawkwind shirts. My pride and joy was a Motörhead T-shirt of the classic "Motörhead, England" design. If you know Motörhead you know the one I'm talking about. Lemmy, the infamous lead singer and bassist from the band, died of brain cancer on December 28th 2015. He set up Motörhead in 1975 after being kicked out of Hawkwind for being caught for possession of drugs in Canada. I think it was the being caught bit that was the problem, bearing in mind that possession of drugs appeared to be a mandatory requirement for members of Hawkwind at the time. After a fantastically hedonistic and gloriously rock 'n' roll life, Lemmy died at the age of 70, still the leader of one of the loudest and longest-lasting rock and roll bands of all time.

All my musical T-shirts generated comments of one sort or another throughout the trip, but the Motörhead T-shirt received the most, and many of them came in New Orleans. Sitting in a bar enjoying a lunchtime pint, listening to some jazz, a chap caught my eye across the crowded room, stood up and said, "We lost Lemmy this year, God rest his soul," whilst making the sign of the cross.

On another occasion as we crossed Bourbon Street, a lady sidled up to me and told me conspiratorially how much she loved Lemmy. "He was a charming man. I used to hang out with him at the Rainbow Bar in LA."

My favourite Motörhead T-shirt encounters in New Orleans happened in very quick succession. We managed to find a seat in the famous Fritzel's European Jazz Pub, in the corner next to the band. I was a little concerned that a rock and roll T-shirt like mine might get short shrift in such an august setting. During a break in the music I nipped to the gents where the drummer gave me a "Nice T-shirt, man" comment. On the way back into the bar, I received exactly the same compliment from the trumpeter, who was enjoying a cigarette in the backyard.

Bourbon Street also features young buskers, tap dancing or playing upturned buckets and bins as though they are drums. The level of talent is variable but at least they are giving it a go, and maybe one day one of them will be talent-spotted and given a break. I'm sure access to the busking pitches is fiercely controlled and expensive, but hopefully the kids make more than a few dollars from their efforts.

We did come across the original New Orleans version of the Pat O'Brien Irish pub we found in San Antonio. It was big and busy, and had a pleasant courtyard at the back with a multi-coloured fountain and bustling staff serving strange cocktails. The speciality in the pub was a Hurricane, not named after Hurricane Katrina as many might think, but after the glass, shaped like a hurricane lamp, in which it was originally served. Apparently it is a rum-based fruit cocktail, made to a special Pat O'Brien recipe. We had a beer each and watched the world go by.

Thankfully, New Orleans' French Quarter consists of much more than just Bourbon Street. Frenchmen Street, a little further north, is where the locals go to see some great live music without being disturbed by the hordes of tourists. It was on our way back from there that we settled onto two stools at the inviting-looking bar of the Golden Lantern on Royal Street, for a quiet beer or two away from the hurly burly. After a few minutes, it became apparent that there was some sort of cabaret going on in an adjoining room, and that the performances were being relayed back into the bar on big TV screens. Not that anyone was paying it much attention. A little further scrutiny revealed that the cabaret performers were all drag acts, and that they were performing to each other. They were taking it in turns to disappear behind a curtain and emerge in full regalia to perform their act to either whoops and cheers or catcalls and jeers. Each act rejoined the audience once they'd finished, until it was their turn to go around again. A little more in-depth watching showed that all the acts were lip-synching to a series of very camp dance tunes. The bar was great and the atmosphere very friendly, and we bounced off a few walls as we wandered back along Bourbon Street, by this time fitting in better amongst the younger drunks. Disappointingly, nobody offered to throw me any beads.

The streets of the French Quarter that surround Bourbon Street contain a fantastic array of post- and antebellum architecture, including some fabulous shops and restaurants. We ate wonderful local Creole food in a touristy restaurant where the service was made dreadful by a waiter who seemed to think that perpetual motion was the equivalent of efficiency.

The fantastic po' boy sandwich is a feature of New Orleans cuisine. It consists of a short baguette, made from an American interpretation of traditional French bread, stuffed full of delicious things like oysters, crawfish tails, blackened prawns or pulled pork. They are called po' boys because they were reputedly invented as a cheap means of feeding striking streetcar drivers in the 1920s and, boy, are they good.

Another attraction in the French Quarter is Jackson Square, named after former US president Andrew Jackson. A wander around on a sunny spring Sunday morning revealed a proper New Orleans jazz band busking with all the traditional tunes. They were attracting large crowds and being well rewarded for their efforts.

THE WARM BREATH OF AN ELECTRIC PIXIE

Also on Jackson Square were a line of four youths – I'll be charitable and call them pretentious twerps – sitting in a line with typewriters set up in front of them. They were charging gullible tourists a few dollars a go to write a short poem around a subject suggested by the mug punter. I suppose you're not that much of a twerp if you can get paid $10 for 30 seconds' worth of typing.

The square leads down to the mighty Mississippi River, where the paddle-steamer *Natchez* plies her trade, giving tourists rides up and down the river. If I wasn't hideously prone to seasickness, I'd say the *Natchez* was a better way to spend your money than on a piece of speedily knocked together poetry.

And it was up the Mississippi to the famously antebellum town of Natchez that we travelled next, leaving New Orleans to recover from its weekend's festivities, and carry on preparing for the forthcoming Mardi Gras superparty.

Before we leave New Orleans, however, I'd like to mention two signs that caught my attention and made me smile. A lovely-looking antebellum home in the French Quarter was up for sale and was being advertised by the real-estate agent with a sign that reassured prospective buyers that the house was "not haunted". Similarly, a house in the Garden District was being worked upon by a firm called "Jesus Is Lord Plumbing Company".

I loved New Orleans, and would go back in a heartbeat, if only I could be assured that it wouldn't be the cause of my last one.

CHAPTER 7
MISSISSIPPI DELTA BLUES

THE WARM BREATH OF AN ELECTRIC PIXIE

For 74 gloriously independent days in 1810, St. Francisville, Louisiana, had the distinction of being the capital of the Republic of West Florida. The events that led up to the formation of this short-lived republic are typical of the politics of the time, and how they shaped America.

Up to 1762, the southern part of America was divided into three territories. Spain owned the bit from the Californian coast to the western border with Louisiana, plus Florida to the east, and the French owned La Louisiane, the bit in between.

The end of the French and Indian War saw France give Spain the western half of La Louisiane, including New Orleans. A year later, in 1763, as a result of Great Britain winning the Seven Years' War, Spain gave us the other half and all of Florida.

So, by this point France was out of the picture and Spain owned everything across the South from California to New Orleans, and Great Britain owned everything east of that to the Florida coast.

Spain was given control of all of it at the end of the American War of Independence in 1783, as a reward for its support of America against the British. However, in 1800, after Napoleon's successes in Europe, Spain gave what had become known as Louisiana back to France.

In 1803, America paid $15 million for all of France's land up to the Canadian border, including Louisiana, in what became known as the Louisiana Purchase.

So, by this point Spain owned everything across the South except modern-day Louisiana, which the Americans owned. I hope you're following all this.

The poor burghers of West Florida didn't know which end was up. They had been swapped like political pawns for the previous 50 years, and were, by now, fed up with Spanish rule. They were mostly made up of immigrant Belfast

Protestants, known as the Scots-Irish, and a few other Brits who had sneaked over the poorly managed Florida border into Spanish territory. In September 1810, they successfully stormed the fort at Baton Rouge and hoisted their new flag over it, declaring it the Republic of West Florida. Ever the ambitious lot, the newly independent West Floridians decided to expand their republic before anyone noticed them, and marched on Mobile, Alabama. Unfortunately for them they overstretched themselves and were unsuccessful, retreating into their original territory.

By now President Madison's nose (he of Square Gardens fame) was firmly out of joint, and he took the opportunity afforded by West Florida's uppity behaviour to seize the land for America, in whose hands it remains to this day.

St. Francisville is an astonishingly pretty little antebellum town overlooking the Mississippi River, and many of its houses commemorate their fleeting taste of independence by flying the flag of the Republic of West Florida. The flag is a simple blue pennant with a single white star in the centre, and is known as the Bonnie Blue. It was used by the Confederate Army during the Civil War, and even has a marching song named after it. The lyricist was an Ulster Protestant called Harry McCarthy. Sadly, but not surprisingly given its Confederate associations, the Bonnie Blue has since been appropriated by far-right groups in the South.

We stopped at the charming West Feliciana Historical Society Museum and tourist information office, where we picked up a walking-tour map that took us past many beautifully preserved properties. After eating a delicious lunch at the Magnolia Café, which doubles as a local live music venue in the evenings, we moved on.

John James Audubon spent much of his life painting and documenting birds in America. He published his masterwork, *The Birds of America*, between 1827 and 1838, and the American equivalent of the RSPB, the Audubon Society, is named after him. He was an immensely important contributor to the documentation of America's natural history, and he spent the summer of 1821 at the Oakley Plantation House, just outside St. Francisville. The town exploits this mercilessly, and very profitably.

Natchez, Mississippi is a strategically important port on the Mississippi River, north of New Orleans and St. Francisville. The Lower Mississippi Valley is perfect cotton- and sugarcane-growing country, and Natchez became the centre for trade and export of these products downriver to New Orleans and the wider world.

Nowadays Natchez is little more than an attractive tourist destination, trading on its renowned antebellum houses, many of which are showing their age and could do with a lick of paint. We stayed in the very lovely Starling's Rest B&B, which sits just above the town on a bluff overlooking the Mississippi River. The views along the river from outside the B&B were sensational, especially when the sun set and burnished the sky in a glorious orange.

The owner of the B&B is charming and friendly, and gave us lots of her time. She is a big fan of Madchester-era Mancunian music, and became quite defensive when I suggested that a few of the Merseybeat bands might give them a run for their money.

Our hostess told us about how she and her husband had bought the house to live in, but its constant need of repairs had caused it to become a bit of an expensive millstone around their necks. They had decided to open the house as a B&B to make it pay for itself. I'm so glad they did, as it is a wonderful place to stay. We slept in a four-poster bed in a beautifully appointed room, and felt like we were in the lap of luxury.

The landlady also has a dangerous selection of fiery chilli sauces in her kitchen that guests are welcome to sample and pass comment upon. Post-it notes hang from every vertical surface, with heated exclamations and scores out of ten.

Our fellow guests were a couple from the Netherlands who had recently landed in New Orleans and were on their own road trip. They had hired one of America's great muscle cars, a Dodge Challenger, without thinking about the practicalities of travelling in a two-seater car with limited boot space. It was mildly amusing watching them trying to squeeze their large and very solid suitcase into the small gap behind the passenger's seat.

As it was Monday night and much of the town was closed, we had limited choices for dinner, and ended up eating in an extraordinary local place called The Pig Out Inn Barbeque. It was an unprepossessing takeout burger and ribs joint, with plastic table tops and paper plates, and it served some of the best ribs I have ever eaten. They were huge, smoky slabs of delight, in a homemade barbeque sauce that the owners describe as Pig Out Heaven, and who am I to disagree?

Natchez is the starting point of the Natchez Trace, an ancient track originally used by Native Americans, and adopted by European settlers to get from the Lower Mississippi Valley upriver to Nashville.

In the early days of trading, boatmen on the Mississippi used flat-bottomed barges to ferry goods downriver to Natchez, using the river's southerly flow to power them. The barges were too big to be transported back upstream, so they were abandoned in Natchez and the bargees walked back upriver along the Natchez Trace.

Nowadays, the Natchez Trace Parkway follows the original route, wending its way north through stunningly beautiful hills and woodlands. Similar to the Big Sur coastal road, the parkway was built by the Civilian Conservation Corps using funds provided by President Franklin D. Roosevelt to alleviate unemployment during the Great Depression. Speed is limited to 50 mph, which means that progress is stately but civilised, and gives you many opportunities to pause and enjoy the scenery.

Our first stopping-off point was the Old Trace Exhibit Shelter, just southwest of the Brandon Hall Plantation. Wandering around, we came upon a heartbreaking little cemetery, surrounded by wrought iron railings. Inside were a number of graves that told the tragic story of a generation of the Brandon family, once owners of the hall. Charlotte and Gerard Brandon married in 1840 and had a total of 12 children, eight of whom are buried in this little graveyard. Their ages at death were 11 months, 4 years, 11 months, 18 years, 11 years, 11 years, 5 years, and 37 years. Three of them, two of whom were twin sisters, died in 1862. The Brandons lived in a small, three-roomed cottage on Charlotte's father's land until the hall was built in 1856, by which time they had already lost three of their children. Thankfully, five of their offspring lived to adulthood and had a multitude of grandchildren for Charlotte and Gerard to dote upon.

Further up the Natchez Trace Parkway, we came across the Emerald Mound, a large, flat-topped ceremonial hill built by Native Americans between the 13th and 17th centuries. It is part of the Mississippi Mound Trail, a network of archaeological sites along the Mississippi Delta, and provides fantastic views across the local tree tops. It was completely deserted when we visited, and we sat enjoying the peace and quiet for half an hour.

Afterwards, we wended our happy way up the Parkway, until hunger struck and we stopped at Port Gibson for some lunch. The town only retains its antebellum status because

Union General Ulysses S. Grant decided it was "too beautiful to burn" after a Civil War battle held near the town in 1863. Nowadays Port Gibson has very little to recommend itself to the casual visitor, apart from the extraordinary finial that tops off the spire of the First Presbyterian Church (a.k.a. the Church with the Golden Hand). As the alternative name suggests, on top of the spire there is a golden hand pointing directly to heaven.

We left the wonderful Natchez Trace Parkway at Port Gibson and made for our overnight stop in Vicksburg, another antebellum town of note, and site of one of the best-preserved Civil War battlefields in the country.

Our digs for the night were at The Duff Green Mansion B&B, which is just as described: a whacking great mansion near the edge of town. And yes, it is antebellum, in case you are wondering.

The mansion is neither duff nor green; Duff Green was the name of chap who built it in 1856. It is a very handsome three-storey home, with verandas all round and magnificently presented rooms throughout. Over breakfast we met a lovely 30-something Goth couple who were on their honeymoon and loved staying in a place so atmospheric. "He's into those 1950s horror films," the newly married lady told us, "and this place reminded him of them so we had to stay here. It's really great, and a bit spooky late at night." I did wonder if they had heard of the mansion's reputation as one of the most haunted places in Vicksburg.

Also at the table were a pair of proper elderly Southern belles, from Texas, who were away together for a few days. Once we had sat down, introduced ourselves, and asked the manager for a cup of tea, one of the Texan ladies addressed a question to me. "So, tell me dear," she began, which caused me to freeze. That is exactly the expression my late mother used when she was about to ask one of her disingenuous questions about the state of my love life or finances. "So, tell me dear, does a cup of tea really solve every problem?" She seemed very happy when I told her it did. I asked her where she got that impression from and she told me that she was an avid watcher of both *Coronation Street* and *EastEnders*, and was curious as to why the first response to every crisis was to make a cup of tea. Now she knows.

Breakfast itself was three courses, with mixed fruits followed by hominy grits and biscuits, followed in turn by pecan pie. I do like the nutty syrupiness of a good pecan pie.

Grits, in case you are wondering, are corn porridge, and are the least appetising thing known to man. Think 1970s school-dinners semolina, without either the sweetness or the raspberry jam that you mixed in to make it go pink. They are widely consumed across the Southern states, normally as breakfast, but sometimes for other meals. Biscuits are scones that haven't risen, and look like they could double as a caster cup or an ice hockey puck. Biscuits are also served with sausage gravy, which is a hideous-looking, flour-based sauce made from goodness knows what. I may be being grossly unfair to some splendid Southern cuisine, particularly as I never did pluck up the courage to try any of them. The hominy grits happened to contain cheese, which gave me the perfect excuse to cop out of trying them.

The caretaker-cum-manager of The Duff Green Mansion is justifiably very proud of his place of work, and took great pleasure in giving us a guided tour after breakfast. During the Civil War, General Grant laid siege to Vicksburg and bombarded the town mercilessly. Duff Green had the bright idea of turning his mansion into a hospital, thus persuading the Union Army to redirect their guns away from the area. One cannonball did hit the mansion, and there remains a hole in an upstairs ceiling and rafter showing where it struck. Thankfully it wasn't explosive, otherwise the mansion would no longer be standing.

The manager did give us a different perspective on the causes of the Civil War. Popular belief is that it was about the right of states to self-determination, which is a way of dressing up the Southern pro-slavery argument against the federal North's imposition of its policy of freedom for all. According to the manager, however, "Nine out of ten Southern men didn't own slaves, so they stood to gain nothing from secession from the Union. But they were prepared to fight to prevent Yankee soldiers from invading their homes and land." It's a Southern view that I'd not heard before, but have subsequently come to understand to carry some weight.

Vicksburg is a pleasant town, although, like Natchez, it has to rely heavily on tourism to keep it afloat, and it could do with a bit of a scrub. There is a Coca-Cola bottling museum behind the old Biedenharn Candy Co. store that lays claim to being where Coke was bottled for the first time, in 1894. There is also the excellent USS *Cairo* Museum, where the resurrected hulk of an ironclad Civil War gunboat can be seen, along with some of the items that were dug up with it.

Vicksburg's main asset is the Vicksburg National Military Park, a superbly well-presented Civil War battlefield, dotted with memorials to the divisions of both the Union and Confederate armies that fought there. You can drive yourself around the site, or hire a docent from the Visitor Center who will drive your car around for you. He or she will stop at all the interesting places, and give you a running commentary of how the battle progressed.

The drive around the battlefield gives you a sense of not

only how close the two sides were to each other, but also how much digging and preparation were involved. Early Civil War battles used War of Independence fighting methods, but with more modern equipment. This led to almost hand-to-hand combat with accurate, fast-repeating rifles, and resulted in hideous slaughter. By the time of the Battle of Vicksburg in 1863, both sides had reverted to trench warfare, which prolonged the fighting but cost fewer lives.

After our battlefield tour, we ate dinner in the excellent Monsour's at The Biscuit Company, a restaurant and blues bar in the middle of town. Thankfully, there were no biscuits involved.

Since we were approaching Mississippi Delta blues country, we were hoping for some good music, and we were not disappointed, although its source was not what we expected.

Parking ourselves at the bar as usual, we ordered a couple of local beers and tucked into a delicious burger and some very good blackened shrimps. The whispers coming from the bar were that the band for the night was a blues trio from Germany that had won a national competition to play a series of gigs in the area. A couple of locals were busy setting up microphones and speakers and fretting over how they would communicate with the band members. They had even gone to the trouble of preparing some phrases on Google Translate, so that they could be as helpful as possible.

The band arrived and, being German, spoke excellent English. They were delighted and very grateful that their hosts had gone to so much trouble to make them feel welcome. Fine Southern hospitality is a reputation well earned.

The band themselves were what you would politely call groundbreaking. They consisted of an excellent young lead guitarist, and an older singer and bass guitarist in the more traditional blues musician mould: middle-aged and portly. The third member of the band provided the beat, in the same way as the busker on Santa Monica Pier, using his voice to imitate an electronic drum machine. The singer led his young charges through a hugely entertaining set of traditional and modern blues. The locals seemed to love it, and everyone kept drinking and applauding, so the bar owner was happy too.

About 90 miles north of Vicksburg is another of the Mississippi Mounds, similar to the Emerald Mound we came across on the Natchez Trace Parkway. Winterville is actually made up of 23 mounds within a 30-acre site, and is believed to be a major political and religious centre for the local Natchez people. The site has been drained and sympathetically landscaped, and the mounds can be clearly seen from the road. For a modest entrance fee you can visit the small museum and wander the site, enjoying the mystical atmosphere and wondering why the mounds were built quite so close to a main road.

The journey north of Vicksburg took us through what one might call stereotypical Mississippi blues country, although that suggests a deliberate effort to make it look the way it does, which I'm certain is not the case.

Similar to our drive through the Coachella Valley in Southern California, the road crosses flat, very rich agricultural land, knitted together by very poor settlements. Roadside houses lack romantic white picket fences, and are surrounded by the detritus of day-to-day life strewn carelessly about. Abandoned pushchairs lie next to children's bikes, broken-down cars, satellite dishes and shattered furniture. Elderly folk sit on rocking chairs on front porches, passing the time of day. The main streets of the towns have few viable businesses, and exist only as truck stops or historical artefacts. Lack of opportunity creates a seemingly unbreakable cycle of poverty that traps people and gives them little hope of escape. You can see why the blues originated in this area.

The road on which we were driving north from New Orleans is Highway 61, the one that Bob Dylan so famously revisited in 1965. Clarksdale sits at the junction between Highways 61 and 49, purportedly the crossroads where legendary blues guitarist Robert Johnson sold his soul to the Devil in return for his musical skills. Robert Plant and Jimmy Page from the greatest blues rock band of them all, Led Zeppelin, got back together in 1998 to create the excellent album *Walking into Clarksdale*.

Clarksdale is the acknowledged home of the blues, and a town that embodies the challenges that communities in the Mississippi Delta face. It is world famous for producing some of the greatest blues musicians of all time, and the roll call of musical alumni who were born or worked here is astonishing: Sam Cooke, John Lee Hooker, Ike Turner, Robert Johnson, Muddy Waters, Howlin' Wolf, W.C. Handy; and these are just the ones that you and I have heard of. The fantastic Delta Blues Museum, founded by the local library, features a cavalcade of local blues musicians, virtually unknown outside of the area, who would knock the socks off most modern-day Johnnie-B.-Goode-come-latelies.

Clarksdale itself is not quite on its uppers but it's not on the up either. A few businesses in downtown seem to be doing well, but others have closed, and there are too many boarded-up shops and bars to make it feel like a place to hang out and enjoy the music scene. Like many American towns, the exodus of businesses to cheaper land on the outskirts has shifted the emphasis from stopping to passing by, and destroyed any sense that the town centre and its community is worth preserving. Clarksdale is justifiably famous for its juke joints, where authentic blues is played by genuine stars of the genre, but there aren't many in evidence on the main streets for tourists to wander into.

Admittedly, we were in town midweek and, as most local blues musicians are amateurs who have day jobs, we may have missed the best bits that occur at weekends.

The Ground Zero Blues Club is situated next door to the Delta Blues Museum, and works in partnership with it to provide a venue for tourists to enjoy some authentic blues without stumbling off the beaten track. One of its owners is actor Morgan Freeman.

Clarksdale does host a number of annual blues festivals that attract large numbers of visitors, and such stellar performers as Robert Plant. They keep the town going, and I would love to spend time at one, enjoying the music and drinking a beer or two.

One shining light in the town centre provided us with another hearty American breakfast. From our table, the Yazoo Pass Espresso Bar, Bistro and Bakery looked like the epicentre of the community, with all sorts of people wandering in and meeting and greeting each other.

Further up the Mississippi, through more of the poverty-addled flatlands of the Delta, is Memphis, Tennessee, the home of great music and the best nightlife we had seen so far on the road trip.

Memphis is very similar to Liverpool. Both cities are important ports on world-famous rivers; both made their fortunes on the backs of slaves and cotton; both suffered economic deprivation on a devastating scale, precipitated by war; both engineered civic recovery via their musical heritage; and both still have some fairly dodgy-looking suburbs.

THE WARM BREATH OF AN ELECTRIC PIXIE

Where Liverpool has The Beatles and all things Merseybeat, Memphis has Elvis Presley, Sun Records and the Stax Recording Studio.

When Áine Two first came with me to Liverpool in 1990 the city was still very much on its knees. A combination of militant left-wing politics, central government neglect, trade with Europe rather than America and the recent Heysel Stadium and Hillsborough football disasters had left the city reeling. Unemployment was in excess of 20% and youth unemployment substantially higher. The only things the city had going for it were its people, The Beatles and the two top football clubs in the country. At the time the city authorities were only just waking up to the possibilities that being the home of the world's greatest pop group created.

The Cavern Club, where it all started, had only recently been rebuilt after having been demolished in the 1970s for a train station that never materialised. Mathew Street itself was a dingy backstreet with a few even dingier nightclubs. The former homes of the Fab Four were ordinary residential houses, not yet the places of pilgrimage that they are now, and the city had a coolness to its own musical heritage that bordered on disdain. Nowadays there are Beatles museums, Beatles bus tours, Beatles taxi rides, Beatles hotels, Beatles shops, Beatles statues and Beatles tribute acts. The city couldn't be doing much more to milk the band's links, other than putting Paul and Ringo behind glass in Lime Street Station and charging £10 a time for Japanese tourists to come and pay homage. The other great Merseybeat acts of the era such as Gerry and the Pacemakers, The Searchers and Cilla Black also get the occasional mention.

The parallels, therefore, with Memphis and its relationship with its musical history are there for all to see. The world-famous Sun Studio, where Elvis made his first-ever recording, had been a car-parts shop throughout the 1970s and early 1980s and only reopened for recording and tours in 1987. The Stax Recording Studio, where the likes of Otis Redding, Wilson Pickett and Sam & Dave all recorded, was demolished in 1989, only to be rebuilt on the same site and opened as a museum 14 years later.

Only Graceland, Elvis' home on the outskirts of the city, made an effort early on, opening in 1982, and it was to Graceland that we headed first for our musical education.

Much of the infrastructure for the Graceland experience, including the box office, restaurants, car museum, private planes, gift shops and other opportunities to squeeze every last dollar out of you, are on the opposite side of the main road from the house itself. After paying the whopping $80 each for the VIP experience, we were loaded onto a bus for the short journey through the famous musical gates to Elvis' home.

Elvis bought Graceland in 1957 when he was only 22, moving his parents in before he had done so himself. He lived there with his family until he died at the age of 42. What struck me about the house was that it wasn't a vast, ostentatious, secluded rock star mansion, but a modest-sized family home with a small garden and a low front wall. It has a reputation for being an icon of 1970s bad taste and the interior design is certainly of its time, but it's hardly the eyesore of clashing colours that some would have you believe.

Another thing that struck me about Graceland was how lonely Elvis must have been living there. I think it was John Lennon who said that the rock star life was tough enough for the four Beatles, but at least they had their three band mates around them who really understood the pressures. Elvis had nobody to turn to in his close circle that was going through the same things as him, and who could properly relate to life as a global icon.

If you watch some of his early interviews, Elvis was a shy, polite, well-brought-up young man who giggled coyly and answered questions with, "Yes, sir" and "No, sir". He didn't have that jokey Scouse self-confidence that characterised The Beatles' public image. He was cooped up in Graceland, hemmed in by fans and the press, bored mindless, watching endless chat shows on the multitude of TVs in every room, amusing himself by racing golf carts and tiny cars around the garden. Apparently he used to wander down to the front gate occasionally to greet some of the fans who were a constant presence there, just to relieve the boredom. He was a humble country boy with endless wealth, and a host of hangers-on to spend it for him.

Having said all of that, visiting Graceland was a really uplifting experience. The house is lovely, and the constant accompaniment of brilliant songs performed in a voice of velvet whilst you marvel at the array of memorabilia on display will cheer up even the darkest of souls. Graceland isn't cheap but it is well worth the money if you are a fan of any music, not just Elvis.

Incidentally, there is even a tenuous Liverpool connection in Elvis' back garden. As you approach his grave on your self-guided tour, your headphones begin to play his version of You'll Never Walk Alone from the musical *Carousel*. This is the world-famous anthem of Liverpool FC, and has been heard being belted out in football stadia all around the world.

The two rooms of Sun Studio are tiny by comparison, but perhaps have even more historical significance than Graceland. Blues musicians such as B.B. King and Howlin' Wolf recorded there, and in 1953 Elvis wandered in off the street and recorded a demo for his mother. A few self-funded efforts later and the studio owner, Sam Phillips, realised he might have something special on his hands. He roped in two local musicians, Scotty Moore and Bill Black, and gave Elvis his first proper recording session, during which he recorded his first single, "That's All Right".

The Sun Studio tour takes you through a small museum of early recording equipment and memorabilia from the genesis of rock and roll and, eventually, into the studio itself. After an excellent talk from the tour guide, you get to stand on the very spot where Elvis recorded "That's All Right" and do silly poses with an authentic period microphone. It made me a very happy little rock and roller.

Sun Studio's other claim to fame is as the place where the Million Dollar Quartet had a jam session. Elvis, by then the new big thing in American entertainment, wandered into his favourite studio just as Carl Perkins and Jerry Lee Lewis were doing some recording. Country and western's Man in Black, Johnny Cash, was also there, hanging around, like you do.

The four musicians sat around the piano and began to chat and jam together, whilst producer and engineer "Cowboy" Jack Clement surreptitiously recorded everything. Sam Phillips tipped off a local press photographer who arrived and took the iconic photograph that now hangs in pride of place on the studio wall. The session lasted for about three hours but, for licensing and legal reasons, the recording is unusable and has never been released in full. Can you imagine how fascinating it would be to hear, not to mention how much it would be worth?

Incidentally, Carl Perkins is the person in the photograph that most people can't identify. He wrote and had a minor hit in 1955 with a little ditty called "Blue Suede Shoes", recorded and turned into a smash hit a few months later by Elvis himself.

Unfortunately, the Stax Museum of American Soul Music wasn't open to the public during our time in Memphis, which left a bit of a hole in our musical education. However, the stroll back along Union Avenue from Sun Studio threw up a few amusing sights.

A sign at the entrance to an office car park left us both bemused. It was in all capital letters, contained no punctuation, and read "ALL DELIVERIES MAKE THE BLOCK RECEIVING LOCATED BEHIND BUILDING". Eventually its meaning dawned on me. The sign was telling delivery drivers to turn left at the end of the block and then take the first left, where they would find Goods Inwards behind the building. I would have driven into the Mississippi River before I'd worked that one out.

The car park of the next building contained a trailer that left us as intrigued as we were bemused by the Make The Block sign. It was the size of trailer that could be towed by a van, was painted all red and proudly displayed a logo of orange and red flames behind a scowling pig's head, above a shield with the legend, "The Norwegian National Barbecue Team". I've seen a few of those American TV food shows and may have been dimly aware that barbecuing is a competitive sport of sorts, but not that it involved teams representing entire European nations. If there was an equivalent UK team, it would arrive with its own umbrella and only be good for burnt sausages and under-cooked chicken drumsticks. If competitive barbecuing is truly an international sport, I would fear being drawn against the Australian, South African and New Zealand teams, but would be onto a certain loser if Fiji, Tonga or any of the other Pacific Island nations were involved. They know how to barbecue things in some very unconventional ways.

The final piece of gentle amusement on the walk back was when we came across AutoZone Park, home of the

Memphis Redbirds baseball team. Liverpool FC uses the city's unique symbol, the Liver Bird, as its crest, so the notion of a "Redbird" as a sporting name tickled me pink. I laughed out loud when I saw, painted on the gatepost of the stadium, an advert for "a proud partner of the Memphis Redbirds, ALDO'S PIZZA PIES". John Aldridge, more commonly known as Aldo, is a very Scouse ex-Liverpool player who I'm sure would be delighted to see his nickname writ large sponsoring a Redbirds team with his Pizza Pies.

The strip of bars and restaurants in Memphis is possibly more famous than any of the others we had visited so far, even more so perhaps than Bourbon Street in New Orleans. Beale Street is where the father of the blues, W.C. Handy, wrote and performed some of his greatest songs. The quality of the music played in all of the bars we visited in Beale Street was far better than anywhere else on the trip. We had three successive evenings there enjoying a fantastic friendly atmosphere accompanied by superb music, great beer and even better food. Áine Two assures me that the ribs she had in B.B. King's bar were the best she had on the entire journey. She gave me a slap on the wrist before I could grab a sample, so they must have been very good indeed.

The company we kept at the bar in B.B. King's was a little different. On this occasion I got the travelling air-conditioning engineer from somewhere in upstate Tennessee. He was pleasant and chatty, if a little downbeat and hangdog, and had the sort of jowly Southern drawl that reminded me of Droopy. He admitted to voting for Trump. "Ah believe blue collar America needs a boost," was his reasoning. Fair enough; at least he'd given it some thought.

Áine Two's companion was a salesman from Louisiana who always stayed away from home, regardless of how close he was to his wife and kids. He seemed to take a bit of a shine to Áine Two and appeared next to us again at the bar of the Irish pub we strolled into after B.B. King's. He wasn't too impressed with me being there but eventually got the message.

On the Saturday evening the local basketball team, the Memphis Grizzlies, played the top team in the country, the Golden Gate Warriors from San Francisco. The stadium is a few hundred yards from Beale Street and as the crowd spilled out at the end of the game they did nothing but add to the happy atmosphere. There was no unpleasant tribal rivalry, despite all the team vests on display: just people having a good time in a great city.

Behind the basketball stadium is the Gibson guitar factory. Gibson is an iconic brand of musical instruments closely associated with blues and rock and roll. B.B. King's famous Lucille is a Gibson, as is the Gibson SG played by Angus Young from AC/DC. The factory has a huge picture window onto the street, so you can stand and watch as the craftsmen go about their business creating musical magic.

The Rum Boogie Café, on the corner of Beale Street and South B.B. King Boulevard, deserves a special mention. The house band was excellent, displaying an encyclopaedic knowledge of local music and the skills to play most of it. Our Saturday evening was spent at an outside table watching the world go by to the accompaniment of great music, delicious food and very good beer.

In the UK, there are some football teams whose shirts are ubiquitous, regardless of locality. Liverpool and Manchester United are the prime suspects, along with – to a lesser extent – Arsenal and Chelsea, and Celtic and Rangers from the Scottish Premiership. All clubs have a core local following, plus a diaspora of supporters who live elsewhere, normally due to parental migrations. I have two nephews who live in Birmingham but who are saddled with supporting Everton because that's their dad's team, poor lads. However, the clubs that have been successful during the Premiership era of the last 25 years have fan bases that defy the rules of birthplace or father's club, and their supporters are widespread, some even global.

It came as a surprise to me, however, that American Football has a similar thing with many of its franchises. I got chatting to a couple at the next table who were wearing Dallas Cowboys jumpers. We had seen several other people in Memphis wearing the same club colours so I asked them whether the Cowboys were playing an off-season game locally. It turns out that the Cowboys and the New England Patriots are the two most successful teams of recent years and are supported across the country. The Cowboys had had a decent season last time around and it had emboldened some of their supporters to dust off their team colours and wear them again with pride. It is called "glory hunting" in the UK, when someone with no connection to a successful club decides to support them. In the interests of good Anglo-American relations, however, and because I liked the guy I was chatting to, I decided not to land him with that sobriquet.

Memphis played a part in one of the sillier episodes of the American Civil War. The city was held by the Union Army under a General Cadwallader C. Washburn. A Confederate officer called Major General Bedford Forrest sent a message to the Union occupiers, purporting to be from their own troops and suggesting that the town had been overrun by the enemy. General Washburn heard the news and escaped in just his nightshirt, allowing Forrest the opportunity to wander in unopposed and capture Washburn's sword and uniform. Forrest escaped with some horses and Washburn's gear and ransomed it the following day. Off South Front Street, the city's main shopping street, is General Washburn's Escape Alley, immortalising his ignominy.

It wasn't far from General Washburn's Escape Alley that we found out how real American drinkers do it. The previous night in Memphis had been a bit of a late one and we had missed breakfast, so we hit the streets at 10.30 am in search of nourishment. We passed over a couple of unlikely-looking places and settled on one that looked about as unlikely as you could get: Bardog Tavern on Monroe Avenue. It was a proper, dark, city dive bar that we only spotted because two ladies stepped out of the door as we passed. Inside were several locals skulking at the bar, nursing coffees or beers. We settled on a couple of barstools, ordered tea, coffee and breakfast and were soon chatting to the well-turned-out couple next to us, who were happily flooring pints of the local beer. It turns out he was an attorney and she his wife and they had attended court that morning for a case, only to find out that the courts were closed for a local dignitary's funeral. So to assuage their disappointment at having a whole day to kill, they'd retired to the bar for an early snifter. An hour later, when we slipped off our barstools, full of scrambled eggs and caffeine, they were on their third early snifter and showing no signs of slowing down. He was Randy (his name; I can't vouch for his state of being) from Texas and was a mad keen golfer, hunter and gun enthusiast; she was his lovely wife, Michelle. He had played most of the good golf courses in Ireland and they were going there again on holiday in August. I told him that he could shoot pheasant in Ireland in August and his eyes lit up. Randy's ambition wasn't to drive coast to coast across his country like we were doing, but to go to Africa on a safari. We thought this very admirable until he explained that his biggest worry was the cost of transporting his guns and getting the animal corpses back so that they could be stuffed. I liked Randy, despite his appetite for destruction of both the animal kingdom and his liver.

Sadly, Memphis is also notorious for one of the greatest crimes against humanity of all time. On April 4th 1968 leading civil rights activist, Nobel Peace Prize winner and Baptist Minister Dr Martin Luther King Jr. was assassinated on the balcony of the Lorraine Motel in Memphis by James Earl Ray, an escaped convict originally from Alton, Illinois.

The Lorraine Motel is now the superb National Civil Rights Museum. It tells the story of the African American community: how they arrived as slaves; fought for freedom and equality before, during and after the Civil War; lived through segregation; suffered lynchings; sat on the "wrong" seats on buses and in milk bars; created the Civil Rights Movement and eventually emerged to see a black president elected in 2008.

There was much to take from the museum but the biggest lesson for me was how much of segregation was ended by a white liberal president from the former slave state of Texas, and how that end had to be forced upon recalcitrant Southern states.

In 1863 President Lincoln issued his famous Emancipation Proclamation, freeing over 3 million slaves across America. The Civil War ended in 1865 but Southern states soon began to implement what became known as the Jim Crow laws, legally instituting segregation of races across the South. It took another 100 years until President Lyndon B. Johnson implemented his Great Society legislation in 1965, finally putting an end to the Jim Crow laws and segregation.

The Jim Crow laws were so named because of the colour of skin of the people they were legislating against. Jim Crow wasn't a real person, but an everyman name coined to represent any black person.

At the end of the walk through the museum is a wall of award-winning campaigners for civil rights around the world. It contains black and white faces and includes the likes of Nelson Mandela, Desmond Tutu, Bono and former Irish president, Mary Robinson. To our national shame, there isn't a single British face on the wall.

On our way to the museum we stopped off in a nearby bar for some lunch. A little plaque on the wall caught my eye. It stated that the bar had been owned in the past by a Frank Liberto and is now run by his grandson. Inside the Civil Rights Museum I noticed Liberto's name for a second time. On a display, he is named as a possible suspect in one of the many conspiracy theories surrounding Dr King's death. Local bar owner Lloyd Jowers claimed that Liberto gave him $100,000 to assassinate Dr King. No evidence to support this theory has ever been found and as far as we know Frank Liberto is entirely innocent.

Something scary happened on the way into the museum itself. A metal detector surrounds the doorway and everyone has to do the usual thing of emptying pockets to go through it. The man in front of us, entering with his family and dressed in a T-shirt and tracksuit trousers, took out his keys, wallet and cash but still managed to set the alarms off. After being challenged politely by the security staff he very carefully pulled a pistol out of his trouser pocket and handed it over, saying that he didn't want to scare people by taking it out in front of them. The security guard gingerly carried the gun away, presumably to store safely somewhere, and the chap was asked to go back through the security gate. Once again he set the alarm off and this time produced his mobile phone from his other trouser pocket. Was he afraid we'd be scared of that too? What sort of person takes a loaded gun on a day out with his family to a civil rights museum, of all places, and then forgets both it and then his mobile phone when asked to empty his pockets for a security check?

We decided, because of time pressures, not to go to Nashville, Tennessee to complete our musical pilgrimage from jazz, through the blues, rock and roll and Southern soul, to country and western. I do regret that decision but maybe we'll make it back to attend the Grand Ole Opry sometime in the future.

We left Memphis, Tennessee via its rather dodgy-looking northern and western suburbs, before turning south towards Tupelo and Elvis' birthplace. On the way we drove under an overhead gantry like the matrix signs that are currently being installed all over the UK motorway network. It informed us that in January 2017 there were 61 road deaths in the state of Tennessee. A quick check shows that that number had risen to an astonishing nearly 500 road deaths by mid-year 2017, in a state of 6.6 million people. These figures are from Tennessee's own Department of Safety and Homeland Security. By comparison, the number of road deaths in the UK in the first half of 2016, according to the UK Department of Transport, was approximately 890, in a population of 65 million. We tiptoed south back into Mississippi.

It was a Sunday morning in Tupelo, and the museum built up around the tiny, preserved shack in which Elvis was born was closed. We could wander around the outside, however, and sit on the swing on his front porch without anyone chasing us away.

The museum had a number of quotes from Elvis' childhood friends and they reinforced the notion that he was an ordinary kid who just happened to have an extraordinary talent. They obviously loved him dearly in his home town.

The drive south of Tupelo included further examples of deep rural poverty, but was otherwise very pleasant, with wide, flat open spaces and views across miles of arable farmland. We spent the night halfway down the state of Mississippi in an entirely forgettable town called Meridian, remarkable only for being mentioned in *To Kill a Mockingbird*. I had to look that up.

We did experience a sad little cameo of American life in the hotel in Meridian. It shall remain nameless for reasons that will become obvious.

We had booked ahead using one of the hotel booking websites, and arrived after a long day's drive hoping for a simple check-in, a shower and a beer from the cool box in the boot. We were met at the reception desk by a sweet lady in her mid-sixties. We gave her the details of our booking which she carefully wrote down before turning to the computer on the desk and nervously and laboriously typing them into the system. After several silent and, for her, very stressful minutes, she went into the room behind the desk and asked her husband for help. He came out and after a polite "Good afternoon" peered at the screen and began to re-type the details.

"Guest name goes there, Mary," he said softly and patiently, "and their address goes there. Is that a London, England address, sir? Yes. OK, so we need to put the city as London."

It was impossible to get frustrated with them, despite our long day, as they were clearly people who were very unfamiliar with technology, and they were trying their best.

Eventually, after about twenty minutes, they found our

booking, confirmed the details that we had given them and we proffered a credit card to pay for the room. This took the confusion to a whole new level as they tried to get the card machine to connect to the internet to process the payment. After another twenty minutes of painful confusion we were sorted and in our room.

As we were leaving later in the evening for something to eat, we wandered into reception to ask about breakfast the following day, and fell into conversation with Mary and her husband Ed.

Mary apologised profusely for the delay during check-in and explained, "This is our first week in this job. We used to run a gas station on the other side of town, but the gas company closed it down and we were out of a job. We have no money behind us so we had to retrain to do something else. This opportunity came up and the hotel company have given us a chance, but we don't like the computers, and the cleaning staff are damn lazy. I'm 64 and Ed is 68, so we are old dogs learning new tricks, and it has been real hard. We get medical cover through the hotel company so we have to make this work or we could be in real trouble."

We reassured them that it would all get easier, and that the computer system will become second nature to them after a while. Despite the "damn lazy" staff, the rooms were perfectly clean and comfortable. We chatted on about life in Meridian and our road trip.

"We've only ever lived in Meridian," Ed told us, "and we've never travelled out of the state of Mississippi. Maybe one day, when we do eventually retire, we could buy a little RV and do what you're doing."

Mary and Ed are lovely, hard-working people who have shown a huge amount of courage to make such a change of direction so late in life, even if it was driven by desperation.

I hope they prosper in their new careers and eventually get their wish to see something more of America.

Equally disappointing was the drive through Alabama, setting for one of my favourite songs of all time, Lynyrd Skynyrd's "Sweet Home Alabama". There's not a lot to see or do if all you are doing is cutting the southwest corner from Meridian to Pensacola in Florida. The road is long and largely straight and goes through mostly forest or arable farmland. Our only stop was at a fast-food restaurant on a crossroads in a nameless settlement, to use the loo and to grab a drink. I walked up to the counter and asked the young lady for a cup of hot tea. I had already encountered the iced tea vs. hot tea misunderstanding, so made sure I asked for it hot. She looked a bit confused and pointed me to the array of large thermos flasks to one side, mumbling something about taking a cup and filling it myself. After a few moments searching for some hot water and teabags, I returned to the counter asking if any of it was hot, only to be met by the same sweet but utterly bemused face. With help from Áine Two, we managed to communicate what we wanted, not only to the poor kid trying to serve me, but all the other staff who were now gathered round adding their two-penneth to the debate. It turned out, after all the patient explanations and equally patient shaking of heads, that all they had were the industrial-sized tea bags used for making large thermos flasks of iced tea.

In the end we worked it out. She gave me a cup of hot water and I popped back out to the car to fetch a normal-sized Tetley tea bag. One day, many years in the future when the next British tourist passes through, our young lady will remember her involvement in the infamous Alabama Tea Compromise of 2017. She will turn to her younger colleagues with a knowing wink, break out the dusty and as yet unopened box of Lipton Yellow Label tea bags, and hand one proudly to the customer, alongside a cup of hot, but not boiling, water.

Whilst I sat in the restaurant supping my hard-earned tea I met a proper, Southern states-accented Tottenham Hotspur supporter. He noticed my Liverpool T-shirt and was begrudgingly complimentary about the team, who only two days before had beaten his beloved Spurs 2–0. He had no idea why he supported them. "It's like a disease that I can't shake off." I know the feeling.

Back on the Alabama roads, it was a non-stop drive to the border with Florida and the delights of Pensacola.

CHAPTER 8
FLORIDA'S WHITE SANDS, BIRDS AND ALLIGATORS

Rather alarmingly, the State of Florida is shaped like a gun. The main bulk of the state is the stock of the gun and the long narrow northwestern part is the gun barrel. Confusingly for this analogy, the long narrow barrel-shaped bit is known as the Florida Panhandle, presumably because in the olden days, pans were shaped like backwards guns. Apparently the correct term for a panhandle is a salient.

Pensacola is perched on the western end of the Florida Panhandle, a few miles east of the border with Alabama. It is a small and very pretty port in Pensacola Bay, and was originally founded in 1559 by the Spanish. It is called the "City of Five Flags", and has an annual Five Flags festival to celebrate the fact that it has existed under Spanish, French, British, Confederate and American control. It was also the nominal Florida state capital during the second period of Spanish rule, sharing responsibilities with St. Augustine on the east coast until someone saw sense and built Tallahassee roughly halfway between.

Almost the entire Florida coastline is protected by what we call sand spits, known locally as barrier islands. There is a natural coastline, an inland coastal waterway, the spit, and then the open sea. Much of the extra land provided by the spit has been built upon but, thankfully, the authorities have been sensible and preserved large parts of it as nature reserves.

Pensacola, like many places in Florida, is also a military town, and as we walked into the centre from our motel in the northern end, we passed a main road junction. Here five painted pelicans preside over the traffic, one for each of the main military services. The red one, representing the US Marine Corps, looked like a jowly liver bird, the symbol of the City of Liverpool.

We stayed at the very pleasant Solé Inn and Suites, a motel much the same as many others we had used, except that the chap behind the desk was from Preston, Lancashire. He had moved to Pensacola with his partner and was happy and settled. He did have the weirdest hybrid Lancastrian/Floridian accent though, like he was the American character on *Coronation Street* who had married the local boy.

Without wishing to labour the point, Pensacola was a pleasant contrast to some of the places we'd driven through in Mississippi, Tennessee and Alabama. It was prosperous and clean and had a cheerful holiday atmosphere. It helped that the weather had changed and we got some proper sunshine for the first time on the trip. Even my blue-white English legs got an airing. The main street had a decent selection of bars and restaurants, and we picked Hopjacks Pizza Kitchen and Taproom to have a beer and dinner. I can't imagine why we did; maybe it was something in the name.

I do love a bar where they hand you a menu of all the beers on tap. Most of the ones on sale in Hopjack's Pizza Kitchen and Taproom were locally brewed, and we sampled many. Purely for the purposes of research, you understand. They were having a special on pizzas to celebrate their third birthday and, to join in the party, we ordered ribs and wings. The stroll back to the motel past the almost-liver bird was wonderfully wobbly.

We did spend some time before dinner on the harbour wall, enjoying the sunset and watching great blue herons and pelicans, and I spotted a great northern diver in its winter plumage. In Canada they are known as common loons, and one appears on the Canadian $1 coin, giving it the charming nickname of a "loonie".

The drive along the Florida Panhandle towards our next destination, Panama City Beach, was a mixed bag of beautifully unspoilt beaches, nature reserves and high-rise tourism. In parts there was just us on the highway driving through white sands, with the Gulf on one side and the inland waterway on the other. We stopped at various beauty spots for lunch, or just to sit and enjoy the peace and quiet.

Other parts were between canyons of identical, grey, 20-storey apartment buildings and hotels. They block out the views and the sunlight and are vast, depressing blots on the landscape.

In one rest stop in a small nature reserve we came across a sign, carefully placed in the inland waterway, warning us not to "feed or aggravate the alligators". "You didn't warn me!" exclaimed the one-armed man.

Eventually we turned off the spit and drove along the inland shore, which was also beautiful and dismal in equal measure.

Panama City Beach sits on the outer shore of the spit, just west of Panama City itself. It is there purely to serve tourists and consists of the same soulless tall, grey blocks besmirching the beautiful white sands of the beaches. We stayed for two nights at the Holiday Inn Resort, a concave edifice facing the beach and built around a pool, bar and kids' play area. All the balconies faced the sea and overlooked the amenities, so that guests could enjoy the sun outside their rooms all day. Sadly, in doing so they could not avoid the cacophony coming from below. A lady set up her steel drums at the rear of the bar at 10 am and committed songicide on unknown or unrecognisable "classic" tunes for an hour. She stopped for a break, but the relief was short lived. Under the cover of her dreadful racket, a pair of musical illiterates had set themselves up on a different stage and immediately struck up a second hour of sonic attack. They batted the honours back and forth from 10 am to 10 pm, an hour at a time, going through the same crappy repertoire over and over. We admitted defeat after a couple of hours of aural misery, and slunk off with bleeding ears to spend the day on the beach.

Almost the entire state of Florida has a frilly hem of pristine white sandy beaches that, despite the vast numbers of holidaymakers, look beautiful at any time of the day or night. Our stroll in pleasant spring sunshine took us past flocks of wild creatures basking in the warmth. Some fluttered and tweeted, others played music and beach volleyball; all seemed happy. We saw flocks of royal and Forster's terns and a few piping plovers, all of which were new to me.

The Holiday Inn Resort had a beachside bar with a happy hour of half-price selected cocktails and draught beers, and it seemed churlish not to participate. So down we went, trying to block out the racket from the "entertainment" by chatting to those around us. One lovely lady, Joy, was in her early fifties and divorced. She had seen her kids through university and into the real world, and then taken a redundancy package from a senior management position in an insurance firm. After her successful life of single motherhood and greasy pole climbing, she was travelling solo on her own road trip, and she was having a ball. Her route was the opposite way from us, down the East Coast, around Florida to New Orleans and then up the Mississippi to Memphis and Nashville, before heading home to North Carolina. Joy knew an awful lot about American craft beers and could floor a good few too. And she was mortified by the notion of Donald Trump being president. "He is the arch-misogynist. He just showed his contempt for all women with his 'grab them by the pussy' remarks."

Joy did give us one of the best hints of the trip. Neither of us had heard of Asheville, North Carolina, but it turns out to be one of the centres of craft beer brewing in the country. It was off our original route but, as we were heading inland in North Carolina to see some friends in Raleigh, we figured we could squeeze it into the itinerary.

Early in the evening, not long after we arrived at the bar, a very drunk couple staggered away, their drinking done for the day. Or so we thought. Once Joy had left, the drunks returned and parked themselves next to us. She immediately assailed to the poor unsuspecting couple on her left whilst he turned his attention to me. His opening gambit, once he'd discovered I wasn't American, Mr Drunk asked, "What do you think of Trump?" I avoided that question so he changed tack and started on a rant about how all the world's problems were down to "the Muslims", and that he would never go to London because there were no-go areas. I assured him that there weren't any such places in my adoptive city and that the vast majority of "the Muslims" in the UK were normal, peace-loving, law-abiding citizens. He nearly fell off his barstool when I told him that I had a good friend who was a Muslim guy who did the same job as me, often better; supported the same football team as me; drove a Porsche 911; was married; had a beautiful daughter and enjoyed life as much as I did, just without alcohol or pork. He was astounded that I would even contemplate working so closely with "one of them", a horribly dismissive expression used when I was a child to deride gay people. I reassured him that, in my experience, the hundreds of members of the Muslim faith who worked in the same office block as I did in west London were just part of the team. They behaved and were treated no differently than anyone else. Somehow, I doubt my efforts got through his thick skull into his drink-addled, bigoted brain, but at least I tried. Thankfully, he isn't typical of all Americans, just some of them.

Eventually I gave up and joined in the conversation Áine Two was having with the group of ladies who were working on an IT installation at a local hospital. My bigoted buddy must have got bored of ranting at my back, because when I turned around again he'd gone off and picked on another victim. I'm pretty sure he was a Trump supporter.

The hospital software ladies were a team who had stumbled upon a formula for being paid for travelling around their country doing a job that they all loved. Sometime in the past they had worked together on a project to implement a new software package in a hospital in California. It had worked so well that the owners of the software offered them all jobs doing it again at the next hospital. Their formula became so successful that it is now a repeatable exercise that they perform all over the country. The great thing is that they are not an ever-changing collection of squeaky-clean young computer consultants, who flit in and out and know nothing of the business in which they are working. These are all very experienced hospital administrators and practitioners, who know the ins and outs of hospitals nationwide, and can apply their knowledge to maximise the benefits of the software for their customers. I spent many years working for an IT consultancy firm and know just how valuable a team with those skills is. They were having a few well-deserved beers at the bar after a very long week completing their umpteenth assignment, and they were due to fly home to California the following morning before heading off on another adventure in a week's time.

From Panama City Beach we carried on east, travelling along Route 98, the Forgotten Coast Highway, and long may it remain so. The road hugs the coast almost all the way, often no more than a few feet from the beach and inches above sea level. It wends its way through picturesque coastal forests, charming towns and beautiful landscapes. We happened upon a local radio station that continually plugged events in the town of Apalachicola. When you hear Apalachicola repeated regularly in a soft, slow, Southern drawl it becomes almost mesmeric, and it was lovely to finally reach Apalachicola and find that it was a splendid little seaside community.

We stopped for lunch in a pretty little seaside town called Port St. Joe. The formerly formal Port St. Joseph adopted the more relaxed title in the early 20th century.

Port St. Joe's spit wraps itself around from the south to form St. Joseph Bay and is host to the St. Joseph Bay Aquatic Preserve. Visitors are allowed to drive along the sparsely populated sand bar to car parks in the long and narrow nature reserve. Climbing a tall sand dune affords you views of both the bay and town on one side and the Gulf of Mexico on the other. It is a truly wonderful, peaceful and relaxing place and well worth the hour's diversion from the highway.

As we drove towards Tallahassee, the current Florida state capital, a song wormed its way into my mind from nowhere in particular. The line, "Today, Billy Joe McAllister jumped off the Tallahassee Bridge" repeated itself inside my head as though on a loop, to the point where I began to sing it out loud over and over again, making Áine Two's life even more of a misery than it most probably was at the time. It caused me to wonder where the Tallahassee Bridge was, and whether we would get a chance to drive over it whilst we were there. I resolved to check the map when we got to our hotel and see if we could include it in our itinerary.

Tallahassee is what you might expect for a state capital. It contains a mixture of politicians, lawyers, lobbyists and university students, but was quite pleasant nonetheless. The city has a delightful park running through the middle, lined with southern live oaks draped in Spanish moss and surrounded by more of the standard antebellum townhouses, now occupied by legal and accounting firms.

Once we had checked into our very pleasant city centre hotel, I dug out the map book and scoured the Internet but couldn't find any mention of a Tallahassee Bridge. Maybe we'll come across it in our wanderings around the city, I thought, and forgot about it.

Dinner that night was in the swanky Harry's Seafood Bar & Grille, where we ate a delicious gumbo at the bar and earwigged on a conversation between an overbearing father and his gormless son. "You've just got to get in here to do it, son," insisted Dad. I hope he was emphasising how the son just had to get into Florida State University to do his masters degree, rather than some hideous crime that they were planning between them. If Dad was anything to go by, the lad's masters might possibly be in how to be a second-generation pushy father. The poor lad looked in his early twenties, and was clearly fed up with his dad's lectures. He seemed on the verge of telling Pops to go take a hike. However, the Old Man was paying the bill, so like the good brow-beaten son that he was he nodded and did his "Yes, sir" act.

Just around the corner from Harry's was what seemed to be the city's only student club, and on the Friday night it made for a very odd spectacle. At 7:30 in the evening, a police car with its blue lights flashing was parked outside, blocking the road. Temporary barriers had been set up across the pavement and into the road, and the coppers were nonchalantly leaning against them. A large gaggle of teenagers who seemed to be first year university students (and therefore too young to drink) were gathered around outside the railings. They were watching a bunch of older male students dressed in basketball vests who were smoking and being very drunk inside the railings. The desperately-trying-to-look-cool-in-front-of-their-adoring-public quotient was off the scale. Since when was all day drinking a spectator sport? And I dread to think why the audience needed a police escort.

Another feature of the early evening performance was an apparent lack of gents' toilets. A steady stream of young lads sneaked around the corner, out of sight of the policemen, and peed against the wall.

We sat on the corner balcony of the next-door bar where we could watch the drinking spectacle whilst the peeing went on below us. We were only allowed to drink half pints of beer, because it was deemed too strong for us. Maybe a 50-year-old Scouser in a Lynyrd Skynyrd T-shirt is indistinguishable from a Tallahassee sophomore in a basketball vest. Maybe I should be flattered.

My very own groupie and I finished our shrunken beers and wandered off for an old person's dinner. Maybe I'm her groupie.

America does great museums in some of the most unexpected places, and they're not afraid to talk about some of the more unsavoury aspects of the country's past. The Florida State Capitol building is a splendidly restored Georgian period mansion that contains the Florida Legislative Research Center and Museum, a surprisingly interesting and informative place to spend a few hours. It shows how colourful Florida's history has been.

Florida was where Europeans made first contact with the continent of North America in 1513, and where some of the first European settlements were founded, in St. Augustine and Pensacola.

As has been mentioned previously, ownership of Florida changed hands quite a few times since then. Once the dust had settled, Pensacola and St. Augustine both had legitimate claims to being the state capital. The first legislative council took place in Pensacola, which meant that the St. Augustine delegation had to sail all the way around the state coastline to get there. Similarly, at the second legislative council a year later in St. Augustine, the Pensacola lot had to do an equally silly reverse journey. There and then they agreed to create a state capital somewhere roughly equidistant from both, and Tallahassee was chosen.

The US Army fought three different wars against the local Native Americans, the Seminole, before eventually driving them from the state.

Like the other Southern states, Florida was a slave state. By 1860, nearly half of the population of around 140,000 people were slaves. After the Civil War, Florida was renowned for viciously enforcing its Jim Crow laws, and its almost 4,000 public lynchings of black people until 1950 was the highest rate per capita of any state.

The State of Florida jumped on Henry Flagler's tourism bandwagon in the 1920s, becoming the East Coast's year-round sunshine playground, and has never looked back. Nowadays it attracts somewhere in the region of 110 million visitors a year, with more coming each year, and these visitors spend over $100 billion per year in the state.

Disappointingly, the otherwise excellent museum made no mention of the internationally famous Tallahassee Bridge and its musical connections to poor old Billy Joe McAllister.

Back on the coast, Indian Shores was a complete contrast to Panama City Beach. It was built up, but most things were relatively low rise. Our little apartment hotel, the Legacy Vacation Resorts Indian Shores, was small, peaceful and faced onto the inland waterway, with its own veranda and dock. Calling itself a resort is a bit of an exaggeration. It was a block of 20 or so one-bedroom apartments on two floors, with a car park underneath and a swimming pool next to the main road. Some of the apartments, including the one next to us, were being refurbished. This wasn't mentioned on the website when we booked it, but we arrived on Saturday evening when the builders were packing up for the weekend, and left again on the Monday morning when they came back, so we weren't disturbed by their hammering. We sat on the veranda drinking beer and chatting to two Canadian gents who were cooking vast steaks on the communal barbie. There was also a Mexican family and a family of blue herons, both fishing from the dock. It was a beautiful evening; we had our feet up with a cold beer (the splendid Dogfish Head 60 Minute IPA), great views, even better company and all was right with our little world.

The Canadians inspired us to cook a steak so the following night we located the local supermarket and bought the biggest, juiciest piece of rump steak I have ever seen. It was more than 2 pounds in weight and cost just $7.99, the equivalent on current exchange rates of about £6.99.

Also on sale in the supermarket was a perfect example of American excess. Supermarkets in the UK sell big spuds as good candidates for jacket potatoes. Sometimes they're sold loose, sometimes in bags and the expectation is that you take them home, stick them in the microwave and bingo, you have a cheap and healthy dinner. In the Publix supermarket in Indian Shores, Florida, they sell single large potatoes under the brand name MicroTater. They are individually shrink-wrapped in plastic and bar-coded, with the strapline, "Ready to eat in 5–7 minutes". Oh, and they're organic.

During a period of repose in our little apartment I decided to resolve the mystery of Billy Joe McAllister and his elusive Tallahassee Bridge. After another half hour of fruitless poring over the map book, I resorted to the Internet again. This time I came across a link to a country singer called Bobbie Gentry who had a 1967 hit with a song called "Ode to Billie Joe". Maybe this is what I was singing and it would give me a clue to where I might find the lost bridge of Tallahassee. Sure enough, the song is about a youngster called Billie Joe McAllister who did indeed jump off a bridge. The bridge, however, was near a small town called Money and spanned the Little Tallahatchie River, until it collapsed into the water in 1972. We had passed within 37 miles of the internationally famous Tallahatchie Bridge off which Billie Joe McAllister jumped when we drove up Highway 61 from Vickburg to Clarksdale, Mississippi.

Just down the coast from Indian Shores is the John's Pass Village and Boardwalk, a diverting little shopping centre with a few bars and restaurants that were gearing up for the forthcoming Spring Break. It was popular with both boat and beach fishermen, and the local birdlife had learnt that these strange humans could be a reliable source of food. A large flock of pelicans was lurking around the small harbour area, waiting for local fishermen to land and clean their catches. They were joined by great blue herons, great white egrets and snowy egrets, all hanging around in anticipation of a free meal. Walking along the beach we saw a number of great blue herons standing behind beach fishermen in the hope of scoring some dinner for little or no effort. Great blue herons are the same as our grey herons but are, like most things American, about 50% bigger.

The drive from Indian Shores to Naples took us around St. Petersburg and across the mouth of Tampa Bay over the astonishing 4.1-mile-long Sunshine Skyway Bridge. It is an elegant suspension bridge that sweeps and undulates gracefully, lifting the road high above the water and affording views of the harbour and the city of Tampa over our left shoulders. As we needed to cover an extended distance in one day, we stuck to the I-75 freeway past Fort Myers and its acres of gated communities, situated amongst dozens of country clubs and manicured golf courses. Many people love these sorts of places and aspire to a long and happy retirement in them. Others avoid them like the plague. We drove past, keen to get to Naples and a cold beer.

Naples is completely different from anywhere else we had seen so far in Florida. It is low rise, manicured and very wealthy and all the properties that overlook the pristine, white beach are privately owned houses, each with its own beach access. The town's spotlessly clean main street is lined with expensive shops, galleries, bars and restaurants, priced to keep the casual traveller on the sidewalk. Much of the art on display was made of glass, blown and formed into the most extraordinary pieces: glass dolphins splashed playfully in glass waves; glass elephants charged through glass jungles; glass Pierrots shed glass tears onto their glass cheeks. It was a veritable spectacle of silicon of all shapes and sizes.

An evening stroll took in several Rolls Royces, a couple of Jaguars, a brace of Ferraris and a Lamborghini or two. This town had a few quid to spend.

We gravitated to Paddy Murphy's Irish Pub, on the basis that we would probably be able to afford a pint. We began chatting to the four elderly gents enjoying a Guinness at the next table. It turned out that they were all of Irish descent, and had all played golf in Ireland. One of them had even played Áine Two's home town course in Co. Mayo, and remembered it well. Maybe the rain wasn't quite as horizontal as it was on all the other days he was in Ireland.

He asked us to explain the famous curse that had bedevilled the Co. Mayo Gaelic football team since the 1950s. The trophy awarded to the winners of the GAA football Grand Final every year is called the Sam Maguire Cup, or

The Sam for short. The last time Mayo won The Sam was in 1951, and they took the trophy on an open-topped bus tour around the county. Mayo is huge and very sparsely populated, so this would be the equivalent of Leeds parading the FA Cup around the whole of Yorkshire. The story goes that the Mayo bus failed to stop for a funeral cortege in the village of Foxford and the local priest cursed them by saying that the county wouldn't win The Sam again until all the members of the 1951 team were dead.

Since then they have appeared in eight Grand Finals and lost all of them, including three in the last four years. In the 2016 final, Mayo were 2–0(6) to 0–4(4) down to Dublin after 30 minutes, but had scored all of the points themselves after putting two goals past their own goalkeeper. Somehow, they managed to draw that game, but then conspired to lose the replay by a single point, 1–15 (18) to 1–14 (17). They really are cursed.

By the way, at the time of writing, two of the 1951 team are still alive.

Dinner was expensive but delicious fish, in a swanky restaurant that reflected the well-to-do nature of Naples. I think the attitude of the proprietors is that if you can't afford to eat there you shouldn't be in the town.

We had a choice to make for the next part of our journey through the Everglades. We could either stay on the quicker I-75, known in these parts as Alligator Alley but properly separated from the wildlife, or the much more interesting Tamiami Trail. This is a slower, unfenced, single-lane highway that would almost certainly get us much closer to nature. It was a no-brainer: Tamiami Trail or bust!

The southern suburbs of Naples stretch for quite some distance and are made up of more manicured golf courses and gated developments, but after a while they fade away and you are in the flat, wet, swampy openness of the Everglades.

The first thing we noticed was the birdlife. The road runs alongside a drainage ditch which is, in turn, parallel to a line of telegraph poles supporting miles and miles of wires. Driving was accompanied by a seemingly endless commentary of "cormorant", "kingfisher", "anhinga", "black vulture", "turkey vulture", "cormorant", "cormorant", "kingfisher". We saw lots of birds.

At the Big Cypress National Preserve's Oasis Visitor Center a number of alligators, turtles, weird-looking fish and herons could be viewed from the safe height of a boardwalk above their drainage-ditch home.

Further along the road was the Everglades National Park's Shark Valley Visitor Center where, for an entry fee, you could walk on concrete paths through the swamps in the hope of catching a glimpse of something interesting. Before we'd even parked the car I was out with my binoculars and camera and had identified several types of herons that I'd never seen before. These included the black-crowned night heron (if it's got no black on it and it's out in the daytime, it's a black-crowned night heron), a green heron (mostly purple), and a tricoloured heron. All these were within 20 yards of one another, along with little blue herons, great blue herons and white ibises. An anhinga (a cormorant in fancy dress) was spearing fish with its beak and then juggling them until it could swallow them whole. Further along there were common and purple gallinules and a glossy ibis hiding in the bushes.

I make no apologies for that list of feathered things. This place was so awesome I was like a dog with two tails.

Seeing your first adult alligator sitting by the side of the path is a bit of a shock. This one was no more than 3 feet away, and there was no fence between us. Alligators are big, cold-blooded killing machines that only eat once a week or so. Unless it was starving, one wouldn't see someone my size as a potential meal. My arm might make a tasty morsel but the trouble of grabbing it and then twisting me around several times until it tore off was probably not worth the effort. We passed at least a dozen, keeping our distance each time, and were just discussing turning around and heading back to the car when there was a commotion from the bushes 20 yards ahead. A great white egret and a white ibis came crashing out making a racket, followed by a massive alligator. It dragged its bulk halfway across the path and then flopped down on the warm surface. I think it was suggesting it was dinner time, so we turned around and retreated.

I was wearing my trusty Motörhead T-shirt that day and had another amusing encounter with a music fan. We passed a group of school kids and the brief exchange, started by the teacher, went, "Lemmy rocks, man!"; "Rocked, past tense"; "Oh, yeah."

Sadly, Lemmy's spirit didn't protect me from the ravages of the local bugs. I had smeared my exposed parts with anti-mozzie gloop, but one or more of the little buggers sneaked under my shirt and gorged themselves on my shoulders, leaving a constellation of bright red bites for me to suffer on the flight home.

The seemingly endless and captivatingly beautiful Everglades eventually morphed into the western suburbs of Miami, a city I dislike only marginally less than LA. We were staying on Coconut Grove, made famous for being Miami's oldest suburb and the subject of a song by The Lovin' Spoonful. It also gave its name to a crappy nightclub in every British town and city in the 1980s.

A selfie in the harbour at Coconut Grove proved that we had literally journeyed from coast to coast, from the cliffs of

Big Sur in the west to the sea at Miami in the east. By way of celebration, a pizza in a local restaurant that evening saw us introduced to a very jealous middle-aged lady and her brow-beaten partner. He got himself into trouble by talking yoga to the young lady sitting next to him at the bar. After a while his other half decided she'd had enough and stomped out in a huff, with him following shame-facedly in her wake. Mind you, Yoga Girl tried to hit on the next bloke who came and sat beside her, so maybe the older lady had a point. I escaped un-chatted-up and the next day, during a tropical rain storm of biblical proportions, we drove to the airport, deposited our hire car and flew home for my sister's Cornish wedding.

CHAPTER 9
EAST OF KEY WEST

Road trips for the over fifties can be exhausting, but it was great to be back on the move after the week-long break in Cornwall. The wedding was a splendid day spent with family, and it passed with only the important hitch. Interestingly, the place my sister had booked for the reception was built around 1500, 13 years before the Spanish landed in Florida.

It seems that car-rental logistics and customer service are

the same on the East Coast of America as they are on the West. We arrived at the appointed place and time, clutching the details of our rental car, only to be told that nothing was available. This time nothing at all was available, and we were one of five or six couples, waiting at a line of desks as the harassed staff chased cars around their computer system. Eventually we were allocated the next vehicle off the washing line, a South Korean Verynice, and off we went.

The Florida Keys are the 114-mile-long, appendix-shaped string of islands that dangle off the very southeast corner of America. Like a human appendix, they seem to attract the indigestible detritus from American society. I don't mean the violent, gun-obsessed nutters; more the charming and harmless ones who just want to be out of the country's mainstream. A bit like our flying-saucer repairman in the Californian desert.

Key Largo is, as its name suggests, the largest and also the most famous of the more northerly keys, primarily because it was the title and setting for a 1948 Humphrey Bogart and Lauren Bacall film. Route 1 south from Florida joins the Keys at the middle of Key Largo. If you turn left at the junction you encounter a long narrow island, covered mostly in wildlife and botanical parks and with an exclusive golf and sailing club at the northern tip. Turning right takes you south past more state parks to the town of Key Largo itself, a narrow strip of bars, restaurants and apartments built around a network of marinas. It is a centre for boating and fishing, and is considered a sea fisherman's Nirvana because of its combination of perfect weather, clear blue waters and plentiful sealife.

The drive down the Keys takes you on a long, slow-moving, single-lane highway through small towns and across endless low-level bridges between the islands. The views from the lower bridges are breathtaking, with the clear blue waters of the Gulf of Mexico on one side and the Caribbean Sea on the other, and they get even better when the road rises gracefully to allow shipping to move around the area.

At one point, at the foot of one of the bridges, we encountered the only traffic jam on the entire trip. Two police cars with flashing lights were parked across the road, and we were held up by officers who were standing with raised hands and fearsome looks. One family pulled onto the hard shoulder and unloaded bicycles for the children to let off steam on until the problem was resolved. As is the way with these things, as soon as the kids were on their bikes the traffic started moving and the parents had to call them back and reload everything. When we crossed the bridge we saw a boom camera and cinematic paraphernalia and realised that we had been delayed because someone was making a film. Sadly we weren't given the opportunity to appear as extras in another *Miami Vice* remake.

Another of the bridges, Seven Mile Bridge, stretches for a few feet short of that distance to connect the middle and lower Keys. It is a little disconcerting driving along something so long that gives you nowhere to go in an emergency. The road to Key West is lined with huge loudspeakers that form part of a hurricane warning and evacuation system. I can only imagine the growing sense of panic amongst drivers stuck in a traffic jam on Seven Mile Bridge, with water on either side and a howling storm approaching.

Alongside the current incarnation of Seven Mile Bridge is its original version, built by a remarkable man called Henry Flagler. Henry made his money in New York as a founder of the Standard Oil Company, and on doctor's orders spent a winter in Florida when his first wife became ill. A few years later he returned to Florida with his second wife, started a sideline in tourism, and put much of his efforts into promoting the benefits of the most southerly state, where he is credited with being the "Father of Miami" and much of the local tourism industry. He also recognised the value of railways in bringing visitors to out-of-the-way destinations, and he invested a significant sum in a line that connected Key West with the mainland.

The remnants of that line can be seen from Route 1 in the form of two sections of low-level bridge running parallel with the road. The more northerly section remains in use as a pedestrian and cycling walkway, and is lined with people fishing over its sides, with the inevitable accompaniment of scrounging cormorants and pelicans. The more southerly section is derelict and is separated from the rest of the world by gaps where segments have been removed. The railway opened in 1912 and closed in 1935, and it is remarkable to see a fantastic piece of transport infrastructure that is only just over 100 years old but has been in disuse for the last 65 of them.

Key West itself is a very pleasant, modestly sized seaside town that began its life as a pirates' stopping-off point. Its famous former residents include our birdwatching friend Audubon, Ernest Hemingway and President Truman. It feels more like you are in the Caribbean than America, and the island is in fact closer to Cuba than the US mainland. The oft-repeated claim is that in Key West you are nearer to Cuba than you are to a Walmart store. If you are in Great Yarmouth your nearest motorway is in Holland, but that's another story.

The town also makes much of its position at the southernmost tip of the United States. There is a heavily photographed painted buoy proclaiming the southernmost point in the US, which is next to the southernmost house in the US, which has been superseded by one built in its garden that is now the southernmost of the southernmost houses in the US. A cabin in the front garden of the southernmost house in the US changes the emphasis slightly by claiming to be the nearest gift shop to Cuba.

If any place in America was going to have to have a main drag lined with bars, restaurants and tourist gift shops it is Key West, and Duval Street doesn't disappoint. There is a thing amongst Americans for buying a T-shirt to remind them of where they are, and Duval Street boasts shops selling garments with all manner of funny and not-so-funny slogans on them. A vest bearing the motif, "I flexed my muscles and the sleeves fell off" is a particularly hilarious example, as is "I'm not gay but $20 is $20". One middle-aged mother seemed completely oblivious to her teenage son's T-shirt that posed the incredulous question, "I shaved my balls for this?"

Needless to say, the famous Motörhead T-shirt was given another outing. It received a smart military salute and a "Lemmy RIP" from one gent in the street, and an accusation of me being German from another. My accuser, a T-shirt salesman, was terribly apologetic afterwards and explained that all Germans are into heavy metal so he just assumed I was one. I've heard a few national stereotypes in my life, but that's a new one on me.

Some Americans live by the T-shirt slogan, "It's not drinking all day unless you have beer for breakfast." I'll drink to that.

We ate and drank on several occasions on Duval Street and enjoyed it enormously, particularly the bouts of extreme people-watching. America is innately very conservative so Key West isn't quite "anything goes", but it would definitely give New Orleans and Newcastle a run for their money on a Saturday night. We spent one very pleasant evening over a few beers with a married couple of middle-aged Bostonian gents who were in town for their annual holiday. They loved the freedom to be themselves that being in Key West afforded them.

True to form, they despised Donald Trump. Of all the people we chatted to on the trip, they were the most vehemently anti-Trump. They complained bitterly about his pro-Christian, anti-Muslim views, his perceived sexism, racism and misogyny, and his stance on climate change. Their biggest fear was what he might do regarding gay marriage. They had been together for many years and had waited and waited for their opportunity to formalise their relationship, and they were terrified that Trump might reverse their rights and put them back where they started.

They were also spectacularly bitchy about some of the people wandering past. It was like sitting with a very camp version of Statler and Waldorf from *The Muppets*, passing comment just loud enough that they might be heard, and then laughing uproariously at their own shocking cleverness.

"Ooh, that's not a good look with that ass!" – about the large woman in the infeasibly tight dress.

"Hasn't she got a full-length mirror?" – about the middle-aged woman with the clashing T-shirt and jogging pants.

"Look at that poor guy, out drinking with his grandmother!" – about the man who was with his slightly older wife.

We enjoyed giggling together at other people's expense and, when the time came for them to move on, they headed to the gay bars at the top end of Duval Street to check out the drag queens.

Key West is justifiably famous for its glorious sunsets, and has concreted over its South Beach to accommodate the thousands of tourists who gather there every evening to admire the view. Apparently, if you believe it exists with enough fervour, you can glimpse a green flash at the top of the sun just as it drops out of sight over the horizon. I spent most of my time trying to capture a photograph of the ever-moving flock of black skimmers that flashed past repeatedly. They proved too fleeting for my skills, but I did get a shot of the two manatees that wandered slowly along the base of the sea wall, and the setting sun that moved sedately enough even for me. You can rent a proper yacht and sail off into the sunset and, in doing so, become the star of a million photographs taken from the quay. Needless to say we stayed on shore with a camera and a beer.

After sunset on the Saturday night we wandered into the Margaritaville restaurant, the original of the global chain of restaurants and casinos owned by American singer/songwriter Jimmy Buffett. Nope, I've never heard of him or his restaurants either, but my musical tastes lean a different way so I'm excused. The story goes that Jimmy had a huge hit with a song called "Margaritaville" in 1977, and invested the money it generated in a bar in Key West where he settled and lived the high life. He has now expanded the chain to cover a host of different states and countries, and has even bought the hotel at the end of Duval Street that overlooks South Beach and its sunsets. We had a very tasty margarita, without the added ville, listened to the house band for a while and then pottered off elsewhere.

Just off Duval Street are two bars that both lay claim to be the infamous Sloppy Joe's Bar, where Ernest Hemingway drank and caroused in the 1930s. The bar on the original site of Sloppy Joe's in Greene Street is now called Capt. Tony's Saloon and is a cool, dark place to lurk over a beer or cocktail. The people who own the Sloppy Joe's brand have a bar of the same name just around the corner on Duval

Street, and they milk its notoriety with Saturday-night live music and general loudness. I know which version of Sloppy Joe's I prefer.

In 1920, the Eighteenth Amendment to the US Constitution enshrined the law of unintended consequences into the statute books, no more so than in Key West. During the early 20th century the small, very conservative and extremely vociferous Puritan lobby set about attempting to spoil the nation's party. In their religiously blinkered eyes, the entire country had turned into Sodom and Gomorrah and the demon drink was to blame. It was wreaking havoc on American society and had to be eradicated before the populace burned in the fires of Hell! They formed the oxymoronic Prohibition Party and their lobbying grew loud and very successful. Congress and the Senate passed Prohibition into law via the Eighteenth Amendment in 1920, banning the manufacture, distribution and sale of alcohol in all American territories.

The ban stayed in place until 1933, and its unintended consequences included a massive loss in tax revenue for state and federal governments, a rise in the uncontrolled market for low-quality home-made moonshine, and the advent of the Mafia. Well done, chaps!

Key West made a fortune out of Prohibition. It was close enough to pre-communist Cuba to run a very profitable and entirely legal trade in seaplane flights to and from the island, where alcohol was freely and legally available. Key West also became the hub of an entirely illegal trade in smuggled Cuban rum, and the town had many speakeasies selling the illicitly imported nectar. Maybe that was why Ernest Hemingway began spending his winters in Key West in 1930.

In a bar somewhere on Duval Street (the one with the really good blues band on), a lady caused a few ripples when she walked in topless with her breasts painted in swirly designs, which apparently is a thing. It must have taken a fair intake of alcohol to drum up the bottle to do it, but she held her head up high and walked through the room exuding confidence. She was with her boyfriend and, whilst a few eyelids were batted, nobody said anything to her and no drunken blokes came over for a gawp or a grope. I bet she wished she wasn't the only girl in town dressed like that though.

The last port of crawl for the evening was the Hog's Breath Saloon, tucked away at the back of Duval Street down a short side alley. The beer was flowing and the band was excellent, so we skulked outside in the warm evening air and enjoyed ourselves. At one point the bouncer stopped three girls from going into the bar and checked their age. None of their fake ID cards passed muster and he wouldn't let them in, but he didn't stop them from buying a pint each at the bar that opened onto the square. They did so and sat under the nearest tree, from where they could hear the music and feel part of the party without compromising the bar's licence. It was nothing to do with him, officer.

On the stroll back to our hotel we encountered an excellent skiffle band, busking for money from the well-oiled tourists. Further down the street we came across Darth Vader playing a fluorescent blue banjo, entertaining the late-night drunks. His sign proclaimed him to be the southernmost banjo-playing Darth Vader in America, which probably made me the southernmost drunk Scouser watching a banjo-playing Darth Vader in America. How's that for a claim to fame?

Despite substantial evidence to the contrary, Key West is not all drunkenness and debauchery. It also has the splendid Fort Zachary Taylor Historic State Park, with its interesting old fort and lovely quiet beaches. The Truman Annex is part of a former naval base and officers' quarters that was used by a number of presidents as a holiday home and out-of-the way conference centre. The rest of the base, surrounding the Truman Annex, is now a very swanky estate for the rich and famous. There is also a Hemingway museum that is occupied by the fabulously inbred descendants of his six-toed cat.

Key West attracts vast cruise ships that berth at the quay at South Beach and disgorge enormous numbers of tourists into the town. They pour off the boat and wander around like disorientated Daleks, determined to spend as little money as possible. Eventually it's time to embark again, and they return to the ship's all-inclusive bars and restaurants. A few T-shirts and fridge magnets here and there is a very poor return for a town that has to put up with such huge, short-term influxes of people. Also, the curmudgeon in me can't imagine anything more hellish than spending my holiday cooped up in a massive floating town, unable to escape from the sorts of people who go on cruises.

Leaving Key West was a bit of a wrench, but the drive out of town did give us an insight into how a visit there is part of the great American Dream. One in every five cars heading south was a new, convertible Ford Mustang, the archetypal American muscle car. They were all in primary colours and were all being driven by men. Sunday morning at the Miami airport car-rental desks must be clogged by people being treated to a week in the Florida Keys in an open-topped 'Stang. I do hope they all got the car that they had booked. Jealous? Me? Damned right I am.

We had to slog our way north of charmless Miami to get to our next stop, an unstaffed hotel next to an anonymous beach in an unremarkable suburb. I won't name the chain of hotels, but when we turned up after a long drive the gates were locked and there was nobody answering the intercom. When we eventually worked out how to open the gates, we walked into a front courtyard containing a pool, a load of rentable pushbikes and a pile of yesterday's unwashed bedclothes. Our room key was in an envelope in a folder hanging by the door of the unattended porter's office.

It wouldn't take much for an entrepreneurial local to open the gates, duplicate the room keys whilst nobody is looking, and then have it away with the guests' gear when they're on the beach. The hotel's rental pushbikes, poolside furniture and TVs are also easy targets. Some might call it efficiency, but I'd call it lazy cost cutting and taking risks with guests' security.

My knowledge of Floridian geography is scant at the best of times, so I had no idea that Cape Canaveral and the Kennedy Space Center were on the east coast, a day's drive north of Miami. For some reason I thought they were in the middle, next to Orlando and all the other theme parks. Similarly, I had no idea that almost the entire southeast coast of Florida is a vast, elongated conurbation, from Florida City in the south, through Miami, Fort Lauderdale and Palm Springs, to Jupiter. Further up the coast are other, shorter ribbon developments of retirement and holiday homes.

The Space Center covers half of a vast section of coast called Merrit Island, about 125 miles north of Jupiter, and welcomes thousands of tourists every day. Thankfully, we were there in the quiet season so the hordes were manageable. We arrived just as the gates were opening and were steered to the bus tour by a helpful member of staff. Apparently the queues become hideous later in the day. The bus tour takes you around the site, past the huge Vehicle Assembly Building, where the rockets are put together. This gargantuan shed can be seen on the horizon from miles around, and leading from its door is a dirt road on which the fully assembled rockets are moved to their launch pads. One of the 6,000 ton, caterpillar-tracked moving platforms that does the lifting and shifting was parked up by the side of the road, and its size took my breath away. The tour also takes in one of the launch pads from which any number of famous expeditions has taken off.

Back in the Visitor Complex we were shuffled into a darkened room in which we were given a brief talk about the *Atlantis* space shuttle. We were told how it was part of NASA's programme to develop and fly a reusable vehicle into space, to launch satellites and service the International Space Station. At the end of the talk the music built to a crescendo and, in a superbly executed big reveal, *Atlantis* hove into view. There it was, right in front of us: the actual been-up-in-space-and-everything space shuttle. It is battered, beautiful and not very big, but above all, completely awesome.

There are other exhibits around the park, including all sorts of rockets and space ships, and there's even a space shuttle simulator that Áine Two loved and I avoided like the plague.

The Kennedy Space Center is superb and somewhere that any self-respecting science or transport geek should visit. The awesome boys' toys quotient is off the scale.

Our hotel that night was in the nearby Cocoa Beach, another of east Florida's coastal developments and famous for being where the Barbara Eden and Larry Hagman TV show *I Dream of Jeannie* was filmed. Just opposite the hotel was a side road called I Dream of Jeannie Lane that led to the beach. The hotel itself was unremarkable other than that it was once owned by NASA's original seven astronauts, including John Glenn, the first American to orbit the Earth, and Alan Shepard, the first American in space and the only one of the original seven to walk – and play golf – on the moon.

On the opposite side of the main road to I Dream of Jeannie Lane was Armstrong Chiropractic ("New spines on back order, let's fix yours"). I made a comment to a passing American lady that I'd worked out what Neil Armstrong did once he'd retired, pointing to the sign. "Oh really, is that what he did?" was her surprised reply.

The lesser known but equally splendid attraction that takes up the other half of Merritt Island is the Merritt Island National Wildlife Refuge. It is made up of thousands of unspoilt and protected acres of swamp and salt marshes, and several miles of driving and walking routes that create the opportunity to get uncomfortably close to alligators, again. There are also roseate spoonbills, which are like pink flamingos with long, flat spoon-shaped bills.

The roads to and around the nature reserve were virtually empty, and it was an unexpected pleasure to have a completely traffic-free day to explore the area.

In America, the phenomenon known as Spring Break is a week-long holiday taken around Easter by many of the country's universities. It has created a tradition of hundreds and thousands of students descending on whichever town is currently en vogue, and drinking and fornicating until they have exhausted themselves and daddy's credit card, or they have burned the town down.

As Florida has the most suitable weather for Spring Break, it has suffered more than most states in having to bear the brunt of teenage excess. Panama City Beach was the place to go until 2016, when the local authorities got so fed up with it all that they banned it. Apparently, part of the Spring Break culture is to emulate the New Orleans boobs-for-beads exposure, but without the beads bit.

Nobody was able to tell us when Spring Break was due to take place in 2017, so we booked our accommodation with some trepidation. Neither of us had any desire to be caught up in the teenage hordes' high jinks. I'm sure the last thing a load of drunken students want to see on their coming-of-age Spring Break is some grumpy old Englishman growling disapprovingly at them at 3 am.

We discovered at my sister's wedding that her new mother-in-law, Margaret, lived in Daytona Beach in the late 1980s and early 1990s and was still very fond of it. We weren't planning on stopping there, but decided to do so on her recommendation. I owe Margaret a pint.

Daytona Beach is famous for a number of high-profile annual motorsport events that take place in or around the town. The hard-packed sand on the beach enabled motor racing enthusiasts in the first half of the 20th century to blast up and down the shore creating as much havoc and having as much fun as they could get away with. Eventually, like Panama City Beach did with its Spring Break guests, the town got fed up with it. However, instead of banning it and losing the tourist income, the local powers-that-were built a racetrack that now hosts the world-famous Daytona 500 NASCAR race.

Daytona Beach is like any other seaside town. Its beachside hotels are built along the ever-present spit and start low rise in the southern suburbs, grow in height until they reach the centre of town and then fall away again at the northern end, creating an architectural bell curve along the coast. The beach itself is vast, clean and safe, with cars allowed to park on certain sections. They even queue up to do so at busy times. State Road A1A, the famous Florida coast road, runs through the town along the spit and the main shopping and drinking streets run at right angles to it.

Bike Week is another famous, or perhaps infamous, annual event. Half a million motorcyclists descend on the town for the Daytona 200 motorcycle race and a ten-day party. It is not often that Bike Week and Spring Break coincide but it seems that these two unlikely bedfellows were about to come to Daytona Beach for the same week, and we were only a few days in advance of them. The bikers were rumbling into town, mostly on Harley-Davidsons, with Britain represented by a sprinkling of modern Triumphs. It makes for a very impressive sight when every inch of available kerb on Main Street is taken up by large motorbikes, reverse parked and on side stands in precise formation.

As with the dune buggies playing on the Algodones Dunes in California, it seems that many of the Harley riders arrive in huge RVs with their bikes in tow on trailers. They camp out of town and burble around on their bikes for the day, before returning to the comforts of their mobile homes at night. Owning and riding a Harley must be an expensive business because the vast majority of the bikers we saw were well into their fifties and above. There were a significant number of female riders, but most were grizzly, bearded men. When they take off their leathers and bandanas, many turn into the mild-mannered retired accountants and bank managers of their everyday existence. It crossed my mind that if most of the present-day Harley riders in America have reached retirement age, who is following along behind them to secure the future of Bike Week, and indeed the nation's leading bike manufacturer?

The tide of Spring Breakers was arriving in equal numbers to the bikers. The youngsters spent much of the morning crashed out on the beach, and the afternoon and evening being refused entry to the town's bars and restaurants. Many of them seemed to retreat to parties being held in rented villas or hotel rooms along the main drag, keeping well out of the way of their scary, bike-riding neighbours.

We started our evening's drinking in the rooftop bar of the restaurant at the end of the town's pier. A DJ was setting himself up so we knew our time was limited. We divided it between staring out to sea at the incoming thunderstorms and watching a group of lads play a barroom game that seemed to involve throwing small bags of rice into a padded toilet seat from 10 yards away. Either they were naturally crap at it or the beer had dulled their capabilities, but I don't think they would make the local league.

We ate a bowl of something unmemorable in the Tiki Hut on Main Street whilst chatting to a guy who had got divorced, sold up his home in the cold north and moved to Miami. He'd bought a nice tidy condo on the edge of Daytona Beach, set himself up doing odd jobs for various people, bought a Harley and settled down to a comfortable semi-retirement in the sun. As his kids were finishing university they were moving south one at a time to join him. It would have been difficult to find a more contented man in all of America, especially since his choice of president had made it to office.

Somehow, later that evening, we managed to get dragged into the Bike Week launch party at Main Street Station, a legendary bar and live music venue. The beer was flowing, the band was very good, even playing a couple of obscure early Lynyrd Skynyrd songs to keep me on my nerdy toes, and the atmosphere was relaxed and friendly. I was fully be-quiffed and side-burned and wearing shorts and a short-sleeved, collared shirt, looking for all the world like a 1950's rock and roller. It was the sort of night I haven't experienced since I drank in the old bikers' bars and clubs in Liverpool in the 1980s, and not the night to be wearing something other than my trusty Motörhead T-shirt.

A couple of Spring Break girls, who couldn't have been more than 19 or 20, plucked up the courage to try to get into the bar. They were flatly refused entry by the bouncers. Maybe they were looking for their granddads.

The drive north to our next port of call, St. Augustine, finally got us away from the high-rise blocks and back to something closer to the natural state of the coastline. It was a lovely, relaxed journey along the coastal spit, with houses and B&Bs lining the inland side of the road and white sands and water the other. Opposite the end of every side road, a set of steps gave safe access over the sand dunes to the beach beyond. Some steps were usable but others had been badly damaged by a recent weather event, presumably Hurricane Matthew. We passed thousands of Harleys and huge RVs heading the other way to Daytona, and even managed to see a frigatebird flying over Flagler Beach, which is the most alliterative piece of birdwatching of all time.

As we travelled through Florida we were advised by many people to make sure we stopped off in historic St. Augustine, so we did and we weren't disappointed. St. Augustine was founded in 1565 and is the oldest continuously occupied European settlement in the continental United States. It was sacked by Sir Francis Drake in 1586, and changed hands several times in line with Spanish, British and American ownership of some or all of Florida.

St. Augustine is now a lovely, historic Mediterranean-style port, built slightly incongruously on the east coast of Florida. It has narrow streets, a big fort and a healthy variety of bars and restaurants. St. George Street, the town's main thoroughfare, is a narrow winding road, with many of its buildings dating back as far as the 1700s. It has been pedestrianised for the tourists, and for a change, isn't lined by bars, restaurants and gift shops, but with proper local craft shops and small museums.

We stayed at the very pleasant Saragossa Inn B&B, where our room had a little sofa on the porch that it shared with the room next door. I was sitting quietly reading a book and enjoying the evening warmth when a voice next to me rumbled, "Are we gonna win tonight then?" It belonged to the man from the next room, who happened to be from Huyton in South Liverpool. William Anderton, who currently lies in a grave in New Orleans, was baptised in Huyton Parish Church on April 4th 1830.

Our neighbour had seen the Liverpool T-shirt I was wearing. He and his wife were on holiday with some friends, and had stopped off in St. Augustine for a night on the way to the airport at Orlando. It was their first time in Florida and they seemed to be enjoying it just as much as we were. We had a good gossip about our favourite football club, and how we were missing a chunk of the season, and he was very impressed with the scale and ambition of our road trip.

The following morning there was much hilarity over breakfast as we were all served the richest chocolate cake imaginable. Mine was minus the double cream and ice cream that accompanied everyone else's. Sadly, Áine Two was unable to finish hers, so I had to step in to save the family honour.

Liverpool beat Burnley 2–1, in case you're interested.

In one shopping arcade we came across a store selling beer and music-related T-shirts and other touristy stuff, and accidentally initiated another Liverpool-based encounter. The shopkeeper was a friendly middle-aged guy who was keen to find out where we were from. On hearing Liverpool he nearly hopped up and down with glee. It turns out he used to be a local radio DJ and quite likes The Beatles. Every person over a certain age from Liverpool can conjure up a Beatles-related connection when pressed, regardless of how many degrees of separation are involved. My grandfather's fruit and veg shop on Wavertree High Street backed onto Arnold Grove, the location of George Harrison's childhood home. George used to come into the shop for his mother's messages. My mum went to school with George's sister, and he and his bus-driver dad used to meet them off the bus on their way home. The road I was born in is a few hundred yards from the top of Penny Lane, and my dad was a customer of both the bank and Tony Slavin's barbershop that are mentioned in the song.

As you can imagine, after hearing of all these Beatles related connections, our DJ friend was having paroxysms of joy, so I held back on the really big one until he'd calmed down a bit, just in case he burst. My mother has a named credit on a Paul McCartney album. Paul wrote a choral piece called the *Liverpool Oratorio*, and it was recorded in 1991 in Liverpool Cathedral. It featured Dame Kiri TeKanawa, Willard White, the Royal Liverpool Philharmonic Orchestra and the Royal Liverpool Philharmonic Choir. My mother was in the choir at the time and when the recording was originally released on vinyl, it came in a box set with a booklet in which all the members of the choir and orchestra were listed. As the choir worked for free, they were each given a signed copy, and my dad still has my mother's somewhere. I think DJ wanted to have my babies after that one.

Also in the city is a fabulously bonkers gift shop called *The House of Ireland* that sells every daft piece of Irishness you can imagine. It wasn't just there for the forthcoming St Patrick's Day bonanza, but is a year-round feature that happened to have its feet set firmly apart in preparation for the expected onslaught of Ireland inspired madness.

The lady owner was delighted to meet a real Irish person and was happy to explain that almost everything she sold was imported from Ireland. Why anyone in sun-kissed Florida would want to buy a real hand-knitted woollen Aran jumper is beyond me, but she had enough to clothe the five-thousand so she obviously had confidence that they would sell. Also on the shelves were Barry's Tea, Tayto crisps, soda bread, shortbread, barm brack, badges, key rings, Irish tricolours and county flags, T shirts, sweat shirts, rugby shirts, tweed hats, tweed caps, tweed jackets, walking sticks, Guinness souvenirs, photographs of the homeland, miniature models of farmhouses, pubs and shops and innumerable other trinkets, likely and unlikely, that a wannabe Irishman or woman could pay their hard-earned dollars to own. It made me realise just how much of a profitable international business Irishness has become. It is a commercial empire that stretches far beyond the British one of which Ireland was once a part.

The shopping bonanza continued in *Pepper Palace*, a store selling nothing but chilli pepper sauces that goes by the strapline, "Over 60 Feet of Free Samples from Mild to Wild". The sauces are arranged in order of heat, with the mild ones at one end and the "playing a prank on your buddies" hot ones at the other. We wandered in to see what was available and came out after a few samples unable to taste anything and with a stinging tingle on our tongues and lips. *Pepper Palace* is certainly not an emporium for the faint hearted.

Castillo de San Marcos, the fort that protects the harbour at St. Augustine, is situated, as one would expect, at the mouth of the local river, providing a perfect view of ships approaching the town through the St. Augustine Strait. It can be no surprise in the oldest European settlement in the continental United States, that Castillo do San Marcos is the oldest stone fort in the continental United States. It was built from 1672 to 1695, and currently hosts a very good museum. The docents are dressed in period Spanish uniforms and give talks on life in the Spanish military at the time the fort was constructed. Five times throughout the day the docents get together and fire one of the cannon on the battlements, demonstrating the rigmarole of loading, priming and firing it to the watching tour groups. It all builds up slowly and then ends with an unexpectedly sudden and loud bang. That'll teach me not to be paying attention when there's a big gun being operated.

A short way from the fort and the riverfront is the oldest church in Florida, the Cathedral Basilica of St. Augustine. The lovely Hispanic building currently on the site was built in the late 18th century and was visited by Pope Paul VI in 1976, when he promoted it from a mere cathedral to the status of a basilica. The interior is very simple, with a red pitched roof and exposed, painted tresses. There are small stained-glass windows, the Stations of the Cross on the walls and a beautifully decorated altarpiece. It is a strange mix of Hispanic and German influences, with a bit of Irish included in the form of a side chapel for St Patrick.

In 1888 our friend Henry Flagler built the Ponce De Leon Hotel in St. Augustine, presumably because there was nowhere else posh enough for him to stay and he wanted to be able to promote the town to his wealthy pals. It was so successful that he also built the Alcazar Hotel directly opposite. They are both Hispanic in style, and today house the Flagler College and Lightner Museum respectively.

It makes a nice change to be able to stroll through the middle of a seaside town and not be assaulted by thumping music and breakfast drinkers. However, that isn't to say that

St. Augustine doesn't have a healthy supply of places to drink; quite the opposite. It's just that they are not conveniently arranged in one place. The tourist in want of a few cold beers is required to wander about a bit and enjoy the town between pints. We stumbled upon one splendid place called The Social Lounge, noticeable primarily because of its variety of football scarves hanging in the window, including Everton, Celtic, Liverpool, Manchester United and, weirdly, Hamburg SV. It turns out that the owner, Scot, is a lifelong Leeds United fan who was brought up in Cambridgeshire, where his dad was in the US forces. After Scot retired from a long career in aviation, he bought something that allows him to participate in his two great loves, drinking beer and talking to people. He is a charming host who runs a tiny pub with an extensive range of craft beers. I can happily say that, of all the bars in all the towns and cities we visited on this road trip, The Social Lounge in St. Augustine was where we had the most pleasurable time, drinking great beer and talking rubbish to friendly folk.

In his aviation career, Scot had worked in military air bases in the same Arizona and New Mexico deserts that we had driven through. He was full of stories of long hot days in the middle of nowhere, and how his thoughts often turned to warm English summer evenings, when the sun didn't set until 10 pm and the warm brown English ale kept flowing until well gone midnight. He considered stay-behinds in pubs in rural England to be one of God's greatest creations. Who am I to argue with that?

That evening we had a very memorable dinner in the Mojo Old City BBQ restaurant, a place renowned for its ribs and onion wings. We ordered big and tucked in to another plate of sticky loveliness, accompanied by a bowl of almost hemispherical onion rings. They were made by simply halving a vast onion laterally and then poking out each ring in turn, before deep-frying them in a glorious crispy batter. Some must have been the circumference of a baby's head and they were absolutely delicious. Unfortunately, my eyes were bigger than my belly (which is some feat, as Áine Two will testify), and we couldn't do them full justice.

As usual, we ate at the bar, and watched in horrified awe as a small clutch of visiting frat boys tried to relive their long lost Spring Break heyday. With much loud and self-indulgent drama, they ordered rounds of pints and shot chasers, ostentatiously downing each drink in one before barking the order for the next one. The bar staff gave them the appropriate attention for a few rounds and then began to take longer and longer to resupply them. Eventually, Head Boy got bored waiting, and they all trooped out to annoy some other people.

Another fun thing to do in St. Augustine is visit the alligator farm. It's been there since the 1890s and houses breeding examples of every flavour of alligator and crocodile known to man, including some albinos. It's also home to a huge nesting site for roseate spoonbills, wood cranes and a variety of herons and egrets. Feeding time for the alligators was an uncomfortable spectacle that generated a proper frenzy amongst the 250 animals in the pond.

Many towns and cities in the USA celebrate St Patrick's Day, or St Patty's Day as it is known around here. Is it just me, or does St Patty sound like he should be the patron saint of fast-food burger joints?

How's this for confusing? St. Augustine is a city in North America founded by Galicians from Spain in 1565. It is named after the Algerian patron saint of, amongst other things, brewers, printers, theologians and Bridgeport, Connecticut. Every year the city holds a parade and festival to celebrate the Welsh patron saint of Ireland, in which it flies the flags of Cornwall, the Isle of Man and Brittany. We couldn't leave town on Saturday morning, as the St Patty's Parade (note the absence of the word Day) had closed the streets. So we wandered along and watched in bemused awe at the variety of green, white and gold on display from just about every institute in town. In the parade were a squadron of kilted *Star Wars* Storm Troopers, a variety of Celtic pipe and drum bands, floats from both the Democratic and Republican parties – kept well apart in case a fight broke out – and a small company of junior army cadets, all turned out in immaculate uniform except one, who came dressed as a leprechaun. The highlight was the lone marcher, not apparently part of any of the other parading groups, entirely encased in an inflatable *Tyrannosaurus rex* costume and wearing a green, tinsel-lined hat balanced on his head at a jaunty angle.

After the parade the entire town decamped to a local park for a shindig, followed by a hooley, two sessions and an almighty hullabaloo. The queues were vast so we retired for the car and headed for some sanity in Georgia.

Getting around the sprawl of Jacksonville, the largest conurbation in America, was looking like it was going to be a bit of a schlep, until Áine Two's navigational genius kicked in. We continued on State Road A1A along the coast almost to the mouth of the St. Johns River at Mayport, where a small car ferry took us to the north shore, thus circumventing the Jacksonville traffic.

I had my doubts about Florida before we came. I'm not a fan of beaches, drunk Brits on holiday (hypocritical, *moi*?), teenagers on Spring Break or theme parks, to name but a few pet hates. However, I loved exploring Florida's coastline and, as long as I can avoid Orlando, I'll be back for more some time.

CHAPTER 10
GEORGIA PEACHES

If, on the off chance, you're into 1970s German electronic music, you'll probably know Tangerine Dream's 1976 album *Stratosfear*, and the legendary instrumental piece "3 AM at the Border of the Marsh from Okefenokee". Okefenokee National Wildlife Refuge is just north of the border between Florida and Georgia, and roughly 100 miles or so from the Atlantic Ocean. Unfortunately, we didn't have time to make a late night detour to it to play the tune in situ.

Georgia stretches approximately 300 miles inland, but we saw very little of it. We stuck to its Atlantic coastline from the Florida border to Savannah, but what we did see was remarkable.

The main road north along the coast turns inland not long after you cross the border, because the coastline loses its spit and ocean geography and becomes very heavily forested. It is also riddled with hundreds of small rivers, tributaries and man-made drainage ditches. These combine to give the coastline the look of the diagram about blood vessels from your O-level Human Biology textbook.

Much of this landscape was historically given over to logging and then, once the land had been cleared of trees, cotton and sugar plantations. *Gone with the Wind*, the Oscar-winning 1939 Civil War epic was set in Georgia. It starred Vivien Leigh as Scarlett O'Hara and Clarke Gable as Rhett Butler, and features Tara, the O'Hara family plantation. It plays on the old Irish notion that everything leads back to "The Land", and at the end of the film Scarlett returns to her war-ravaged home to try to rebuild her life. During the film she owns and runs a very successful logging business and sawmill, reflecting the dominant industry in the area during the Civil War period.

Further inland, Georgia now grows peaches and peanuts; former President Jimmy Carter used to be a very successful peanut farmer from Plains, Georgia.

Georgia has an ignominious history when it comes to its black population. It relied heavily on its enslaved workforce to make its economy financially viable, and after the Civil War it took grim and spiteful revenge on its freed Negroes. In 1877, at the end of the enforced post-war Reconstruction Era, during which time black men were granted the vote, Georgia introduced a poll tax, forcing all citizens to pay to live in the state. This punitive tax disenfranchised most of the poor population, both black and white. They couldn't afford to pay it and, consequently, lost their right to vote. Margaret Thatcher's attempts do the same thing in 1989 caused riots in London, and brought about the end of her tenure in office.

This state-sponsored discrimination against almost half of the population carried on until 1965. It is hard to believe that some parts of America were operating a system similar to South Africa's apartheid until only two years before The Beatles released *Sergeant Pepper's Lonely Hearts Club Band*.

Our first stop after St. Augustine was an extraordinary place called Jekyll Island, off the coast of southern Georgia. One of the Golden Isles, it once housed the Jekyll Island Club, a fiercely private institution whose members included J.P. Morgan, the Vanderbilts, the Rockefellers and Joseph Pulitzer of Pulitzer Prize fame. Each owned a stake in a 5-star hotel, plus a plot of land on which to build a summer retreat for themselves. At its peak, it is estimated that the members of the Jekyll Island Club owned a sixth of the world's wealth. The island must have been like the Davos of its day, with many of the world's richest people gathering to make conversation and do business away from the prying eyes of the media. We saw our first cardinal bird and a beautiful Carolina wren in the grounds of the Jekyll Island Club.

For a lot of your own hard-earned dollars you can now stay at the still 5-star Jekyll Island Club Resort. For many dollars fewer you can stay at a dreadful national chain hotel a few miles up the road, and wander around its posher neighbour for free.

Some of America's cheaper hotels are stuck out of the way and can't get decent management or staff. They run the same sort of system for preparing and allocating rooms as the car-rental companies do for their vehicles, except without the instant-upgrade bit. We arrived at our hotel midway through a Saturday afternoon and were given our room keys. The room hadn't been cleaned and there was a pile of dirty bedclothes heaped on the floor. We returned to reception to be told that there were no other rooms available yet. We weren't the only people in this situation, and as we waited we watched as cleaning staff moved slowly around the hotel, stopping to rest and gossip in full view of their frustrated customers. Once a room eventually became available it lacked its most essential ingredient: a working coffee machine. Áine Two rang reception to ask for one to be delivered, waited half an hour for nobody to turn up, and eventually stomped down there in full Irish-woman-on-the-warpath mode to pick one up herself. When she got back to the room clutching her trophy, it became evident that there were no pods with which to fuel the replacement machine, so off she went again, this time to be told that the hotel had actually run out of them. Rooms not being ready is routine, as are broken coffee machines, but this was a national chain of hotels on the East Coast tourist route, and someone had forgotten to order the coffee.

Over beers and dinner that night in the equally badly run bar, we met another lovely group of fellow travellers. First up were a couple from Indiana who were on their way south for some winter sunshine. We learned from them the expression "snowbirds", meaning the people who escape the harsh northern winters and migrate south to warmer climes for a few months at a time. We had already met many snowbirds on our trip, without knowing that they had a collective name.

Mr Indiana was a very pleasant, hard-working guy who ran a business drying out flooded basements and had a very dry sense of humour; a fact that he acknowledged was ironic. He had watched the BBC coverage of the 2015 floods and subsequent repairs in places like Somerset and York, and couldn't believe how long it was taking to dry the buildings out. "I could do the job in a week," he reckoned.

His wife expressed a fear of going to Europe because of the terrorist threats, and we had a very lively but friendly conversation about the relative numbers of deaths across America and Europe caused by crackpots with guns or bombs. America won hands down, or maybe Hands Up! In fact, California beats the whole of Europe for gun-related deaths on its own. Their opinions were probably based on America's appallingly biased and ill-informed TV news coverage, rather than on any sort of prejudice, and they were nothing like the bigoted drunk in Panama City Beach. I'm not sure we managed to change their views all that much though.

We were joined after a while by a splendid lady from Atlanta called Camilla. She was a tour guide, down for a weekend in her holiday home on Jekyll Island, and was full of amusing tales about guiding the uneducated, uncomprehending and plain stupid around her home city. Camilla gave us another one of those invaluable pieces of advice and suggested we stopped at Beaufort in South Carolina.

Interestingly, all three of our drinking buddies voted for Donald Trump: Mr Indiana because he liked what Trump stood for, and both ladies because they couldn't bring themselves to vote for Hillary Clinton. This was the first indication we'd had that Hillary was as much part of the country's electoral dilemma as Trump. In a choice between allegedly crooked and demonstrably sexist, misogynistic and racist to boot, in their minds the latter was the better bet.

A footnote to our Saturday-night session at the bar in the unnamed crap hotel was the appearance of the bartender's Black and Tan turtle. When I was doing my drinking apprenticeship in 1980s Liverpool, a Black and Tan was a cheap way of disguising rubbish beer; a half pint of Guinness or dark mild was poured into a pint glass that already contained a half pint of bitter. There was no messing about trying to keep the two drinks separate to distinguish the colours; it was, "Pour, pour, plonk. There you go, son. That'll be 50p please."

The name Black and Tan comes from an infamous group of British Army WWI veterans who were sent to Ireland to help the local police fight the IRA. Their thrown-together uniforms were two-tone, with black police tunics and tan army trousers.

In their bid to romanticise all things Irish, Americans also drink Black and Tans, and some barmen take great pride in being able to keep the two halves separate for long enough for the drinker to see the effect. Our man in Jekyll Island brought out a special implement to enable him to do this: his Black and Tan turtle. The four legs of this little chrome creature sit on the rim of the glass and the domed carapace allows the Guinness to flow slowly enough to settle on top of the beer below. A similar back-of-the-spoon method is used to keep the cream separate in an Irish coffee. We all watched his demonstration in drunken awe, whilst his customer unsuccessfully tried to persuade everyone in the bar to join in the round.

Further up the coast from Jekyll Island is Darien, a small but interesting town at the mouth of the Altamaha River.

In the 1690s, Scotland put half of its cash into a hare-brained scheme to set up a colony in Panama. It failed spectacularly, bankrupted much of the country and led directly to the Acts of Union of 1707.

New Inverness was established in 1736 by a shipload of Scots who were sent over to settle and protect the southern reaches of the nascent British colony of Georgia. They succeeded in becoming a permanent fixture, but almost blew it in 1739 by attempting to attack St. Augustine during the oddly named War of Jenkins' Ear. They took a fearful thumping from the Spanish in the process, but clung onto their settlement.

There is a plaque in the town celebrating the original Scottish settlers. They were led by a Captain John McIntosh Mohr and had proper Scottish surnames like McDonald, McClean and McCloud. The town is in McIntosh County.

The failed attempt at a Panamanian colony was known as the Darien Scheme, and the town's name was changed from New Inverness sometime in its early existence to commemorate it.

Paying for anything in America on a credit card still requires a signature, although it is never compared to the one on the card. Recently, banks tried to introduce chip and PIN technology, but it wasn't thought by users to be as secure as an unchecked signature, and was quietly dropped. Some traders continue to use the chip and PIN-enabled terminals, which only ask for the number when a correctly set up card is entered. The cards we were using are chip and PIN enabled, and it caused any amount of confusion in some of the more remote parts of the country. On a number of occasions our cards were rejected because the person operating the machine was overriding the PIN, expecting the machine to default to a signature. We had to step in a few times to prevent our cards from being cancelled on the grounds of suspected fraud, and more than once were asked to enter our PIN and then handed the receipt and a pen so that we could sign it anyway. After a while we gave up explaining the process, and did both like it was normal. We had just such an experience trying to pay for our lunch in a roadside café in Darien.

We took a very pleasant post-lunch stroll around the town, taking in its early churches and antebellum houses, eventually wandering into its excellent little museum, set up in the old police station and town jail.

According to our map, just south of Darien are Rhetts Island and Butler River. Putting two and two together, I wondered aloud to the lady in the museum what came first, the name of the character in *Gone with the Wind* or the place names. She didn't know, and didn't seem the least bit curious. Maybe my mind works in peculiar ways (there's no maybe about it), but wouldn't you want to know? An eight-Oscar-winning Hollywood epic is set around and about you, it depicts your history and you have such place names on your doorstep, and you don't make the connection. I think the town is missing a great opportunity to cobble together some tourist-attracting piffle to boost its economy.

The number of eccentric roadside attractions so beloved of American travellers drops the further east you go. Most of them seem to have sprung up in the Wild West, where distances between sane people were much greater, and the combination of heat, open space and solitude led to more off-the-wall thinking. On the East Coast they are fewer and further between, but do occasionally rear their heads to distract the unwary traveller. A few miles north of Darien on Highway 17 is the Smallest Church in America, a tiny 12-seater shed with a separate bell tower, painted white and properly consecrated. Officially called Christ's Chapel in Memory Park, the original was built in 1949 by a local grocer, Mrs Agnes Harper. When she died, Agnes left the chapel to Jesus Christ in her will, thus ensuring its future. The little building burnt down in 2015 but was rebuilt with the help of donations and is open to visitors again. It is non-denominational and is used for baptisms, regular services, weddings and funerals.

Georgia is proper Bible Belt country, where evangelical Christians hold sway in religion, education and politics. Many of the smaller towns on our route were service centres for widespread rural communities, and consisted of only those businesses required to keep residents stocked up on essentials. On entering such a settlement, we would pass a café, a bar and restaurant, a doctor's surgery, a hardware store and at least five churches. Two would represent the different flavours of the Episcopalian church, and the other three would be Baptist. This may be a slight exaggeration to make a point, but there were certainly many towns where churches of the same Christian sect outnumbered the businesses.

Savannah, Georgia is the star in the Deep South firmament; the veritable Southern Belle of the Ball. It is a small, compact Georgian-era colonial city, laid out by its founder, General James Oglethorpe, in a symmetrical grid pattern. It is peppered with 22 squares, most with a statue commemorating a famous son, daughter or Civil War hero of the city. Each square is lined with fabulous southern live oaks, and surrounded on four sides by glorious antebellum architecture. To wander around Savannah is to be transported back to the Deep South of the early 1800s, with wide boulevards, pony and trap combinations and massive skirts.

It is astonishing that so many of Savannah's original buildings still exist. It was besieged for a month during the War of Independence, and in the Civil War, Union General William Sherman (of Sherman tank fame) made Savannah his objective in his March to the Sea. This was a scorched earth campaign that laid waste to Atlanta and all points along the way to Savannah. It is Atlanta that can be seen burning in the background of the famous *Gone with the Wind* posters. Thankfully, the Savannah authorities saw sense and negotiated a truce before Sherman could raze it to the ground.

Savannah is a prosperous port at the mouth of the Savannah River, and was critical to the military efforts of both the Confederate and Union forces during the Civil War. It was blockaded by the Union Navy from 1862 until the end of the war in 1865.

At the start of the Civil War the Confederacy didn't have a navy to speak of. More than 90% of shipbuilding and naval capability was in the North, and the Confederacy needed ships to run Lincoln's blockades and bring in vital supplies. They sent a wily old Savannah native called James Dunwoody Bulloch to Liverpool to orchestrate the purchase of ships and provisions and the running of the Union blockades. Britain didn't officially recognise the Confederacy as a nation, and James Bulloch became its de facto ambassador to the UK. Bulloch and his team worked from offices in Rumford Place in Liverpool that now carry plaques commemorating those connections. My younger brother once had a desk in Bulloch's former office in Rumford Place.

Incidentally, Bulloch was the uncle of President Theodore Roosevelt and great-uncle of Eleanor Roosevelt, who went on to marry her distant cousin and future president, Franklin D. Roosevelt.

Britain had strict neutrality laws that prevented it from supporting one side or the other in an ally's internecine war, so it effectively supported both, turning a blind eye to ships, arms and uniforms being made and sold to both Union and Confederate agents. Liverpool was very much a Confederate city. It had made its fortune on slavery and cotton, and wanted to maintain its successful trading relationships with its Southern partners. The Confederate Navy's most famous and successful battleship, the CSS *Alabama*, was built and fitted out at the Laird shipyard in Birkenhead, and was crewed largely by Scousers. In *Gone with the Wind*, Confederate gun runner Rhett Butler claims poverty in America with the quote, "My funds are in Liverpool, not in Atlanta." Coincidentally, the blue half of Liverpool might like to know that the Bonnie Blue flag of the Republic of West Florida also gets a mention in the film. Rhett Butler and Scarlett O'Hara's daughter is described as having eyes "as blue as the Bonnie Blue flag", causing Rhett to give her the name "Bonnie Blue Butler".

Our old friend the CSS *Shenandoah* turned away from sacking San Francisco in August 1865, after the captain heard that the war had ended several months earlier. Throughout the war, the *Shenandoah*'s crew had carried out attacks on Union ships, and captured cargo was sent to Liverpool to be sold by Bulloch to raise funds for the Confederacy. The *Shenandoah*'s captain, Lieutenant Commander James Iredell Waddell, feared that he and his crew would be arrested and hanged for treason or piracy if they put into an American port, so he turned south from San Francisco and fled. The *Shenandoah* was pursued by Union ships as she sailed down the coast of South America, around Cape Horn and up the Atlantic to Liverpool, where Waddell's commanding officer, James Bulloch, was still living.

The *Shenandoah* turned up at the Mersey Bar, the mouth of the river, in November 1865 but was told by the river pilot that she couldn't come up river to the port unless under a recognised flag. Waddell hoisted the Palmetto flag, the state flag of Confederate South Carolina, and sailed up the Mersey. He surrendered to Captain Paynter of HMS *Donegal*, anchored in the river off the Toxteth shoreline.

The government in London didn't know what to do with the crew. Americans didn't come under British jurisdiction, and word came back to Liverpool to free any American citizens and arrest any British ones on charges of piracy. Rumour has it that a large number of Liverpool, Glasgow and Bristol accents suddenly changed to a Southern American drawl when that news came through. Nobody was arrested, and the CSS *Shenandoah*'s short journey up the River Mersey was the last act of the Civil War, and the last time a flag of the Confederacy was flown as part of it.

James Waddell returned to America and carried on his maritime career sailing ships down the East Coast of America and through the Panama Canal to trade with Japan and the Far East.

James Bulloch remained in Liverpool as a successful businessman. He died on January 7th 1901 at the age of 72 and is buried next to his brother, Irvine, in Toxteth Cemetery in Wavertree, Liverpool. His grave is a few hundred yards away from that of Alice Prior, wife of William Anderton of Earnscliffe, Blundellsands.

Liverpool has a difficult relationship with its slaving history, but has opened a brilliant International Slavery Museum as part of its equally brilliant Merseyside Maritime Museum. James Penny, after whom Penny Lane in Wavertree was named, was a prominent Liverpool slave trader. The Beatles weren't celebrating him in their song; just the lane that bears his name.

Savannah has no discernible relationship with Ireland or St Patrick's Day, but it plays host to what is reputed to be the second biggest St Patty's Day parade in America, after Chicago's. History suggests it grew from a parade carried out on March 17th 1824 by a small branch of the Hibernian Society, and the tradition has stuck. We heard all this as we worked our way north through Florida, and idly wondered if we could or should participate. That idea was put to one side as soon as we saw that hotel rooms in the town for the days around the parade were going for $400 a night.

Official estimates are that the population of the city doubles to 300,000 for the day of the parade, and the authorities have to operate a $10 a wristband system to limit the numbers of celebrants in the centre of town.

We turned up a few days before it all kicked off and enjoyed the increasing buzz as celebrations started to ratchet up. Savannah is a well-to-do town with plenty of upmarket shops, and every single one of them, without exception, was selling something green. If you knew nothing of St Patrick's Day you would think that this agonisingly pretty Southern city must be having a harvest festival for cabbages, or maybe a seasickness parade. The water in the fountains in Forsyth Park had been dyed green so that the stone swans and mermen were vomiting emerald bile for all to see.

Down on the riverfront, a row of historic warehouses has been converted into the requisite strip of bars, restaurants and tourist shops. Each one of the latter was selling an extraordinary array of green. Who in their right mind buys a green and white, squid-shaped hat to celebrate the patron saint of a small country 4,000 miles away? I'm glad we weren't staying for the actual day, because the overdose of such paddywhackery could have been fatal.

The lovely receptionist in our hotel had strongly recommended a bar on the riverfront called Kevin Barry's, which had apparently recently been voted the Irish pub in America that bore the closest resemblance to a proper one back home. We'll be the judges of that, we thought, and strolled off downtown to test her theory.

Whilst the Kevin Barry's Irish Pub is a splendid place to drink and chat, there's nothing that makes the drinker think of your average pub back in Ireland, other than maybe the Guinness pumps and posters. It has a long, U-shaped bar that faces you as you walk in, surrounded by the usual barstools, and a number of tables and booths around the walls. The ceiling is low, creating a nice, dark, close atmosphere and the walls are covered in an array of pictures of old Ireland and old Savannah. We came to the conclusion that Kevin Barry's was actually the Irish pub in the Deep South that possibly bore the closest resemblance to an Irish pub in Chicago or New York.

We got chatting to a Boston Irish couple who were returning north after their snowbird winter, and had stopped in Savannah to see what all the fuss was about. The pub had employed a new bartender in the build-up to St Patty's Day, and Boston Man and I set about instructing him in how to pour a proper pint of Guinness. I'm sure the last thing he needed was a couple of fat drunken know-it-alls making his life difficult, especially as neither of us was actually Irish, but he took it with good grace and could pour the best Guinness in the room by the end of the night.

Another bar recommended by the hotel receptionist was the Crystal Beer Parlor, just behind the hotel. Reputedly a speakeasy during the Prohibition era, it was the first bar to officially sell liquor in the city once the ban was lifted in 1933, and has been doing so continually ever since. It has a very long bar and an equally long beer and food menu, and all of the items we tried from them were excellent.

We fell into conversation with an electronics salesman from Sacramento, California, who was doing his regular tour of his customers in the South. He was full of dark tales of the incompetence of low-cost internal airlines in America, and how he was forced to use them by his cost-cutting bosses. We compared war stories, and he was appalled by the sheer chutzpah of Michael O'Leary and Ryanair in squeezing every penny out of customers through outrageous pricing tricks. Apparently none of the American equivalent airlines have gone quite as far yet.

Like all the other Californians we met on the trip, he voted for Hillary Clinton. His reasoning was that he simply couldn't bring himself to vote for Donald Trump. "Trump is a bully. He reminds me too much of my boss." Our new friend was working out his last few years before he'd retire to the golf course.

An outstanding feature of the Crystal Beer Parlor was that there was no evidence of St Patty's Day anywhere. It was a most welcome oasis of not-green.

Savannah boasts the atmospheric, gothic Bonaventure Cemetery and we strolled around it, partly because we could, and partly to see if there were any interesting graves we could investigate. Some of the statuary is morbidly fascinating, and the mixture of Jewish, German, Irish, Dutch, English and Scottish surnames on display shows how Savannah developed throughout the latter half of the 19th century. Alongside the striking in-full-bloom purple azaleas lining the pathways, another feature of note are the Irish graves that had been decorated in green, white and gold in preparation for the St Patty's Day celebrations. Who says the dead can't join the party?

Leaving the Bonaventure Cemetery, we struck east for Tybee Island, Savannah's seaside resort. London has Margate and Southend, Newcastle has Whitley Bay and Savannah has Tybee Island, and they are all much the same. The island sits at the mouth of the Savannah River and has miles of lovely Atlantic beaches but very little else. It has a locally famous restaurant called The Breakfast Club which, true to its word, serves breakfasts but only until it closes at 1 pm sharp. Anyone looking for an even moderately ill-timed lunch is sent elsewhere.

The small row of seaside shops scraping a living in what acts as the town centre were all valiantly flogging the obligatory green faux Irishness, but I fear that the town missed out on any spin-off revenue as the local taxi firm was offering $10 return trips by minibus into Savannah for the big day. After an undistinguished lunch in a local bar, we strolled along the beach in a stiff, cold spring breeze, huddled into our overcoats and hats, having our hangovers blown away for free.

CHAPTER 11
MY CAROLINAS

We decided to take Camilla the Tour Guide's advice to stop off in Beaufort, South Carolina on our way north. Pronounced Bew-ford, as in Sheriff Buford T. Justice from *Smokey and the Bandit*, Beaufort is a small picturesque antebellum port hidden in a tangle of rivers and inlets a few miles north of the South Carolina state border. It is next door to the historically significant Port Royal, but wouldn't appear out of place along the south coast of England. We wandered around the town for an afternoon, ooh-ing and aah-ing at all the lovely properties and views across the various waterways that surround it. Each waterside property has an extended jetty that reaches across the reed beds to the nearby creek. Houses have wide verandas and picture windows, so that views are available all year round.

We spoke briefly to a retired Marine who had served all over the world, and who was quietly pottering around his pristine front garden. He could have retired to anywhere in the country, and chose Beaufort because, "It is so peaceful. And because I can go fishing from the end of my garden." He gave the impression of being a very contented man.

My younger brother wastes far too much of his life cruising the internet, admiring places and properties from a distance on Google Street View. Beaufort is the sort of town that would keep him enraptured for hours on end.

Our B&B, The Beaufort Inn, is another antebellum masterpiece in the centre of town. It has given up on serving breakfasts, and hands out vouchers for a selection of local restaurants for guests to choose from. Everyone plumped for the excellent Blackstone's Café over the road, where the food is very filling and the tea and coffee bottomless. The busy, bustling room was hung with university and military flags from all over America, plus some interesting oddities from elsewhere.

Above our table was a British Union Flag that seemed to

be missing something. We eventually worked out that it was the red diagonal cross representing Northern Ireland that wasn't there. We discovered later that it was the British flag that was in use in the colonies during the 18th century, prior to the War of Independence, and only shows the Cross of St George and the Scottish Saltire. Ireland wasn't added until 1801. Versions of this early Union Flag appear throughout the historic sites of the East Coast of America.

A couple at the next table were discussing another unusual flag hanging over them, and asked us what we thought, as it had a British element to it. This flag was a black ensign: a white cross on a black background with the Union flag in the top left-hand quadrant. They were Americans who had lived in Reading for a number of years, and they recognised what they thought was the black and white Cornish flag. However, they couldn't reconcile it with what appeared to be a flag of a mythical Cornish Navy.

The Blackstone's Café has so many enquiries about its flags that it has a crib sheet for the staff, and we were informed by the new owner that it was indeed a Cornish Ensign. He had only bought the restaurant a few weeks beforehand, and had no idea where the previous owner had acquired the flag. Perhaps it was a prop for a production of Gilbert and Sullivan's *The Pirates of Penzance*.

Also on the wall of the Blackstone's Café was an old tourist poster showing the seven flags associated with Beaufort.

Like a number of East Coast towns and cities in America, Beaufort has a long and interesting history of discovery, settlement, war, conquest and eventual stability. A fort was built in nearby Santa Elena by the French in 1562 (Flag 1). They were kicked out by the Spanish in 1565 (Flag 2), who, in turn, were replaced by the British in 1670 (Flag 3). Scottish settlers arrived around 1684 to farm the land (Flag

4). The Stars and Stripes in its various early guises flew over the area from 1777 (Flag 5) until the Civil War broke out in 1861, when the Confederate flag took over (Flag 6). This flew alongside the Palmetto flag of South Carolina (Flag 7). It makes for a fascinating story, especially as the original French and Spanish forts have recently been excavated, and it knocks Pensacola's measly Five Flags Festival into a cocked hat.

We learned all of this from the superb Santa Elena History Center, situated in the old federal courthouse in downtown Beaufort. It had recently been refurbished and the docents were justifiably proud of it.

The Port Royal Experiment is an interesting piece of local history. It was an attempt by Northern charity workers to set up former slaves with land to see if they were capable of making a go of it without their white masters. Well meaning, definitely; patronising, possibly; successful, sadly not. Northern Civil War forces took control of the area around Port Royal and Beaufort in 1861 and the white landowners fled, leaving their slaves behind. The former slaves were given parcels of land to work, and the freedom to make their own decisions and to sell their excess produce within their local community. As you would expect, they were highly successful and within a year things were going well enough for the experiment to be considered a viable model for post-war reconstruction. Unfortunately, after the war ended, President Andrew Johnson killed off the idea and gave the land back to its previous owners, thus ending the first real chance at post-war equality between blacks and whites.

There are two additional features of Beaufort that are worth mentioning. The promenade has large bench swings where romantic couples can sit on pleasant evenings and watch the boats in the harbour sail by. I'd love to see something similar in seaside towns in the UK. Also, the bartender from the local bar was originally from Cork, and was battening down the hatches for the forthcoming bonanza of blarney.

The southeast coast of America was battered by Hurricane Matthew in 2016 and much of the area is still recovering. I wonder how many local residents see the irony in their town having the same name as the scale that measures wind strength. We took a drive from Beaufort out to the Hunting Island State Park, only to find that all the picnic spots and walking trails were closed due to the damage caused by Matthew. Even the bridge over to Fripp Island was shut, and the State Park Pier had taken a fearful hammering and was also fenced off.

Charleston, further up the North Carolina coast, has the dubious distinction of being where the first shots of the American Civil War were fired.

I've tried to keep the history lessons short whilst writing this book, but it is impossible to ignore the Civil War. Its causes go to the very core of the American psyche: the great dichotomy between federal government oversight and the rights of individual states to make their own laws. It is the same debate that lies behind the UK's Brexit referendum: federal European government versus UK sovereignty.

In the first half of the 19th century, America was divided into three sections, largely for geopolitical reasons. The northeast quarter was economically, industrially and commercially advanced. It had over 90% of the nation's industrial capacity and a largely paid workforce. These states had either outlawed slavery or had so few slaves that any trading of them was negligible.

The southeast corner was made up of slave states. Here

most manual work was performed by slaves, and the internal slave trade flourished. The South was economically backward, with very limited industry and an economy based on cotton, sugar, tea and tobacco that were kept at competitive prices by its free workforce. The South had few means of manufacturing anything from its produce, and exported much of what it made to the North or to Great Britain. It then had to buy back finished goods, made from what it grew and exported, at a higher price than it had sold the raw materials for in the first place.

The western half of the continent, west of Texas in the south and the Missouri River in the north, was largely unchartered territory, with a few sizeable settlements like San Francisco beginning to take shape.

It was easily demonstrable that the North benefited from a paid workforce that saw opportunity and betterment resulting from hard work. By contrast, the South's economy was retarded by its use of a slave workforce for whom getting through the day alive was their primary motivation. Through no fault of their own, slaves were in no position to better themselves, unless through escape and freedom.

A federal law existed that obliged all states to allow slave owners to recover escaped slaves from within their borders. Many Northern states chose not to enforce this law, turning a blind eye to those who harboured escaped slaves from the clutches of their Southern owners.

The balance of power between the slave states in the South and the free states in the North was precarious. In the years between 1816 and 1848, 12 states joined the Union: six each in the free and slave state camps. This reflected a deliberate federal policy to pair new states entering the union, to maintain the balance. After 1848, the South began actively lobbying for new territories and states to become slave states, in order to tip the balance of power in their favour.

These moves were blocked by the federal government. The four states that joined the Union between 1850 and 1861, including California and Oregon in the west, were all free states.

The South cried foul and accused the North of interfering with their rights to self-determination over the issue of slavery and the retrieval of lost property. The North claimed not to care about slavery within the then boundaries of the South, as long as it didn't expand beyond them. The assumption in the North was that slavery would run its course anyway, and would eventually be abandoned in the South.

Things bubbled up, with the existing anti-slavery Whig Party being replaced by the new and more robust Republican Party. Members were referred to as Black Republicans by Southern Democrats because of its anti-slavery, pro-freedom stance. The Democrats of the time represented the hard right, pro-slavery voters and were most prominent in the South. In 1860 Abraham Lincoln was elected as the first Republican president, with the North and its western free state allies holding sway over the South in Congress.

Seven slave states seceded from the Union after Lincoln's election, forming the new Confederacy under President Jefferson Davis.

In his inauguration speech, held in March 1861 beneath the dark clouds of an inevitable civil war, Lincoln vowed to keep hold of all the federal land, property and arms in the South. Fort Sumter, in the harbour at Charleston in North Carolina, was one such property.

Resupply and reinforcement of the Union garrison at Fort Sumter was prevented by the threat from Confederate guns stationed on the harbour wall. A stand-off prevailed for a short time, until, on April 12th 1861, the Confederate guns began a bombardment of the fort and the garrison surrendered.

After this opening act of war, Lincoln issued a call to arms for 75,000 Northern men, and four further slave states seceded almost immediately afterwards.

Civil War battles took place mostly across the South, with Confederacy foot soldiers justifying their personal involvement as a fight to the death to protect their land and families from the invading armies of the North. For the privates from the Union Army, it was about preserving the Union and freeing slaves.

Eventually, after almost exactly four years of fighting, General Robert E. Lee surrendered the Confederate Army of Northern Virginia to General Ulysses S. Grant on April 9th 1865, after final defeat at the Battle of Appomattox Court House in Virginia.

Five days later, on April 14th 1865, President Abraham Lincoln was shot by John Wilkes Booth and died the next day. Lincoln was the architect of the Union victory and the man many believed most likely to be able to rebuild a shattered nation. Booth escaped and was chased down and shot on April 26th, in a barn in Port Royal, Virginia (not the Port Royal near Beaufort, South Carolina).

According to the US National Park Service, the total number of soldiers killed in action during the Civil War is estimated at just under 235,000, with a further 450,000 people dying of disease, starvation or in POW camps. That is more than the total number of American soldiers who have died in all the other wars the country has fought up to the present day.

Charleston is as lovely as Savannah, but feels more like a proper port city. The streets are less well ordered and there are more original buildings from the 1700s, especially in the French Quarter and port area. They predate the traditional antebellum style, and are more like the plain and ordinary terraced dockside houses of a Cornish fishing village. It is a splendid place to wander down the little back streets and alleyways, seeking out original churches and other interesting buildings to explore.

The city is dominated by the mysterious Citadel, the Military College of South Carolina. Residents will proudly tell you that their sons and daughters are Citadel cadets or Citadel graduates. The town boasts many very smartly turned out youngsters in spotless cadet uniforms and fierce haircuts, often accompanied by their equally fierce parents and mini-me siblings.

The main tourist attraction in the city is the Charleston City Market: a narrow, quarter-mile-long 18th century market hall that stretches from the old dockside almost to the city centre. It originally sold meat, fruit and vegetables produced by local farmers, but is now a vibrant, modern food and craft market selling fantastic tea, coffee and sticky buns as well as a wide variety of trinkets. The night market was just kicking off again for the spring when we were there, and looked like it could be a great place to spend an evening. The market buildings are surrounded by a host of interesting-looking bars, cafés and restaurants, and we felt obliged to try a few out to make sure they were up to scratch.

Charleston was almost the epicentre of the American slave trade, and as early as 1708 the city had a majority black population. It was the northwestern tip of a triangular trade route that took sugar, tobacco and raw cotton to Europe; textiles, metal goods and guns to Africa and slaves back to America. Liverpool was the primary northeastern point of that triangle. It is estimated that half of the 3 million slaves shipped to the Caribbean and America were transported on

Liverpool-owned and registered vessels. That is not something that I am proud of, but it happened. I'm a firm believer that history should be commemorated, with the good things celebrated and the bad things remembered as lessons for the future. The South is currently agonising over whether to retain the statues of Confederate Civil War heroes in many of its major cities. Some have already been torn down, either officially or by local people.

Charleston emphatically hasn't torn down Ryan's Mart, but has turned it into the Old Slave Mart Museum, a small but brilliant depiction of the local involvement in slavery and how slave markets worked. Thomas Ryan began selling slaves there in 1856. In 1859 auction master Z.B. Oakes bought the property and built the market structure. It was closed at the end of the Civil War in 1865.

The museum depicts slavery in all its horror, with a particular focus on how the process of buying and selling human beings worked. Displayed on a map of the world, Liverpool and Bristol were the only two British cities highlighted (although Bristol has managed to migrate to Exeter for some reason). A panel about prominent slave owners uses George's Dock in Liverpool for its background, and highlights Thomas Golightly, a former mayor of Liverpool, as a slave trader.

We arrived in Charleston on the afternoon of St Patrick's Day, after a morning in the superb Charleston Tea Plantation, the only business of its type in the whole of North America. Out of town on the exotically named Wadmalaw Island, the plantation is a peaceful oasis of carefully trimmed bushes cultivated in ordered rows. It gives bus tours around the site on reconditioned old city trolley buses, as well as self-guided tours around the processing facility. There is also the obligatory gift shop which was a genuine pleasure to potter around, sampling the different teas as we went.

For some reason, the gift shop has a blackboard on the veranda on which they ask visitors to write their home state or country. Áine Two put down Ireland and the place nearly went into hysterics. You would imagine that the presence of a real Irish person on St Patrick's Day was the equivalent of a visit from the Pope or John Wayne. They had also dressed their tin frog, Waddy, up in a "Kiss Me I'm Irish" T-shirt for the amusing photo opportunity.

We saw wild turkeys at the tea plantation; the first new bird we'd spotted for weeks.

After checking into another hopelessly inadequate hotel, this time under renovation with rooms not ready, a closed bar and a lobby full of people wanting to get on the green beers, we got on the green beers.

One of the plethora of Irish pubs in Charleston is Tommy Condon's. It was, as you would expect, rammed with people dressed in green, white and gold, swilling back green pints and having a ball. Until that point I had only heard of green beer on St Patrick's Day. It is one of those urban myths that incredulous Irish people bring back from their early expeditions across the pond. However, after a night in Tommy Condon's I can confirm that it is not a myth. Green food colouring was being liberally administered to glasses of Bud Light to create a lurid, almost fluorescent emerald pint. By this stage, I think the horse was beyond ill and was on the tumbril to the knackers' yard. One of the quotes from the road trip was a voice that came from behind me whilst I was standing at Tommy Condon's bar. "Four green beers and a Guinness, please." I nearly wept as the bartender handed me my resolutely yellowy-brown pint of local craft beer.

We sought sanctuary in a quiet corner and immediately disproved Áine Two's theory that she was the only real Paddy in the place, by stumbling across two young lads from Belfast. They were both 21 and were on a student exchange from Queen's University to the University of Charleston, and they were agog at how Americans celebrate Ireland's patron saint's day.

One of them was studying history and told of how he attended two lectures on the same subject, one to a class of mostly white students and the other to a class of mostly black students. He was staggered at how the same subject could be taught so differently from two opposing perspectives. We gently pointed out that he was from one of the most divided cities in the world, and that the history he was taught in his Catholic school would be very different from that taught to his Protestant neighbours.

It turned out that, not only were our two new friends strangers before they came to Charleston, but they were also from the opposite sides of the religious divide in Belfast. They had hit it off as mates immediately, and only realised their supposed differences too late for them to care. They were the first people we had met from Northern Ireland who had grown up after the Good Friday Agreement had been put in place, and with the peace that it eventually brought. Whilst it will take generations for the hatred and mistrust to dissipate, their friendship, struck up outside the context of their home city, gives hope that it will eventually happen.

Their opinions on Guinness in America are unprintable, but they were resolutely sticking to their native product.

And on that basis, as the Saw Doctors song goes, we had a session.

During our St Patty's Day adventures, a lady we were chatting to in a bar was a bit shocked to find out we were a mixed British and Irish marriage. She asked us how that worked. I resisted the, "Well, when a man loves a woman..." response. She would have gone into meltdown to find a Belfast Protestant and a Belfast Catholic sharing beers together in an Irish boozer in the Deep South.

We met one of our drinking companions the following day, as we wandered into the city to find a hair of the dog. In contrast to our hungover state, he was depressingly chipper and was heading off to the university to do some work.

During our befuddled wanderings, we happened upon the excellent Lagunitas Charleston Taproom and Beer Sanctuary in the city's French Quarter, where we stopped for some afternoon refreshment. I love the notion of a beer sanctuary, as it seems to offer so much more than your common or garden pub. Swimming against the tide of pointlessly high ABV beers, Lagunitas brew DayTime Ale at 4.65%. At last, we had found a delicious and sensible session beer for which big trousers are not required. If it wasn't for the pipe-smoking redneck youth who insisted on spitting on the pavement next to our table every 30 seconds, we would have stayed for a few more. Stereotypes are exaggerations based on fact, and all this guy was missing was a straggly red beard and dungarees and he would have perfectly fitted the image we have of hillbilly Southern folk.

Leaving Charleston we cut inland, having decided to take Joy's recommendation to visit Asheville in North Carolina.

En route we stopped off at Columbia, the South Carolina state capital. It was fairly non-descript, with a modest high street and a pleasant capitol building, much the same as Tallahassee and on a smaller scale to that of Austin. A plaque outside the capitol building casually conveys the initial enthusiasm with which the city tackled its construction, why it was stopped, and their less-than-eager completion of the job:

"Construction of this state house was begun in 1855 and continued uninterruptedly to February 17, 1865, when Sherman burned Columbia.

Work was resumed in 1867 and carried on irregularly to 1900."

The guy manning the hotel reception desk pointed us to a restaurant in the student quarter called California Dreaming for our Sunday dinner. After walking for a couple of miles we came across it in a converted railway station by the university. The place was rammed, with queues stretching out of the door of people waiting for tables. We spotted two empty seats at the bar and swanned to the front of the queue to claim them. Sure enough, we were able to sit down straight away, avoiding all of the waiting around. My guess is that California Dreaming was not only the best place in town, but quite possibly the only place in town open on a Sunday afternoon. The food was very good and we left happy.

National Football League and National Basketball League games are often beyond the reach of your average sports fan; tickets are expensive and very difficult to come by. Combine that with a strong attachment to and identification with the local university or college, and you get a popular and very lucrative college sports scene. There is nothing in the UK that I can liken it to by way of illustration. In Seattle a number of years ago, we met a middle-aged couple who had travelled from Sacramento in California to watch their local college football team play. Neither they nor any of their kids had gone to the college, and they knew nobody in the team. However, they were prepared to travel the length of the

West Coast to watch the team play, and they insisted that they were typical of many fans. That would be the equivalent of several thousand Falmouth University football fans flying to Inverness to watch their team play against the University of the Highlands and Islands.

In Columbia we became conscious of basketball's March Madness. It isn't a sale of players at knockdown prices, but a national college basketball competition between 68 university and college teams. They are divided into four geographical regions and play a knockout competition, after which the four regional winners play two semi-finals, the winners of each going on to play the final.

This in itself is not particularly remarkable. After all, many countries have national university sports competitions. However, this being America, the hyperbole and consequential advertising revenue generated by the television companies is astonishing, and the coverage is widespread. Of course, we got hooked and followed progress on hotel and barroom TV screens. The South Carolina Gamecocks were doing extremely well, generating a degree of excitement in Columbia, and they won their Eastern Region. The North Carolina Tar Heels, directly north of them on the map, won the Southern Region. The Gonzaga Bulldogs from Washington State won the Western Region, and the Oregon Ducks, on the West Coast immediately south of Washington State, won the Midwest Region. I think the regional divisions may benefit from a reorganisation.

Sadly, we didn't get the two Carolinas in the final, although both of the semi-finals were incredibly close affairs. The Tar Heels eventually beat the Bulldogs 71–65 in an exciting final.

In the UK, Tottenham Hotspur FC fans shorten their club's name to Spurs, and display their abbreviated name and proud cockerel emblem on all manner of clothing. South Carolina Gamecocks fans do a similar thing.

Georgia and South Carolina are wonderful states to travel through, and have helped us put slavery, the Civil War and the innocent use of the word "Cocks" into context.

CHAPTER 12
IN THE BLUE RIDGE
MOUNTAINS OF VIRGINIA

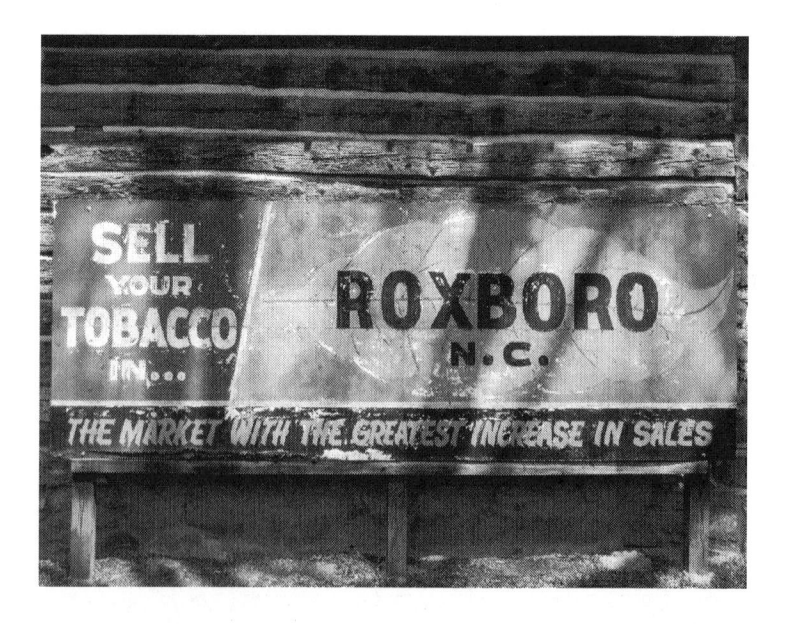

The drive from Columbia to Asheville, North Carolina, took us along a section of the immensely popular Blue Ridge Parkway, another special road built by the CCC using

Roosevelt's New Deal funds. As its name suggests, it runs the length of the Blue Ridge Mountain range, parallel with the border between North Carolina and Tennessee, and it takes in some of the most glorious mountain countryside imaginable.

To get to the Parkway we drove through Spartanburg and Hendersonville and up an astonishingly twisty and challenging road into the mountains. It was proper driving, and the automatic gearbox of the poor rental car was giving off some very odd smells by the time we reached the main road. We had a near-death experience as we arrived at the T-junction with the Parkway. A local *The Dukes of Hazzard* wannabe in his battered Honda turned left off the main road, taking the racing line around the corner so that he cut across the oncoming traffic. As we pulled up to the junction to turn right he careered past us and howled off down the hill, missing the front of our car by millimetres. I half expected to see a cop car with flashing lights and Sheriff Rosco P. Coltrane at the wheel whizz by in hot pursuit. Unfortunately, he failed to materialise, and the dangerous twerp got away scot-free with his stupidity.

The section of the Parkway that took us to Asheville wasn't very long, but was a tantalising foretaste of what was to come. The speed limit is 45 mph, and there is a stunning view across mountain peaks and deep valleys around every corner. It took us far longer than intended to navigate our way into Asheville because we kept stopping and gawping at the scenery. The mountains really are blue, with each set of peaks becoming a shade closer to grey the further away they were, until the distant ranges were a lovely soft, smoky mixture of light blue and grey.

The driving itself was as much fun as the Big Sur road, but without the ocean backdrop and Matt Monro soundtrack.

Asheville has an unremarkable past, an interesting present and a great future. Initially, it grew reasonably wealthy on local industry, and borrowed heavily against its future success. The Wall Street Crash of 1929 and the Great Depression put an end to the fun, and left the town wallowing in debt. It stagnated for more than 50 years, until things began to pick up again in the 1980s.

Riding on the back of the American craft beer revolution, Asheville has become an important centre for brewing, and is also a favourite place for men to take their partners for romantic weekends away. I can't think why.

There are almost 40 breweries in or near Asheville, many of them within easy walking distance of one another in the town centre. We made the effort to visit several of them in the interests of research, with some very mixed results. The brewers ranged from the enthusiastic amateur who inherited his grandfather's home-brew kit, through the mad scientist bent over steaming vats of foul-smelling liquid, past some with long and prosperous careers in the brewing trade ahead of them, to the big boys like Sierra Nevada, who have just moved into town and are busy recruiting all the good young talent from around and about.

On our initial brewery crawl we discovered that there is a lot of experimentation taking place, resulting in some weird and wonderful flavours and colours, not all of which work. Several of the most highly recommended breweries are amongst the least impressive that we visited. The Asheville Brewing Company and Wicked Weed Brewing Pub are both worth a mention for brewing some decent beer, and for selling it in reasonably attractive surroundings. The Asheville guys had a pleasant bar done out a bit like a traditional American diner, with a large covered area outside where most of the drinkers congregated. It served food and caught some of the townsfolk returning home from work, so had a steady early-evening trade. Their beer was very good, especially their Shiva and Perfect Day IPAs. Wicked Weed's main premises on Biltmore Avenue is a large, modern, airy room with a very long bar and a mural of Henry VIII. Apparently he coined the phrase "wicked weed" to describe that most life-giving of plants, the humble hop. Wicked Weed are guilty of going over the top with the ABV of many of their beers, and of giving them some very silly names, but the Napoleon Complex I had was very good. I did draw the line, however, at visiting Wicked Weed's Funkatorium, where they specialise in a godforsaken brew called sour beer. I do have my standards, and a bar called The Funkatorium is for people with far more style and far less sense than I have.

The best beer we drank in Asheville was at Ben's Beer, on sale in their little surf shack next to their sake brewery and concert venue. Ben's has been brewing Japanese rice wine for several years and only started on beer when it became an obvious sideways move. Their music hall also contributes to Asheville's reputation for being a great place to see live bands, although sadly there was nobody on the night we were there. We settled into the bar at Ben's over several excellent pints of IPA, and chatted happily to the deputy head brewer and acting bartender. He was intent on hoovering up as much information as he could about the beers we had tasted along our journey, on the pretext of blagging a research trip to California from his boss. He was also a bit of a music fan and asked about the Hawkwind T-shirt I was wearing that day. He was very impressed when I told him that they were the band Lemmy played bass guitar for before he formed Motörhead. That got me a free pint.

Our research concluded that the best places to drink beer in Asheville are actually the independent tap rooms in the centre of town. Barley's Taproom & Pizzeria on Biltmore Avenue had a superb range of local draught beers, all of which had gone past the experimental stage and were actually in production. They do very good lunchtime burgers and, if time had allowed, would have been a splendid place to lose an evening.

The Biltmore Estate, on the southern edge of Asheville, was built in the late 1800s by George Washington Vanderbilt II, as a mountain retreat to compete with his siblings' more cosmopolitan efforts. It is built in the Châteauesque style, and for a vastly inflated sum, you can wander around and see how the other half lived. We gave it a miss.

Back on the Blue Ridge Parkway we continued northeast, crossing for a short time into the State of Virginia. This gave me the brief opportunity to serenade Áine Two with my version of Laurel and Hardy's "The Trail of the Lonesome Pine", from their 1937 classic film *Way Out West*. I assure you, their version is a lot better than mine.

Further up the Blue Ridge Parkway from Asheville, Blowing Rock is a town built around a single tourist attraction. It is a ski resort, although a very mild winter meant that all the snow had gone as early as mid-March and the town was quiet. We stayed in a strange static caravan done out with the look and feel of an alpine cabin, in a line of six such buildings placed next to a small creek and opposite a main road. They were part of an extraordinary set-up that included a sub-*Ripley's Believe It or Not!* house of strange things, called Mystery Hill, which seemed far more popular than it really ought to be. Mystery Hill is just down the valley from the Tweetsie Railroad, a Wild West theme park featuring, amongst other things, a proper old steam train. Sadly it hadn't opened for the spring, so we couldn't enjoy the wonders it no doubt contained.

None of these were the tourist attraction around which

the town of Blowing Rock was founded. That is called The Blowing Rock, and is up on a high ridge behind the town, off a road that was being widened and from which all useful signs had been removed. It is privately owned, and has a pleasantly done out gift shop that leads to a walkway and viewing points. The Blowing Rock itself is a small convex rocky outcrop that sticks up above the top of a narrow ridge at the peak of a 3,000-feet-tall cliff. Wind hitting the side of the mountain is channelled by the shape of the cliff up to The Blowing Rock, where it creates the illusion that snow, rain and other light things thrown over the side can rise on thin air.

The owner's ability to milk a piece of rock for money is far more impressive than the rock itself. However, the views are spectacular and there are two very friendly black and white cats to play with, and the bonus of a number of slate-coloured dark-eyed juncos to see. A slate-coloured dark-eyed junco is a small grey bird, in case you're wondering.

It is not immediately apparent what our next stop, Mount Airy, was originally built for, but it has also milked its claim to fame for all it is worth.

Andy Griffith was the lead actor in an iconic American TV sitcom called *The Andy Griffith Show*, which ran from 1960 to 1968. It was set in the fictional town of Mayberry, North Carolina with Andy playing the town's sheriff, Andy Taylor.

Griffith was born in Mount Airy and the town has taken on the mantle of Mayberry, emulating some of the TV show's businesses. Unlike Truth or Consequences in New Mexico, Mount Airy hasn't changed its name to reflect the show, but it does continue to live off its popularity, which is some going considering the show finished its regular seasons nearly 50 years ago. Thetford, a pleasant market town in Norfolk, manages the same trick, exploiting the fact that the popular BBC TV series, *Dad's Army*, was filmed in the surrounding area in the 1960s and 1970s. Mount Airy's ongoing prosperity is in part a memorial to Andy Griffith's talent, as is the fact that his shows are constantly rerun on daytime American TV.

Whilst driving through Texas, we had been unable to make a detour to a town that bears Áine Two's surname, which felt like a bit of a missed opportunity. So when we saw a town on the map of North Carolina that bears the same name as her junior school, we couldn't resist. Our intention was only to stop for an hour in Roxboro, North Carolina, to have a wander around and grab a sandwich before moving on, but, as is the way with these things, it all got a bit extended.

In the absence of a visitors centre, or indeed a town centre of any description, we popped into the small local museum to ask for a pointer to a café or diner. Whilst we waited for the lady in charge to deal with some other guests, Áine Two signed the visitors' book, including "Roxboro, Co. Mayo, Ireland". The nice lady was by now a little flustered, as there were two groups of people needing attention, but she found time to glance at Áine Two's entry and nearly fell over.

Just then, another helper arrived and the excitement ratcheted up a notch. The other guest, a teenager who just wanted some blurb on the museum for her school project, was looking a bit bemused by all the fuss.

We managed to get ourselves organised and the original lady took the teenager off for a tour, whilst we were left with the latecomer. Despite only popping in to pick up some stuff, she gave us over two hours of her time and a very detailed tour of the museum, which uncovered some weird and wonderful coincidences.

The commander of the HMS *Roxsborough*, a Royal Navy ship whose bell hangs in the museum, was a chap called Lt Cdr V.A. Wight-Boycott. The common expression to "boycott" someone comes from how the locals ostracised a land agent called Captain Charles Boycott, in the next town to Roxboro, Co. Mayo, Ireland.

There were two local Roxboro, NC, people on the *Titanic* on its fateful maiden journey; one survived, one didn't. A display in the museum tells their stories. The survivor was picked up, like all the other *Titanic* survivors, by a Liverpool ship called the RMS *Carpathia*. Its captain, Arthur Rostron, lived in the same road in Great Crosby on which I was brought up. I used to walk past his house every day, and even went to view it when it was up for sale not long before our trip.

The final coincidence is that just north of Roxboro, NC is the town's reservoir, Mayo Lake. The town was named after Roxburgh in Scotland and has no link, other than the coincidental, with Co. Mayo, Ireland.

Our wonderful museum guide told us about Roxboro's tobacco-growing history and her own family's involvement in it. She is also a retired schoolteacher and educated us on how in 1965 she, as a young African American teacher, suffered the indignity of white parents removing their children from her class because of the colour of her skin.

After the coincidental Roxboro and its excellent museum, we headed for the twin cities of Raleigh and Durham to spend a weekend with friends.

The drive there took us through miles and miles of arable land and dozens of small farming settlements. The grinding poverty isn't quite as evident here as it is in the Mississippi Delta, but there are enough of the typical unfenced, detritus-strewn gardens to suggest that we weren't in the wealthiest part of the nation.

Having said that, the Raleigh–Durham conurbation plays host to Research Triangle Park, a vast business park that houses companies like IBM, Cisco and GlaxoSmithKline, amongst others, so the area isn't short of a bob or two. Presumably little of that wealth trickles down to the poorer elements of the community.

We spent Friday night in the rural outskirts of Zebulon, a railroad town named after Zebulon B. Vance, a former Confederate officer who served his second term of office as Governor of North Carolina during the Civil War. Our hosts were an old friend who I worked with several years ago, John, and his lovely wife Caroline. John likes his beer, particularly English ale, which he developed a taste for after spending time working in the south of England. His weekends were spent wandering around London doing vital research into the pubs and beers of the capital city. For the two years we worked together we somehow managed to have important meetings in London that he *just had* to attend that coincided with the annual week long CAMRA Great British Beer Festival held there every August.

John and Caroline live in a beautiful house set in an acre of woodland in the countryside surrounding Zebulon. Their gardens are neatly manicured and their privacy is ensured by having trees on three sides of the property. There are no disused bits of furniture or machinery lying around, although John did proudly show off his huge hog roasting trailer that was parked up and chained to a tree. He regularly wheels it out for family or church dos, and it is so vast that it can cook an entire pig carcass in one piece. It was the best and most pleasing example of American Excess that we saw on the entire trip.

John has a preference for run of the mill American pick-up trucks, whereas Caroline has far better taste in vehicles. Sitting quietly and discreetly in the garage were her lovely 1999 Chevy Corvette Convertible and her Harley Davidson Sportster motorbike.

John had taken the Corvette to the local garage that morning for some work to be carried out on it, and he confessed to having a bit of a blast around the local backroads as a reward to himself for being a good husband.

"What do you prefer, Caroline's Corvette or my Jag?" I asked.

"My pick-up truck." he replied.

"Philistine!"

Alas, we were not to see either vehicle or the hog roast in action as, on the Friday evening John dragged us kicking and screaming into the nearby town of Wendell for a few beers. The establishment he took us to is called Wine & Beer 101, and is more like a beer and wine shop that happens to have a pub attached than a conventional bar. It consists of two North Main Street properties that have been knocked together into one, and you can sample the wares on offer in one half and then buy them in bulk in the other to take home with you. It seems to me that the term "convenience store" was coined for just such an emporium of joy. We were introduced to a few of John's friends and work colleagues, some of whom I knew from previous transatlantic telephone encounters.

North Main Street in Wendell exhibits an excellent car parking convention that is alien to the UK and can only be applied where the width of the road allows. Parking spaces are outlined either side of the road at a 45-degree angle to the kerb. The driver is required to park nose first and can only do that by entering the space from the right-hand lane, going with the flow of the traffic. When leaving the parking space, the driver is required to reverse into the moving traffic. The same convention is in use in Australia, New Zealand and Canada, all places where ample space is available to make it work. The thing is, it does work really well. It reduces traffic holdups whilst drivers make multiple failed attempts to parallel park, it does away with the risk of idiots bumping your car forward a few inches to create enough space for themselves, reduces incidents of people being blocked in at both ends by inconsiderate berks, protects car doors from dings by stupid or distracted people exiting their cars with unnecessary force, and stops parents from unloading children onto the road, with doors wide open and vast arses protruding into the traffic.

I like nose-in, angled parking. It is very civilised.

The following day John and Caroline took us to the Double Barley Brewing Company in nearby Smithfield to sample a few of the excellent brews on offer. Afterwards we said our goodbyes, promising to meet up at the next GBBF, and headed around the Raleigh ring road to Morrisville for a night with more friends, Dianne and her husband Paul. Dianne was John's boss and predecessor when we all worked together, and she recently retired after a very successful 40-year career. She and Paul have had a wonderful family set up over the years. Paul has a passion for music and has turned it into a successful career by practicing during the day and working in the evenings. This means that he has been able to look after the school and household activities whilst Dianne did the international businesswoman thing.

Dianne retired recently to their lovely home on an executive estate, and, as is the way with these things, was soon bored and causing trouble. She admitted to being the perpetrator of *Scoopgate*, a household scandal to end all household scandals. Over the years, Paul has swept the house and scooped up the dust using a now well-worn little plastic dustpan. Dianne, in her newly retired vigour for all things household, decided that they needed a replacement for the rather battered old shovel, so she went out and bought one without consulting Paul. On returning to the house with her new trophy, she installed it in the broom cupboard and threw the apparently knackered one in the trash. Paul didn't notice for a few days, until he went about his usual weekly sweeping routine, only to find that the leading edge of the new scoop was way too thick to be effective, leaving a line of dust on the floor where the previous one would have scooped it up with aplomb. He wasn't a happy bunny, especially after he found out that the trash had already been collected and the old, much loved predecessor had been consigned to the cleaning cupboard in the sky. "I'll know not to do something like that again," said Dianne, hanging her head in shame.

Paul was working on the Saturday night so we had a lovely, comfortable evening catching up with Dianne over several bottles of red wine and a fantastic meatloaf, an American delicacy that I'd never had before. She told us that they were contemplating their own road trip and Paul was very keen to pick our brains over breakfast the following morning.

As has been confirmed by a number of the people on this journey, a road trip for most Americans has to be carried out in an RV. The couple we met in the Old School House Inn B&B in Bisbee suggested it might be something to do with a cultural memory of travelling west in covered wagons, and Paul agreed. He was dead keen on selling up, packing a few worldly goods into the back of a vast pantechnicon, and taking off on a wild and wonderful adventure across the country. He was a bit disappointed when we told him that all we had was two weeks' worth of clean clothes and a cool box in the trunk of a rental car. That wasn't the romantic story he was hoping for to persuade Dianne that he was on the right track. We did discuss the route and some of the weird and wonderful things we had encountered, and he was impressed with the distances we had covered. He was, like many we have spoken to before, during and after the road trip, vehemently against driving across Texas. It seems that the Lone Star State bears an unearned burden of being the state that everyone hates. It's a bit like Lincolnshire; flat, forlorn and forsaken. For the record, we loved driving across the vast open expanses of Texas.

The good Southern hospitality that our friends in Zebulon and Morrisville afforded us was welcoming and limitless, and we loved every minute of it.

Spits and barrier islands begin to reappear on the coastline halfway up North Carolina, and the Outer Banks are not only a popular holiday destination for North Carolinians, but also the site of two events of major global historical significance. The first is the Lost Colony of Roanoke, where Virginia Dare became the first English baby to be born in America, before mysteriously disappearing along with her mother and the other settlers.

The second is a modest town called Kitty Hawk, 4 miles south of which, in a big flat field, the Wright Brothers made their first ever heavier-than-air, powered flights. The field is preserved, and is the site of an excellent museum and a huge memorial, shaped like the tail of an aeroplane, that dominates the flat landscape for miles around. A famous photograph was taken of the historic first flight, and the scene has been reproduced in 3D using life-sized bronze sculptures of the plane, the brothers and their local helpers. If you'll pardon the pun, it is a truly uplifting place to visit.

Incidentally, next door to the field and museum is a small modern airfield called First Flight Airport, which must be a great place for aeroplane enthusiasts to land.

Predictably, a town has grown up around the site and it goes by the splendidly macabre name of Kill Devil Hills. Its neighbour, Nags Head, got its name from the local wreckers who used to tempt ships to flounder on the shore. Their method was to hang lanterns from their horses' necks to convince navigators that their bobbing motion indicated ships in a safe harbour.

We stayed overnight in Kill Devil Hills in another incompetently run national chain hotel. Again, no room was ready when we arrived in mid-afternoon, apparently because they had been full the night before. Áine Two managed to persuade the management to pull their collective finger out by parking our overloaded luggage trolley in the middle of Reception, and politely refusing to move. Oddly enough, a room become available straight away.

Later that day, a member of staff threw a dramatic wobbly in the corridor outside our room, causing a huge racket and scaring the living daylights out of one of her colleagues. Management and security staff arrived and carted both women away. The following morning, five coaches parked below our window at 7.30 am, and noisily warmed up their diesel engines for two hours.

What the Outer Banks lacks in competent hoteliers, it makes up for in some fantastic local cuisine. Breakfast was served up in the excellent Bob's Grill, where the quality of both the welcome and the food belie the strapline of "Eat and get the hell out!" The staff in Bob's Grill suffered from the familiar inability to cope with chip and PIN technology, necessitating the entry of a PIN followed by a completely unnecessary signature, which wasn't checked against the card.

Dinner was in the rough-and-ready Red Drum Grille & Taphouse, where the seafood platter was delicious and the bartender was full of entertaining tales of summer excesses and winter weather. According to him, it is not uncommon for power to be cut off for days at a time on the Outer Banks, leading to impromptu parties, accidental pregnancies and any number of near-misses for the local Fire Department caused by misplaced or forgotten candles.

From Kill Devil Hills, we drove south for the afternoon to the Pea Island National Wildlife Refuge, along a road that is under such constant threat from sand that it employs a digger to keep it useable. The dunes and beach were beautiful, and included views of the funnel of the Union Civil War troopship, *Oriental*, that ran aground there in 1862 and, weirdly, gave its name to a town about 100 miles southwest, near the original Roanoke settlement.

The nature reserve consists of a parking lot and visitor centre, and two huge lakes on which a wide variety of migrant and permanent birds flaunt their feathers for the binocular-wearing masses. Actually, it was just us and two snowbirders from up north, braving the blistering heat. We observed the very weird behaviour of a flock of American coots that moved around the lake in formation, as though they were practising for the changing of the guard. We also ticked off an American black duck and a Northern shoveller, which is just like the shoveller that we get in the UK, but northern: "Ay up, me duck!"

Birdwatching is one of those very male pastimes, like trainspotting and beermat collecting. It must be something to do with competitive list-making and collecting things. The snowbirds we met in the Pea Island National Wildlife Refuge were a middle-aged couple who turned the tables on this particular truism. She was mad keen on birds, and her long-suffering husband sat quietly on a bench whilst she rushed around looking for new feathered things through her expensive binoculars. We happily compared notes on some of the birds we had seen recently whilst our spouses sat talking about other, more mundane things.

The return drive north from Pea Island, once we had passed Kill Devil Hills and the Wright Brothers National Memorial, took us inland through lovely, bucolic farming country dotted with mysterious purple fields, possibly of indigo. Entering Virginia we had to skirt the cities of Norfolk, Portsmouth and Suffolk and cross the harbour on the Monitor–Merrimac Memorial Bridge–Tunnel. This, as its alliterative name suggests, transforms halfway across from a bridge into a tunnel. It felt like we were driving into an episode of *Thunderbirds*, or a scene from a James Bond film. *The Spy Who Drove Across America*, or *Casino Cheapskate* perhaps. The tunnel emerges on dry land at the tip of the Virginia Peninsula in the oddly named city of Newport News. Nobody knows why the place is called that.

The Virginia Peninsula, named because it is a peninsula in Virginia, is at the mouth of the vast Chesapeake Bay, between the James and York Rivers, and holds an unbelievably important place in British colonial and American history.

On the southern shore of the peninsula is Jamestown where, in 1607, the British Empire took its first tentative colonial steps. Three ships carrying 104 settlers and 44 sailors arrived on the American mainland on April 26th 1607, faffed about a bit and eventually plumped for a nice secure-looking location 40 miles from the ocean. The original settlers were all men and boys; no women had travelled with them. To compound this extraordinary error, a number of the men were gentlemen, who couldn't and wouldn't turn their hands to anything as demeaning as manual labour, leaving the heavy lifting to their serfs.

The colonists, or at least some of them, built a fort and settled in, whilst the mariners took the ships back home, promising to send further supplies when they got back.

Unfortunately, a few critical details had been overlooked, such as that April was way too late in the year to be planting crops. This meant that there was no grain to see them through the harsh winter months. Also, the area was buzzing with disease-carrying mosquitoes, and there was no fresh water where the party had settled.

By the time the resupply ships arrived in 1608, 60% of the original settlers were dead, probably out of frustration at the lack of women. The new ships brought supplies, additional settlers and women. Mysteriously, the ships also carried a team of German glassmakers, who set themselves up outside the township and began making poor-quality glass out of poor-quality raw materials that, when shipped back to England, made no profit at all for the settlers.

Despite their setbacks, the settlers fought on bravely to become England's first successful permanent settlement on mainland America. By 1620, when the Mayflower tiptoed its way to Plymouth with its cargo of Pilgrim Fathers, Jamestown had been going for 13 years and was already successfully trading its newfangled crop of tobacco with London.

The foundations of the Jamestown fort were discovered in 1996 and are still being excavated today. The outline of the fort has been plotted and partially rebuilt, a brick-lined well has been uncovered and a number of graves identified, some to the extent that the archaeologists are confident they know who is in them. Next door is the Jamestown Settlement, a living-history museum with reenactments of various aspects of early settler life, and replicas of the three ships in which the original settlers arrived. These three tiny vessels illustrate the courage and pioneering spirit of the 148 people who set sail in the spring of 1606, with little or no idea of what fate would befall them. That they even made it across the Atlantic is a miracle in itself. The living museum is hugely successful and was heaving full of happy, noisy and remarkably well-behaved children when we visited.

On the opposite side of the peninsula lies the site of the rather ignominious end to Britain's colonial involvement in America, and the drive between the two sites is on the Colonial Parkway, another charming and relaxed 45 mph route through beautiful woodlands.

By the 1770s, Britain had 13 colonies covering almost the entire East Coast of America. They were seen by the British as assets to be sweated mercilessly for profit. Taxation on trade was punitive and levied to enrich the Mother Country, causing simmering resentment amongst the colonies, none of which were represented in Parliament at Westminster.

Britain fought France in the Seven Years' War from 1756 to 1763, leaving the country skint and leading to more taxes on the American colonies, and more resentment.

In December 1773 the simmering resentment boiled over and the Sons of Liberty, a shadowy underground movement of colonial politicians and businessmen, threw a shipload of tea into Boston harbour in protest at Britain's tax regime. Three notable Sons of Liberty were Samuel Adams, John Hancock and Paul Revere.

Not only did Sam Adams spark the American Revolution, but he had a beer named after him that sparked the American craft beer revolution. John Hancock signed the Declaration of Independence in such flamboyant fashion that a person's signature in America today is known as their John Hancock. Paul Revere famously rode through the night to inform American forces of the British approach before the decisive battles of Lexington and Concord.

Britain's response to the Boston Tea Party was further punitive measures that made life very difficult for

Massachusetts, and led directly to the Declaration of Independence of 1776 and George Washington being given command of the Continental Army.

After the "shot heard round the world" was fired in Concord, New Hampshire, France joined in on the side of the Americans in the hope of winning back lands they lost in the Seven Years' War. Spain threw their hat in by supporting France, in the hope of winning back their possessions in Florida, as well as Gibraltar, among others. Things also go a bit hot in India, and even the Dutch had a go.

In 1781, General Charles Cornwallis led a British army on a campaign across America, culminating in Yorktown in Virginia. The French navy, with support from Spain, defeated the British navy in the Chesapeake Bay and took control of access to and from the Atlantic Ocean, preventing Cornwallis from reinforcing, resupplying or evacuating his troops that way.

The Continental Army, boosted by 5,500 fresh French troops, arrived from New York and laid siege to Yorktown, where the hapless Cornwallis and his battle-weary army were holed up. The siege lasted for 19 days until, on October 17th 1781, Cornwallis sued for peace. He officially surrendered on October 19th but didn't attend the handover ceremony in person, leaving his junior officers and troops to suffer that indignity without their commanding officer.

Yorktown proved to be the final land battle of the war on American soil, and Britain opened peace negotiations that eventually led to the Treaty of Paris of 1783. America formally took control of its 13 colonies and Spain got their possessions in Florida back, but not Gibraltar. Despite their decisive intervention on behalf of America, France got nothing; neither did the Dutch, and things stayed as they were in India.

Yorktown itself was founded in 1691 as a customs port

to enable the British to levy taxes on tobacco being exported to overseas markets. Today it is a very pretty little town, largely unchanged since its 18th century heyday, with many original buildings and parcels of land still in evidence. A vast column, the Yorktown Victory Monument, was erected in 1884 on the bluff above the harbour to commemorate the Continental Army's defeat of the British.

A battlefield site museum explains how the siege unfolded and where the decisive events took place. Many of the original trenches and earthworks still exist, with tours available to take visitors around.

Yorktown wasn't just the scene of the decisive final battle in the War of Independence, but also an important Civil War battle, and the museum shows how the original 1781 earthworks were reused by troops fighting nearly 100 years later.

Williamsburg sits between Jamestown and Yorktown as the final point in a triangle of historic American settlements. It was founded in 1632 and served as the capital of the Colony of Virginia between 1699 and 1780. It now exists, preserved in aspic, as a model of life in the early colonial years. Beautiful brick-built buildings line a wide, unmetalled central boulevard called Duke of Gloucester Street. Presumably, most Americans will be as bemused by the pronunciation of Williamsburg's Duke of Gloucester Street as they are with London's Leicester Square. The exquisite early-18th century Bruton Parish Church sits at the entrance to a long green that culminates in the spectacular Governor's Palace. The church is named after the town of Bruton in Somerset, where my sister, of Cornish wedding fame, used to live and work.

The church was originally Anglican, but changed denomination, in name at least, at the end of the War of

Independence. The new constitution officially separated church from state, and the former Anglican Church of America is now the Episcopalian Church.

Williamsburg isn't just a museum piece, however, and is dominated by the historic and thriving College of William & Mary. The institute exists as a direct result of the royal patronage of King William III and Queen Mary II and was established in 1693, making it second behind Harvard in the pantheon of oldest education establishments in America. It is now a university and its alumni include three of the first ten presidents of the United States, a host of federal and state politicians and legislators, military figures, sportsmen and sportswomen, film and TV stars and writers.

Our B&B for the night, called A Williamsburg White House, was opposite the university and was a charming, elegant white house set in its own grounds. Its name and the parking spaces, labelled after government cabinet positions, should have forewarned us of its eccentricities.

Each room in the house, including the elegant lounges downstairs, were named after former US presidents. We stayed in the extremely comfortable Washington Suite and had afternoon cookies and a glass of wine in the Bill Clinton reception room, which led into the JFK library.

We chatted happily to Mike, the very welcoming proprietor and proud fifth-generation Marine, who gave us the full rundown of his appreciation for some, but not all of the former presidents, and how he valued the support given to America by British prime ministers like Margaret Thatcher and Tony Blair. He was looking forward to Donald Trump's four years and hoped he lived up to his promises to Make America Great Again.

I think I worked out Mike's political opinions before his Trump discourse when, looking around the Clinton room, I noticed that all the references were to Monica Lewinsky and Clinton's impeachment. The JFK library was there because, despite him being a Democrat, Mike saw him as one of the good guys.

At breakfast in the morning, our table settings were for George and Martha Washington, and our eating companions were Thomas and Martha Jefferson. In reality, they were a charming retired couple from Illinois, heading south on the snowbird trail for a bit of spring warmth. Inevitably, the conversation turned to Donald Trump, and we accepted with good grace their apologies on behalf of America for him, silently hoping that Mike hadn't overheard them from the next room.

Williamsburg has a good selection of bars and restaurants, either in the historic buildings of Duke of Gloucester Street or in the more modern back streets. We took Mike's recommendation and ended up in Berret's Seafood Restaurant and Taphouse Grill.

The restaurant was full and there was a queue outside, but as usual, we strolled past it and settled onto a couple of barstools in time for some happy-hour beers and superb crabcakes. Opposite us were two chaps, in town for a monthly sales meeting, who were tucking into plates of $1 oysters and large vodkas and lime, and looking like they were having a wonderful time of it. At 6.55 pm, five minutes before the end of happy hour, a burly, elderly man with a weird hybrid accent burst into the bar looking a bit flustered, grabbed a barstool and quickly ordered a plate of the happy-hour oysters and a pint of happy-hour local beer. Once his order was placed, he calmed down a bit and joined in the chat around the bar. It turned out that he was Canadian of Northern Irish decent, hence the strange accent, and had driven all day from somewhere up north, arriving in town just in time for the end of happy hour. He had abandoned his wife to park their car so that he could grab a discounted meal and beer. It was noticeable that he hadn't ordered anything for her.

She eventually joined us, and it was only several beers into the evening that they admitted that they hadn't got anywhere to stay for the night. They left the bar a few hours later, both several pints to the good, to drive to the out-of-town strip of motels and a well-earned, but as yet unbooked, bed.

Moving on from Williamsburg meant that we were finally leaving the South, after eight glorious weeks of amazement and education. The place is dripping with history, some of it significantly earlier than many in Britain understand or acknowledge, much of it ignominious in its treatment of other human beings, and a great deal of it still barely concealed beneath a veneer of civility and equality. A museum docent who shall remain unidentified spoke to us very frankly and openly, saying conspiratorially that we "weren't like other white folks". That person's opinion was that the genie of equality had been let out of the bottle by the Civil War, but it wouldn't take much for some people in the South to put it right back in there and revert to the old ways.

CHAPTER 13 TAXATION WITHOUT REPRESENTATION

There is a city in America of over 600,000 people who pay their federal taxes, but who have no voting representation in Congress. In UK terms, that is a city roughly the size of Sheffield that has no MPs in Parliament. That is extraordinary in itself, but it is even more so when you find out that the city in question is the country's capital, Washington, D.C.

"No taxation without representation" was a phrase used by our old friends the Sons of Liberty to express their dissatisfaction at being charged tax by a distant country in which they had no voting rights and no MPs. Today, many residents of Washington, D.C. carry a similar slogan on their car registration plates, expressing their equally unsatisfactory current status, "Taxation Without Representation".

For the pub quiz aficionados, Washington, D.C. is not one of the 50 states that make up the United States of America, but its residents do get to vote in presidential elections.

At the end of the 18th century, America had booted out the Brits and created itself a parliament in the acting capital, New York. Congress asked the states of Maryland and Virginia to contribute a parcel of land each to create a permanent one around the settlements of Georgetown and Alexandria, northeast and southwest of the Potomac River respectively. This formed a diamond-shaped area of 100 square miles that straddled the river.

As the area, known as the District of Columbia, was established with the purpose of housing Congress, its governance fell exclusively under Congress' control. Therefore, to avoid any accusations of turkeys voting for or against Christmas, the city's founding fathers eschewed the rights to representation.

By the 1830s, it was becoming apparent to the Virginian half of the city that Maryland's anti-slavery stance was beginning to hold sway, meaning that the very profitable trading of slaves was likely to be banned in D.C. in the near future. On top of this, all the investment in government buildings and infrastructure was taking place in the Maryland half of the district, leaving the Virginia half as the poor neighbour.

In 1846 Virginia's general assembly voted to take back their contribution to D.C., in an act known as retrocession, or a fit of pique, depending on your viewpoint. This left the Maryland portion northeast of the Potomac to form the country's capital city on its own.

Manufactured capital cities tend to be fairly soulless places. Canberra in Australia and India's New Delhi are the two examples that spring to mind. They are occupied by politicians who have constituency homes elsewhere to go to at weekends. The bureaucrats, lobbyists, management consultants and other sundry hangers-on who also live there couldn't give a city a soul if they formed a mass James Brown tribute act. I have been a management consultant, and there is nothing more soul destroying than having a few after-work beers with colleagues who talk only of work and office politics, and who have that easily recognisable and hideously ambitious glint in their eyes.

Washington, D.C. flies against that stereotype and is a proper, lived-in city with character and soul. Like London, it has its government and museum quarters, both full of tourists such as us, and also like London, it has parts of the city where real people live real lives away from the blue-suited political and corporate world.

We stayed in a perfectly pleasant corporate hotel amongst all the other perfectly pleasant corporate hotels, just north of the city centre and not far from the busy bars and restaurants of 14th Street NW. We found sanctuary in the excellent Stoney's on P Street NW, where the beer was local and the ribs and wings were excellent.

One thing that became apparent in D.C. was that more people sat at bars engrossed in their mobile phones, and fewer were willing to talk to their fellow drinkers. However, we did share a few rounds in Stoney's with a friendly local who was interested in our travels and what we had seen. He was very non-committal about what he did for a living but was prepared to admit, with a nudge and a wink, that he worked within the political world. He did say that D.C. was quaking in its boots awaiting President Trump's impact on the city, and the swamp he had promised to drain. According to him there was fear that people would lose their jobs, countered by that classic civil-servant arrogance that "the machine" would be able to tie Trump's administration in enough knots that all their attempts at change would be scuppered. We suggested he watched the classic BBC TV programmes *Yes, Minister* and *Yes, Prime Minister* for perfect examples of what he was suggesting.

The bartender at Stoney's gave us an excellent recommendation for a good breakfast at the Commissary two doors down. We stopped in the next morning and she was spot on with her suggestion.

A stroll along P Street to the west of 14th Street took us into a wealthy neighbourhood of renovated townhouses and 21st century apartment blocks. A walk in the other direction goes through the fantastic Logan Circle, named after Major General John A. Logan, hero of the Union Army during the Civil War. The circle itself is a huge roundabout, surrounded by beautiful original Victorian residences and with a park in the middle of which a statue of Logan surveys his domain, sitting atop his mighty steed. He was not only a Union war hero, but initiated what was to become Memorial Day, the national public holiday on which America remembers its war dead.

We asked our friends in Raleigh where the South ended and the North began. Their answer was that it is roughly halfway up Virginia, somewhere to the south of where the Washington, D.C. conurbation begins. It is noticeable once you get north of that imaginary demarcation line that Civil War statues celebrate Union heroes rather than their Confederate counterparts. A short distance from Logan Circle is Thomas Circle, named after George Thomas, another Union Army general.

The area around 14th Street and Logan Circle was the scene of extensive race riots in the immediate aftermath of Martin Luther King's assassination in 1968. Since then things have slowly but surely improved for locals, not all of it the sort of gentrification that prices original residents out of an area. East of Logan Circle remains a typical inner-city neighbourhood, with schools, local shops and pockets of social housing. Our barroom companion in Stoney's told us that the area began to go up in the world when the Whole Foods Market opposite opened its doors in 2005. Waitrose, eat your heart out.

We walked through the Logan Circle district and then turned south to the magnificent Pennsylvania Avenue and the Capitol Building, the superb white, domed building situated at its eastern end where Congress is housed. Its construction was completed in 1800 to a competition-winning design that was buggered about with by an embittered losing architect, appointed to oversee construction. The fabulous dome that we see on our TV screens today was added in the 1850s, after the building was extended for the umpteenth time as the federal administration grew in size.

On Pennsylvania Avenue, a few blocks west of Capitol Hill, is a modern building called the Newseum, a very popular museum of the First Amendment and free press. On its front wall, four storeys high, is the First Amendment itself, writ large for all to see, including presumably the president as he is whizzed past in his presidential cavalcade.

The UK doesn't have a written constitution, and so doesn't have such protection so clearly and unequivocally stated and so easily quotable by anyone who can memorise it. America can't make laws preventing Catholics from being the head of state, for example, or preventing the head of state from marrying a Catholic, or silence the media, or stop people peacefully protesting against the government. Equally, it cannot ban people from entering the country simply because they are Muslim. Apparently.

The Capitol Building is an imposing sight all by itself, but when you can drag your eyes away from it and turn around 180 degrees you take in the astonishing view along the National Mall to the Washington Monument and the Lincoln Memorial in the distance. Paris has the Champs-Élysées and London has the view of the Houses of Parliament and Big Ben from the River Thames, and this is up in their league. The only bugbear is that cars are allowed to park in the streets that cross the Mall, adding an unwelcome distraction to the otherwise splendid vista. The views from the foot of the Washington Monument, the vast obelisk halfway along the Mall, back towards Capitol Hill and forwards to the Lincoln Memorial are in some ways even better, because you get a perspective on the size of the buildings at both ends.

It is possible to ascend the Washington Monument, as Dan Brown demonstrated in *The Lost Symbol*, but it has been closed for some time for repairs to its lifts.

Washington and Lincoln are the undisputed giants of American history and deserve their memorials in the country's capital. Washington was the brilliant military leader who defeated the British in the War of Independence and became the nation's first president. Lincoln was the outstanding politician of his day who, as president, oversaw the North's victory in the Civil War and ended slavery, emancipating over 3 million black people in the process.

The Lincoln Memorial, the neo-classical Greek building with its 36 columns and 19-feet-tall seated statue of the president, was crowded with people and being used by citizens as a place of public celebration. On its steps to one side of the main entrance, a young soldier was being awarded a medal by his commanding officer, surrounded by his very proud family and friends. Afterwards, the crowd inside the building stood respectfully to one side so that he could be afforded his photo opportunity in front of Lincoln's statue. Also on the steps were a school orchestra, spotlessly attired and enthusiastically blasting out the national anthem, with only the odd misplaced parp to add to the occasion.

The statue of Lincoln is certainly imposing. He would be 28 feet tall if he stood up, but would still be able to do so comfortably within the interior, although his legs might be a bit stiff from all that sitting down.

The National Mall is lined with museums housing a tiny fragment of the astonishing collection of the Smithsonian Institution, and we chose the National Museum of American History for shelter on a very damp morning. The museum is a great place to learn more about American's maritime, military and transport history. Liverpool received several mentions, not all of them related to slavery. Its pièce de résistance is the original Star-Spangled Banner, the huge flag that flew over Fort McHenry at the Battle of Baltimore in the War of 1812. It was the inspiration for a young lawyer called Francis Scott Key to write the lyrics to what would become the national anthem. The words are an evocative account of how, through "the rockets' red glare, the bombs bursting in air" of an overnight naval bombardment of the fort, the stars and stripes of the flag could still be seen when dawn broke. In Britain we tend only to hear it played when we've lost to an American at the Olympics, or when it is being wailed appallingly by some minor C-list pop princess at the start of the Super Bowl. Americans, however, are hugely proud of it and give it the respect it deserves. It is certainly a damn sight more stirring and interesting than our national dirge.

The White House is off the National Mall, a few hundred yards to the north, with the traditional frontage view facing away from the memorials at the bottom of the road. Initially, we were prevented from getting close by stern-looking security guards who held us at the edge of Lafayette Square. Eventually, we were allowed to cross the park to the kerb of Pennsylvania Avenue to take photos and be quietly respectful.

The White House is not quite what you might expect. It is a modest-sized building, like Number 10 Downing Street or Graceland, but it is a global icon and interesting to stand and stare at for a while.

The building was surrounded, as one would expect, by armed Secret Service officers. You can spot them because they wear black military uniforms and have the words "SECRET SERVICE" emblazoned across their bullet-proof vests, which I think rather gives the game away. Maybe the all-black squirrel we saw on the lawn was involved in covert activities; a secret squirrel perhaps?

Approaching the White House from the Mall we came across a plaque commemorating another of America's wars. It began "During the War of 1812, in 1814 ..." which made me and the other English guy standing nearby laugh out loud. When we read even further we both sniggered childishly, upsetting the American between us. It turned out that during the War of 1812, in 1814, the British Army sacked Washington and burnt down Congress and the White House. The story goes that President Madison had time to write an urgent letter to his wife, Dolley, telling her to vacate the building as it would soon be under attack. Apparently, she also had time to write a reply confirming her actions. Things moved at a more considered and polite pace in those days.

The walk along the east bank of the Potomac River took us past the impressive memorial to Martin Luther King Jr. and to the shores of the Tidal Basin, ringed by the beautiful cherry trees that were in full bloom in honour of our visit. The weather was overcast so they didn't sparkle as they might under a blue sky, but the sight of the lake entirely encircled by soft pink blossoms was lovely nonetheless.

I've mentioned the remarkable President Franklin Delano Roosevelt a number of times so far, and his memorial is also on the shoreline of the Tidal Basin. FDR won an unprecedented four terms as president between 1933 and 1945, and he is remembered for leading America through WWII, for starting the atomic bomb programme and for dying in office. However, his greatest achievements, those that created his most lasting legacy, were initiated during his first 100 days in office.

He came to power in 1933, when America was deeply entrenched in the Great Depression. Within his first three months in office, he provided funding to put 250,000 unemployed men into jobs via the Civilian Conservation Corps, stabilised and regulated the banking industry, provided huge capital funding to spark an industrial recovery and, most popular of all, ended Prohibition.

Continuing his reforms, FDR oversaw economic security for the disadvantaged and sick, introduced a minimum wage, and reduced unemployment by 40%. His efforts paved the way for America to be the dominant post-war global political power, and he certainly worked out how to make America great first time around. Today FDR would be considered by many to be a dangerous socialist, but he is held in the highest regard by most Americans, and deserves his place alongside Washington and Lincoln on the National Mall.

Further round the shores of the Tidal Basin is the impressive Jefferson Memorial. Thomas Jefferson has the distinction of being both the main author of the Declaration of Independence and the third President of the United States. He also appears carved in giant profile on Mount Rushmore in South Dakota, alongside Lincoln, Washington and Theodore Roosevelt. His memorial is another neoclassical edifice, and contains an imposing statue of the late president, as well as excerpts from the Declaration.

We wandered northwest in the rain to see Georgetown, the settlement around which Washington, D.C. was built. It was a relatively prosperous river port until it was subsumed by the Washington urban spread. Nowadays it is a very pleasant Georgian suburb, with some charming original houses, shops and coaching inns.

On our walk back I had the most bizarre of my Motörhead T-shirt encounters. The weather was damp, and I was wearing an overcoat and was sporting a decent quiff-and-sideburn combination. A guy walking towards us obviously mistook me for a teddy boy of some sort. He accosted me with great enthusiasm, asking me about my tastes in rock and roll. He expressed his love for my Motörhead T-shirt and assured Áine Two that, "This n***** is the real deal." Not many middle-aged white Scousers can claim to have been called a "n*****" in Washington, D.C., or elsewhere I presume, especially by a white bloke with a proper East End of London Cockney accent.

We retreated from the weather and weird conversations to the excellent Irish Whiskey Public House for a few happy-hour warmers. The beer was good, the bartender was talkative and the rain took just long enough to stop for us to settle in nicely.

Unfortunately, after visiting so many interesting cemeteries, we couldn't find time to pay our respects at the most important of all, America's National Cemetery, across the river at Arlington. However, Washington, D.C. was such a pleasant surprise that it definitely warrants more investigation in the future, so we'll be back to see it then.

CHAPTER 14
UP NORTH AND PERSONAL

> ENTERED INTO REST ON THE
> EVENING OF MARCH 15, 1886.
> JAMES IREDELL
> WADDELL.
> LATE COMMANDER OF THE
> CONFEDERATE STATES' STEAMER
> "SHENANDOAH."
> BORN IN PITTSBORO, N.C.
> JULY 13, 1824.
> GRADUATED FROM THE U.S.
> NAVAL ACADEMY IN 1848, AND
> RESIGNED TO ENTER THE CON-
> FEDERATE STATES NAVY IN 1862,
> SENDING IN HIS RESIGNATION ON HIS
> RETURN FROM THE EAST INDIES.

In 1767, over 100 years after Annapolis was first settled, a ship called the *Lord Ligonier* sailed into its picturesque harbour and offloaded its cargo of slaves. In 1976, Alex Haley published a fictionalised version of his family history called *Roots: The Saga of an American Family*, in which his ancestor, Kunta Kinte, disembarked from the *Lord Ligonier* in Annapolis harbour into a life of slavery in America.

Today in the same Annapolis dockside is the emotional statue of Alex Haley, enthralling children with his tales. It contrasts markedly with the expensive ocean-going yachts of the wealthy local elite, moored in the long narrow channel next to it known as Ego Alley.

The American TV mini-series of *Roots*, first broadcast in the UK in 1977, changed the popular understanding of slavery and, perversely, gave thousands of black kids around Britain the racist nicknames of Kunta Kinte, Kizzy and Chicken George.

The State of Maryland was founded by George Calvert, the first Lord Baltimore, in the 1630s as a refuge for Catholics suffering persecution in England. The state flag of Maryland is the crest of the Calvert family, and we discovered that it is illegal to fly it unless the ornament on the tip of the flagpole is a gold cross bottony. Once we'd worked out what one of these is, we had great fun spotting the flags that were being flown illegally, of which there were lots.

Like all of the major colonial East Coast seaports we have visited on this trip, Annapolis is a delightful and well-preserved city. It sits atop a raised bluff on a short peninsula between the Severn and South rivers. Roads lined with original 18th and 19th century houses and shops slope gently down to a very pretty dockside that is surrounded by many interesting bars and restaurants.

Annapolis is the state capital of Maryland and dominated by two important structures: the Maryland State

House and the United States Naval Academy. The historic Maryland State House is the oldest state capitol remaining in continuous use in America, and sits strategically on the peak of a central hill, overlooking the town and its port. It was here during the Continental Convention of 1783 that General George Washington resigned his commission as commander-in-chief of the Continental Army, to return to his life as a Virginia plantation owner. The Treaty of Paris that formally ended the War of Independence was also ratified in the Maryland State House in 1784.

Roger B. Taney is a well-known Marylander of equal fame and infamy who is commemorated, through gritted teeth, in the grounds of the Maryland State House. As Chief Justice of the Supreme Court, he oversaw the 1857 case of *Dred Scott v. Sandford*. Dred Scott was a slave whose master moved him around the North, settling eventually in Wisconsin, a territory in which slavery was banned under the Missouri Compromise. He sued for freedom on the basis that he was enslaved in a place where slavery was illegal. Justice Taney ruled that Scott had no rights to sue for freedom because, as a negro, he was not a citizen of the country. Bizarrely, the judge interpreted the US Constitution as meaning that black people "had no rights which the white man was bound to respect; and that the negro might justly and lawfully be reduced to slavery for his benefit". He also declared that the Missouri Compromise, which enshrined the freedom of slaves in the Northern states in law, was unconstitutional.

After a life successfully serving his country as a politician, legislator and noted abolitionist, who even freed the slaves he inherited from his father, Taney rather blotted his copybook with quite such an unexpected and outrageous judgement. It shocked and surprised many, and was seen by some in the North as an attempt by the South to expand the slave states. It was a major contributor to the start of the Civil War.

The United States Naval Academy, founded in 1845, is a huge university-style campus on the northern edge of the city and produces about 1,000 graduates a year. Similar to Charleston's Citadel, Naval Academy undergraduates are only allowed into Annapolis in their spotless uniforms, and make quite a sight as they make their way through the city centre.

The Academy has an astonishing list of alumni, such as Georgia peanut-farming President Jimmy Carter, one of two graduates who went on to become Nobel Prize winners. The list also includes eight astronauts, one of whom is former Cocoa Beach hotelier and moonwalker, Alan Shepard. My personal favourite on the roll of honour is science fiction author Robert A. Heinlein, who wrote the brilliant *Stranger in a Strange Land* and the very right-wing *Starship Troopers*.

For our weekend in Annapolis, we stayed with some friends, Bill and Maria, in their beautiful, recently refurbished late 19th century townhouse. In one of those odd coincidences that have dogged us along our road trip, the house next door to theirs used to belong to Francis Scott Key, the lawyer who wrote the lyrics to "The Star-Spangled Banner".

On arrival, Bill kindly offered us a hot drink. Áine Two asked for a coffee and was pointed to the pod-based contraption in the corner of the kitchen. I asked for a cup of tea and we had a conversation about the appropriateness or otherwise of making tea through a flushed-out coffee machine. We decided that it would be easier to boil some water on the hob, which we set about doing once Bill had searched the cupboards for a saucepan. Maria wandered in at this point and gave us both a withering look as we stood waiting for the water to boil. I'm not sure what was worse for her, a fussy Englishman and his search for a decent cup of tea, or the fact that there were two large men in her spotless kitchen in the process of making tea and a mess.

Bill was very keen to take us on his boat, and had recommissioned it from its winter hibernation in time for our visit. I don't do boats – I've been sick on the ferry across the Mersey – but as Bill was being so generous I thought I'd better give it a go. I dosed myself up with Dramamine and off we went.

Maria very kindly drove us and their crazy chocolate Labrador, Josie, across the vast Chesapeake Bay Bridge to the marina at Stevensville, where she left us to our boating after a delicious lunch. We boarded the 37-feet twin-engine monster, and Bill blasted us back across the bay. The bridge casts an enormous shadow over the bay, and looks even bigger from below than it does when you're crossing it. Being driven at speed in a powerful motorboat and a powerful sports car are very similar: the wind in your hair, the sense of freedom, the long bonnet stretching into the distance as it banks around a corner, Matt Monro on the stereo ... sorry, I've set myself off again.

We drove up the Severn River past Annapolis, to a pleasant inlet where we dropped anchor and Bill spent an hour throwing a toy into the water for the dog to chase. The weather was lovely and we passed the time chatting and gently bobbing up and down. Once Bill had finally exhausted the mad canine, we set off back to harbour, with Áine Two taking the wheel for an entertaining high-speed cruise. Thank goodness for Dramamine.

Once Bill and Maria had decided to move to Annapolis, Bill made sure he bought himself a berth for his boat long before they had decided on which house to buy. As it happens, he picked correctly and we moored the boat at the end of his road. Áine Two and Maria rolled their eyes at the notion of buying the berth before the house, but I can sympathise. One of the main reasons we bought our house was because it had a garage in which I could store The Jag.

We ate some excellent meals in Annapolis, including one at the top-end Osteria 177 and another at the more homely Chick & Ruth's Delly (sic). In the latter, I had another T-shirt encounter, although this time it had nothing to do with Motörhead, or any music for that matter. The shirt in question depicts three fish swimming in a line. The first two have bubbles coming out of their mouths, whereas the third wears a self-satisfied smirk and has bubbles coming out of its rear. I know it's childish, but it makes me smile. The waitress spotted it and broke into a rendition of Dr. Seuss: "One fish. Two fish. Three fish. Four fish." Her colleague then pointed out that she didn't think that's what the T-shirt was about. The waitress took a closer look and shrieked in mock horror at the farting fish. She gathered all the staff around and I suddenly became the most popular person in the place. The waitress knocked my lunch off the bill and gave me a big kiss on the way out.

In contrast to places like Clarksdale, Mississippi, the selection of shops on Annapolis' Main Street reflected the fact that the city centre is lived in, and not usurped by out-of-town malls. There was a healthy mix of the tourist and the everyday, including a splendid Irish shop selling an astonishing collection of Celtic clobber, including Tayto Crisps and Barry's Tea.

There was one last piece of a certain jigsaw I wanted to find before we left lovely Annapolis, and it meant a short walk from Bill and Maria's house, across the centre of town, to the graveyard of the historic St. Anne's Church. We very quickly found the headstone we were looking for. On it were carved the words, "Entered into rest on the evening of March 15, 1886. James Iredell Waddell, late Commander of the Confederate States Steamer *Shenandoah*".

This finally tied together the twin strands of William and Alice Anderton of Blundellsands, and their resting places in Lafayette Cemetery in New Orleans and Toxteth Cemetery in Wavertree, with James Dunwoody Bulloch, his Confederate colleague James Iredell Waddell, and the last act of the American Civil War, in the River Mersey, off the shore of Toxteth, Liverpool.

The highlight of the journey from Annapolis to Philadelphia is another drive over the Chesapeake Bay Bridge. The bridge consists of two separate 4.3-mile structures, and spans the Chesapeake Bay between Annapolis in the west and Stevensville in the east. From its western end it sweeps through a long elegant left-hand curve before straightening out and rising gracefully to its peak, about 190 feet above the water. It then drops gently back to ground level on the eastern shore. The bridge operators offer a driver service for people who can't face being so high above water for such a long distance.

Once on the eastern shore we drove through farmland that was largely hidden by trees lining the highway. When we hit Wilmington and the I-95 into Philadelphia, the scenery changed to suburban sprawl and the remains of that city's industrial past.

Grid-pattern cities are generally easy to navigate, unless they are riddled with roadworks, in which case they are a nightmare. It seemed that every road in Philadelphia was being dug up simultaneously. Each time we turned down a one-way street, we were redirected to one going in a different direction, forcing us further and further away from our destination. Eventually, after much swearing and driving around in squares, we found our hotel.

The car park takes up the first and second floors of the building, is shared with a major car-rental company and has a very well-concealed entrance that confused more than one driver. We were required to abandon the car that we had carefully nurtured up the East Coast from Miami, paranoid about expensive insurance claims. We handed over the keys to someone we had never met, and weren't even sure worked for the hotel, in the hope that the car would come back unscathed in a few days' time. Valet parking may be the norm in America, but it's not something that comes naturally to your average Brit.

As it turned out, a genuine complaint about an odd smell in the room just before we were leaving secured us a no-quibble discount that added up to the car-parking costs, which was a bit of a bonus. The car, of course, was returned to us completely undamaged.

I knew nothing about Philadelphia before this trip to America and had no idea of its place at the pinnacle of the history of the nation, to the point where it is the only city in America with UNESCO World Heritage status. Liverpool's got that too.

Something dawned on me as we arrived in the city. The Tom Hanks film *Philadelphia*, about a gay man with HIV who is represented by a homophobic lawyer, could have been set anywhere in the US. It took place in Philadelphia because the city's name means "brotherly love" in Greek.

In 1682, a Quaker called William Penn landed in the New World from the Home Counties of England, clutching the documentation signed by King Charles II that handed him modern-day Pennsylvania and Delaware, in lieu of the king's debts to his father. Just in case, Penn also bought the land from the Lenape people, effectively paying for it twice. Penn set about naming his wooded colony after his old man, and established Philadelphia as its capital in the same year.

In 1776, during the War of Independence, the Founding Fathers of the United States got together in Philadelphia and commissioned Thomas Jefferson to draft the Declaration of Independence. He did so in a house in the city centre owned by one Jacob Graff Jr. The original house was pulled down in some past piece of redevelopment zealotry, and a reproduction was built on the same spot in 1975 and is now a museum.

The Declaration was formally approved by the newly formed Congress in a building around the corner, and a handwritten copy was signed by 56 men representing the 13 original colonies. You will most likely recognise such names as Benjamin Franklin, cousins John and Samuel Adams, John Hancock and Thomas Jefferson. It was also signed by lesser-known but no less heroic revolutionaries with names such as Robert Treat Paine, who wasn't a doctor; Richard Henry Lee, who may have been the great-great-grandfather of the founder of a Liverpool department store; Richard's brother, Francis Lightfoot Lee who may have been a good dancer; and Button Gwinnett, about whom much is known, but little about whether he blamed his father or mother for his silly name.

Four of the Sons of Liberty, the revolutionaries behind the Boston Tea Party, were signatories to the Declaration of Independence: Samuel Adams, John Hancock, Oliver Wolcott and Benjamin Rush.

Another signatory, Benjamin Franklin, was an interesting character. He could turn his hand to pretty much anything and make a decent go of it. He wrote books and edited newspapers, and then set up a printing works to produce them. He was the postmaster for Philadelphia and then the US Postmaster General. He was a scientist and also invented things, including the remarkable glass harmonica, a sort of formalised way of rubbing a wet finger across a half-filled glass. For some 20 years before the War of Independence, Franklin lived in London as the unofficial ambassador for the 13 colonies to Britain, lobbying constantly on their behalf. During that time he travelled extensively in the British Isles, including in Ireland where he saw widespread poverty caused by the same exploitation and tax treatment that was being meted out in America by the British government. At the start of the war he was sent to France, again as unofficial ambassador for the colonies, and was instrumental in persuading the French to join in the war on the side of America. He may well have been the best president America never had, and his personality rests gently over Philadelphia like a comforting blanket.

In 1752, the city authorities ordered a bell to be cast by the Whitechapel Bell Foundry in east London. It was to be hung in the city's new State House. It duly arrived and was rung for the very first time with much ceremony. It immediately cracked with a dull clunk. The dud bell was melted down and recast by two local metalworkers. Their first effort, again unveiled with much public hoo-ha, sounded dreadful and they were told to go back and try again. Finally, bell three was deemed acceptable and hung in the State House bell tower in 1753.

Legend has it that the bell was rung on July 4th 1776 to celebrate the signing of the Declaration of Independence, but this myth has subsequently been debunked. It may very well have been rung on that day for a more mundane reason, but no public announcement about the signing ceremony was made then, so no bells were rung in celebration on that date. Despite this historical hiccup, it was dubbed the

Liberty Bell and has become a symbol of American independence ever since.

Nobody knows when the third bell cracked, but by February 1846 it was properly knackered and no longer in use. Stories of its history increased its iconic status, and it was regularly carted around the country for people to see, touch and cut bits off for souvenirs.

The Liberty Bell now hangs in an excellent museum in the middle of Philadelphia, where it can be properly revered. We chatted to one of the National Park guards in the museum who was heading to the UK on holiday with his wife. He was desperate to visit London to see where the original bell was cast. Sadly, I fear he may have missed his chance because, after casting bells for 450 years, the Whitechapel Bell Foundry closed its doors in May 2017. Its last owner was retiring and had been unable to find a viable buyer for the business. His family had only owned the foundry since 1904, so they were virtually newcomers to the trade. The original pattern for the Liberty Bell, amongst those of many other historic bells, including Big Ben, has been donated by the company to the Museum of London, so at least it will be preserved.

Amongst Philadelphia's many other claims to fame is that it is where the Constitution of the newly formed United States of America was drafted and approved. Since then, the Constitution has had 27 amendments, the two most contentious being the First Amendment – the right to free speech, a free press and freedom of religion; and the Second Amendment – the right the bear arms. As mentioned earlier, the First Amendment appears prominently on a wall in Washington, D.C. The Second Amendment appears on the T-shirts of people all over the country, particularly in the South.

Our hotel room in Philadelphia was one of those apartment jobbies, so to save a bit of cash and enjoy a little domesticity after all the travelling, we headed for a local supermarket to find something to buy for dinner. Our target was a Trader Joe's in Downtown, a dozen blocks west of the hotel. With hindsight, our error was less about the timing of our visit, and more about the simple act of trying to buy some food there. When we arrived at the modest-sized supermarket at around 6.30 pm, the queue for the tills wended its way around all of the aisles and was beginning to double back on itself. This not only meant that the wait to pay was half an hour long, but also that the act of picking items off the shelves would necessitate half a dozen excuse-me's, and probably result in some inappropriately hasty food selections. The company even employed staff to manage the queuing system, with some poor unfortunate soul on "Back of the Queue" sign duty. His job was to stand next to the last person in line, moving ever backwards as more people joined.

Shopping like this may be the norm for the residents of downtown Philadelphia, but my patience wasn't robust enough to cope with it. We repaired to the likely-looking Liberty Bar & Grill over the road, to pass enough time for the queue to recede. It was my AC/DC T-shirt that drew the attention of the gent next to me at the bar, giving him the inspiration he needed to load the juke box with a bit more cash and pick a few of their finest songs.

"I'm Scottish, you know," he stated in the blunt way that Glaswegians do, but with a local Philadelphia accent.

"Whereabouts?" I asked.

"Not me obviously," he replied. "I'm from here. My mother's mother was from Aberdeen."

"Was she? I've been to Aberdeen. It's a nice place.

Famous for its oil and granite. Did you know that Donald Trump's mother was Scottish?" I asked.

"Was she? Oh fuck!" he replied.

During our short visit to the pub we saw another example of your average American's respect for other people. A young couple were sitting at the end of the bar on the seats closest to the front door, huddled together in private conversation. A very elderly gentleman shuffled in, clutching a six-pack of cans of beer. He paused on the threshold to locate the closest free seat, and the young couple, without hesitation or being asked, hopped from their perches and moved over to let him sit down. It was a simple, everyday occurrence of politeness and respect for the elderly, but it made me think about how often it would happen in a city centre pub in London.

We secured a couple of recommendations for good places to go drinking from the bartender and headed back to the supermarket. The queue was still laughably long and we were starving, so we gave up and headed for the Irish bar underneath the hotel. That'll teach us.

A stroll from the hotel towards the Old City area took us through the excellent Reading Terminal Market, a huge covered area inside a former train shed, in which real food was served by real people to real people. There were a few of the artisan breadmaker types that you find in London's Borough Market, but there were no stupid moustaches or beards on display, and it was largely proper local stuff on offer. The Philly cheesesteak is a culinary legend, and we watched, mouths agape, as skilled stallholders fried onions and shredded beef, packed them into soft, white half-length baguettes and then smeared them with liquid cheese that oozed into the gaps in the hot filling, like a politician at a party. Thankfully, they were off the menu for me, otherwise I might have been forced to try one.

Beyond the market are the city's historic buildings and artefacts, including, amongst others, Independence Hall where the Declaration of Independence was signed, the Liberty Bell and the elegant Carpenters' Hall, built in 1775 as the HQ for the city's carpenters' guild. This was where fire-insurance rates were set by the people who knew how much wood was in every house that they had built.

During our wanderings we stumbled across Elfreth's Alley, a narrow thoroughfare of two- and three-storey terraced houses, the earliest of which was built in 1728. The houses are still occupied, and many display the original fire-insurance plaques that used to indicate to the fire brigade which ones had been blessed by the carpenters' guild to receive their services. No insurance meant no plaque, and your house would probably burn down.

On the riverfront, at the junction of Chestnut Street and South Front Street, is the Irish Memorial, a haunting sculpture commemorating the many thousands of Irish people who were forced to emigrate from their home country by famine or economic necessity. It depicts a tableau of people moving from digging a grave for a lost loved one, through the voyage across the Atlantic to the point of disembarkation in America.

Philadelphia's early history is characterised by its willingness to accept migrants, particularly from Europe. Not only were there thousands of Irish people in the city, but Italians and Germans as well.

Country Wexford-born Commodore John Barry, revered as the "Father of the American Navy", is celebrated with a statue outside Independence Hall, and is buried in St. Mary's Roman Catholic Church.

Two other remarkable churches in Philadelphia are Christ Church and Old St. Joseph's. Christ Church was founded in 1695 by the Church of England, and was one of the first to change to the new Episcopalian denomination after the War of Independence. Its current elegant building was completed in 1744 and contains the oldest baptismal font in the country, used to baptise William Penn in 1644 at All Hallows-by-the-Tower, one of the oldest churches in London. All this was told to us by a young cleric who was leading a group of schoolchildren on a tour of the church. We quietly latched onto the back of the group, and I don't think he noticed us. During the question session at the end, a little girl put up her hand and asked in a tiny voice, "Is the church haunted?" All her schoolmates giggled, but she looked genuinely terrified. My guess is that she had never been in such an old and atmospheric building in her short life. The tour guide's answer seemed to put her mind at rest.

Old St. Joseph's is the first Catholic church in Pennsylvania, founded in 1733 and still in regular use today. The present building isn't particularly old but it remains on the same site as the original, tucked out of the way down a short alley, allegedly to protect the building from attack by Protestants.

Philadelphia doesn't have an obvious strip of bars, restaurants and loud music, but one of the roads the Liberty Bar & Grill bartender recommended was South Street, which aspires to be the hipster part of town, but hasn't quite made it yet. There were some great places to buy hippy chic, vinyl records or have a pint, including a tremendous heavy metal bar, and it reminded me very much of Camden Town in north London, before the market brought the ravening tourist hordes to its streets.

The other side of downtown has its own trendy area, known as the Northern Liberties. Formerly the place where new immigrants would gravitate to for cheap accommodation, the Liberties had a degree of independence from the rest of the city, with responsibilities for self-policing and raising taxes. Similar areas used to exist in ancient London. The Liberty of Norton Folgate, in present-day Shoreditch, is the most well known of them, and was also the name of a 2009 album by Madness. Heaven only knows the sort of choleric hellhole the Northern Liberties must have been in their day.

Nowadays, as is the way with gentrification, the Northern Liberties are halfway to becoming the new trendy part of town, where hipsters can show off whatever new fashion the magazine editors create for their own cruel amusement. If I was a betting man I'd put my money on this part of town growing into Philadelphia's version of the ubiquitous strip of bars, restaurants and tattoo parlours.

We did find an interesting Irish pub in which to sit down and ride the free wifi for an hour so that I could fret over the score of an ongoing Liverpool match. The pub was imaginatively named Irish Pub, without the definitive article and also without the normally ubiquitous Guinness. The story goes that a number of long established Irish pubs in Philadelphia have been in dispute with the North American distributors of Guinness for a number of years. Their problem is that Guinness effectively sponsor new Irish pubs by providing ersatz Irish pub interiors and training for staff in how to pour a good pint. According to their owners, this puts established businesses at a disadvantage because they can't compete with the mighty Guinness corporation.

As it was, we had a cup of tea each and I watched the

score tick over on the BBC website as Liverpool threw away a 2–1 lead with 3 minutes to go to draw 2–2 with the mighty Bournemouth. Sometimes I wonder why I bother.

It is not possible to go to Philadelphia without running up the steps of the Philadelphia Museum of Art, striking a victorious pose and declaring your everlasting love for Adrian, which is probably fine in the City of Brotherly Love. Of course, when we got there the steps were closed, apparently to allow for the stage set for the TV coverage of the NFL Draft.

All this meant that our efforts to imitate Sylvester Stallone were limited to the very top steps. Once I had regained my breath from the climb, I stood ready to be photographed in my heroic pose, just as a police motorbike pulled up and parked directly in the middle of the shot. The officer dismounted, walked a few steps away and took half a dozen pictures of his bike, all powerful and gleaming in its PPD livery. Once he had finished he smiled at us, said, "I've always wanted to do that," then clambered back on board and buggered off.

The walk back towards our hotel took us past the superb Rodin Museum. It houses a collection of the French genius' sculptures, accumulated over a number of years and bequeathed to the city by an impossibly wealthy chap called Jules Mastbaum.

Just around the corner from our hotel was Mace's Crossing, a pub into which we dived when the rains came. Two seats at the bar started two separate conversations, mine with a construction worker who was in the process of building a new 40-storey skyscraper in the city. He was the union representative responsible for health and safety of the team putting the steel girders in place several hundred feet above ground. He was so confident that rain would stop play the following day that he was drinking the night away without fear of failing tomorrow's possible alcohol test at work. He was full of tales of Irish workers on building sites, how his mother was from County Cork, and how he had built some of the tallest towers in the country. He was also pleasant, friendly and generously buying rounds, and wasn't a Trump supporter at all. He didn't hold with Trump's rhetoric about creating American jobs. He believed that much of it would take the country backwards, not forwards. Plus, Trump was a New Yorker, which was anathema to a man from Philly.

I'm afraid Áine Two's companion took a bit of a shine to her. He was a middle-aged city type, with a job he hated and an expensive wife who hated him. He loved Donald Trump and couldn't wait for him to clean up the country and Make America Great Again. He'd had quite a few pints by the time he got up to go, and as he staggered past me he patted me on the shoulder, and whispered to me conspiratorially, "You have a wonderful wife. You should cherish her always." It was lovely of him to say so, and I'm sure his intentions would have been entirely honourable if I hadn't been around.

CHAPTER 15 THE TWO ÁINES AND THE BIG APPLE

New Jersey is the home of the redoubtable Áine One, and the only sensible route to her house is along the New Jersey Turnpike. The road was made famous by a Simon & Garfunkel song about looking for America.

The Turnpike is split into four separate but connected motorways, two northbound and two southbound, with trucks and cars segregated. Anything with 18 wheels is restricted to the right-hand road, leaving the left-hand road free for smaller vehicles. Slip roads on and off have been built to allow access to and from the middle lanes, and everything works remarkably smoothly. It was almost a pleasure to drive along a busy urban freeway without having to contend with the big trucks. Mind you, truck drivers are professionals who know what they are doing, which is a far cry from some of the New Jersey and New York car drivers, who seem to have learnt their driving skills on a PlayStation.

New Jersey is officially the name of the state that sits west of New York City. It encompasses the vast urban sprawl opposite New York on the western shore of the Hudson River, also known as New Jersey, and which is made up of any number of separate cities and towns. This conurbation is made up of places with evocative names that anyone with Irish connections has heard many times: Piscataway, Newark, Hoboken, Hackensack, Jersey City, Union City. However, they create a false romance that masks a rough, industrial metropolis that acts as an overspill for Manhattan, and sports vast petrochemical and pharmaceutical factories.

A constant flow of immigrants has fuelled New Jersey since it was first settled by the Dutch in 1623, and it grew into the industrial heartland of the northeast, providing many of the armaments and other military requirements for the Union Army during the Civil War, and the American Army for both World Wars and Vietnam.

Much of that heavy industry that was built close to the

Hudson River has gone, leaving a tangle of post-industrial dereliction that is gradually being reclaimed and reconstructed. However, the train ride from Newark airport into Manhattan must leave the more timid tourist wondering what they've let themselves in for.

For a brief period from the mid-1990s until 2008, before the world's financial systems collapsed, Ireland was a net importer of people for the first time in recorded history. Families stayed together rather than dispersing around the world, and immigrants from Eastern Europe moved to Ireland, not for the weather, but because it was a thriving modern economy. Before that brief golden age, Ireland supplied much of the manual labour force that built the infrastructure for both the British Empire and America. In more recent years Ireland has supplied high-calibre graduates into established industries around the world.

Áine One is Áine Two's aunt on her father's side. One of six siblings born in the west of Ireland, she initially moved from there to London just after World War II, sharing a flat in Clapham with one of her sisters. A third sister was already established in Melbourne, Australia, and one of their brothers was set up in New York. The two sisters in London, intent on taking a further step from Ireland, tossed a coin to see who would go in which direction. Áine One ended up with New York, where today she is the kindly elderly aunt to her late brother's children. Her other sister went to Melbourne and is still there, the matriarch of a large and wonderful Australian family. Incidentally, a second brother ended up in Auckland, New Zealand, leaving only Áine Two's father back in Ireland. This was a typical distribution of an Irish family at the time, and means that Áine Two has cousins handily placed in some of the world's best countries.

Unlike her father's generation, Áine Two is the only one of her family who left Ireland to live elsewhere. All four of her siblings live within a few miles of where they were born. The post-financial-crash generation are moving out again, but to a far lesser extent than others have done in the past.

Áine One is the second of four consecutive generations of the family that are known to have attended the small, two-roomed school in Roxboro, Co. Mayo. Áine Two is the third generation, and several of her nephews and nieces are continuing the family tradition.

In the mid-1990s I was privileged to be party to a family reunion of Áine One and her three surviving siblings in their Irish birthplace. As with any such get-together, the love is unspoken and the bickering is loud. I walked into their rented house and was immediately invited to settle a debate, held loudly between the four elderly people who haven't been together as a family for 50 years or more. "Now James," began Áine One with another of my mother's favourite starters for ten, "do we have to wait for the washing machine door to open, or should we be able to open it immediately?"

Áine One is well into her eighties and lives on her own in a very pleasant apartment in a suburb just north of Newark. She had a successful career as a legal secretary in New York, only retiring in her mid-seventies, and professes not to miss the job at all, although she does miss the buzz of Manhattan. She has lived in the same flat for many years, and benefits from the protected rent scheme that operates there, where rent rises are subject to a reasonableness test and landlords are bound by strict laws regarding services and maintenance. Áine One wouldn't move back to Ireland for all the tea in China. Sky News is a constant backdrop on the TV.

We brought a box of teabags from the Charleston Tea Plantation as a little present, and between the three of us managed to use all of them in less than 24 hours. How's that for cementing the Irish reputation as the world's greatest tea drinkers? Áine One was delighted with them and grateful it wasn't a box of Ireland's premier brand of tea, Barry's, that everyone brings over when visiting and that she hates. She has a stack of the familiar red boxes in a cupboard in her kitchen. We were lucky we didn't pick some up in the Irish shop in Annapolis. By the way, Áine One has a proper kettle that you put on the gas hob and that whistles when it's ready. No electric pixies for her.

Over one of the many cups of tea, we were discussing where she had lived in London and managed to find the very house on Google Street View. It was a top-floor maisonette on what was then a fairly scruffy side road near Clapham Common. She nearly fell off her chair when we found a similar three-bedroomed flat two doors down for sale for £1.1 million.

Our time with the wonderful and unique Áine One was all too short, and we left her and her warm and welcoming hospitality for our final destination and one of my favourite cities, New York, but not before returning our faithful rental car to its owners at Newark Liberty International Airport. I loved seeing the look on the guy's face when we rolled into the garage with a car on Miami plates. He was impressed with how far we'd driven and that we'd seen so much of his country.

New York needs very little introduction. It is big, loud, busy and fantastic and one of a small, select group of true world cities. I think London, Paris, Rome, Tokyo and maybe Delhi are the others. They are cities on such a scale, and with such global attraction and cultural and economic importance, that they belong to us all.

When Áine Two was a university student in the mid-1980s, she spent her first summer holidays in New York, staying with Áine One and earning money working as a waitress. Not in a cocktail bar as the song might suggest, but in a local burger joint. It still makes me shudder to think that the first major city she visited anywhere in the world, after leaving the family smallholding in the west of Ireland, was New York. She was a slightly-built teenager, and New York was at its lowest and sleaziest ebb. It comes as absolutely no surprise that, not only did she survive but she thrived, and she has been back many times since.

New York's history as a Dutch colony and a magnet for immigrants is well documented, but not many people may know the role it played in both the War of Independence and the Civil War.

A month after the Declaration of Independence had been signed in Philadelphia, the British and Continental armies fought the largest battle of the entire War of Independence on Long Island, across the East River from Manhattan.

George Washington, commander-in-chief of the Continental Army, had just beaten the British in Boston and needed to keep them from securing the strategically important port of New York. The British built up a large number of troops across the bay on Staten Island, and eventually landed some of them on Long Island in full view of Washington. This distraction enabled them to land more troops further east and sneak up behind the Continental Army, outflanking them in the process. The Americans were beaten and retreated to the northern half of Manhattan Island, before abandoning New York to the British altogether.

A few days after the British took control of the city there was a massive fire, the Great Fire of New York, which burned a third of the city to the ground. Nobody knows who started it, with both sides of the conflict blaming the other, but it did make life very difficult for the occupying British Army and the thousands of Loyalist refugees and freed slaves who made their way there throughout the war.

Britain returned New York to American control after the war, and from 1785 it took the mantle of the new country's capital city, until Washington, D.C. was established five years later. After that, New York prospered and grew into the great world city that it is now. By 1860, half of the city's population of more than a million people were either Irish or German, with the Irish performing much of the manual labour, in competition with the large number of freed slaves and their offspring who shared the city.

During the Civil War men were being drafted into the Union Army, with a buy-out clause enabling the wealthy to dodge their call-ups. This caused riots in 1863 amongst the poor Irish community, who were hit hardest by the draft. The Irish were also blamed for attacks on black people competing for work, which escalated into more full-scale riots and even lynchings, until many members of the black community moved out of the city in fear of their lives.

The Manhattan of today bears no resemblance to what it was like in the 1980s, when Áine Two first arrived. Mayor Rudy Giuliani took office in 1994 and scrubbed the city to within an inch of its life, with a regime of zero tolerance for drug dealers, sex workers and rough sleepers. Some might say that these groups of people were merely shifted into someone else's patch to become their problem, but to be fair, New York is a cleaner and safer place now than it ever has been.

A consequence of the cleansing of a city is that it removes some of the character that makes it such an interesting place. Soho in London is a perfect example of this, and the knock-on effect on New York is that many of the best parts of the city no longer hold the same attraction. Areas like the Meatpacking District, Greenwich Village and the Lower East Side have been gentrified to the extent that few of their original residents can afford to remain. A film like Alan Parker's 1980 dance-school epic *Fame* wouldn't make sense in New York nowadays, because it is too expensive for all those aspirational performing-arts students to live there. In effect, Manhattan has become an island for the wealthy elite. Those whose efforts make the city tick, like the emergency services, nurses, shop workers and waiting staff, live in the outer suburbs and commute for hours to do their jobs. London is going the same way.

The shopping district of New York seems to be a breeding ground for scaffold monsters. Most of them are not fully grown, and only reach to what we call the first floor – our lifts go G, 1, 2 ...; American elevators go 1, 2, 3 ... – and they squat in front of the store entrance, apparently feeding off the advertising hoardings adorning their sides, like slow-release nicotine patches. They block the pavements and the views and generally make the place look crap. Anyone who starts a scaffolding-monster extermination business would be showing true American entrepreneurial spirit, and could make a proper fortune.

In one of Bill Bryson's first travelogues, *Notes from a Small Island*, he brilliantly sums up 1980s Liverpool with a devastating putdown, describing the city as being in the throes of a "festival of litter". New York is currently suffering from an outbreak of potholes and roadworks that cover the city with a painful rash, and leave unsightly scars on the highways and byways. In one particularly graphic open sore, it was possible to see the city's subcutaneous veins and arteries, only inches below the road surface, exposed to the open air like one of Leonardo da Vinci's anatomical sketches. If New York is serious about making itself the squeaky clean, post-Gotham metropolis, it should consider how its streets look to the average visitor.

New York has an extensive subway system, similar to London's Tube network but with aircon and an incomprehensible map. But why travel underground? The city is famous for being tall, and has a road layout in which it is impossible to get lost. New York should be seen on foot with many of the best views found when you look up. It is peppered with fabulous skyscrapers from the greatest era of tall buildings; the Empire State, Chrysler Building and Rockefeller Center are three of the finest examples of Art Deco architecture anywhere in the world. The new One World Trade Center, built to replace the twin towers destroyed in the terrorist attack of 9/11, is a graceful glass edifice. When you view it from the correct angle, it fills the end of Fulton Street like a perfectly fitted door. As we stood gazing up at it, a family walked up next to us and the young son said, "Look Dad, the new Twin Tower."

I don't want to dwell on the horrors of 9/11, but would like to pay tribute not only to those who died or who had to live with the aftermath, but also to those who designed and built the memorial fountains in the footprints of the old towers. They are a suitably elegant and respectful way to remember that dreadful event.

The grid-pattern street layout of Manhattan is very simple to remember: avenues run north–south with the lowest numbers on the eastern shore; streets run west–east with those north of Houston Street having ascending numbers. The original city at the southern tip of the island, south of Houston, is more higgledy-piggledy and doesn't follow these rules.

A stroll around Central Park is a real pleasure and, once

you've escaped the other tourists, gives you an idea of how the residents of a crowded city use their only real open space for leisure. Softball diamonds can be hired for local league games, and small crowds gather to watch unfit middle-aged men huff and puff their way around the field. Very little goes on in softball, the neutered version of baseball. One player tosses a large white ball underarm to a batter with a full-sized bat, who hits it to a fielder who, in turn, catches it in a great big glove. This happens nine times until the teams swap places and it all goes around again. The most appealing element of the entire performance was the umpire, who delivered his lines with vigour and authority. I have no idea what he was shouting, or the meaning of his gesticulations, but it livened up a procession of batting hopelessness and catching practice.

The park is laced with roads, and people whizz around them on wheels of a dizzying array of sizes and configurations. There are bicyclists, unicyclists, BMX-ists, scooter-ists, roller-bladers, roller-skaters, wheelchair users and babies in racing pushchairs. A number of people manage to combine multiple disciplines in a remarkable display of skill and dexterity: roller-bladers push pushchairs; roller-skaters pull young scooter-ists on short leads; dogs tow all types.

In some cases, bicyclists tow specially adapted carts containing their offspring, perilously low down and at the mercy of the vast cars and trucks that occupy New York's streets. These people may have perfectly legitimate concerns for the environment, held to secure the futures of their children. However, they put the lives of those same children at risk by cycling around busy city streets with them in contraptions that can't be seen by other road users, however carefully everyone involved proceeds. That doesn't make sense to me. A child killed in a cycle-trailer by a perfectly innocent lorry driver today, has had less of a future than an adult killed by the man-made elements of global warming in 40 or 50 years' time.

It is said that Central Park contains over 230 species of birds, but they must have all gone to a birthday party, or the opening of a highly anticipated packet of seeds, because all we got to see were sparrows, starlings and pigeons.

Central Park also contains its eponymous zoo, made famous as the meeting place of lovers and baddies in any number of movies and TV shows. There are also lakes to boat upon, rocks to climb, fields to lie around in, and queues to join to buy overpriced coffee or chocolate-coated nuts.

At the southern entrance to Central Park, at the top of 6th Avenue meets W 59th Street, tourists are assailed by the army of touts offering rides around the park in buggies drawn by very smelly horses. To be fair to them, they are just trying to hustle a living in the place where hustling was invented, but they are bloody annoying when all you want to do is cross the road safely and get into the park. Hong Kong has its suit makers and hooky watch sellers, Delhi has its street kids and New York has its carriage-ride touts. I guess they are a fact of life and give the city a bit of character.

A short walk south from Central Park down 5th, 6th or 7th Avenue takes you to a myriad of the city's landmarks. The recently refurbished and gloriously sparkling St. Patrick's Cathedral and the magnificent Rockefeller Center are opposite each other on 5th, Radio City Music Hall is behind the Rock on 6th, and Times Square is on 7th, all between 43rd and 51st Streets. Broadway and its theatres slice diagonally through Midtown from the corner of Central Park and 8thAvenue, through Times Square to Union Square Park on E 17th Street.

At the junction of Park Avenue (4th Avenue) and E 42nd Street is my favourite building in New York, Grand Central

Terminal. The outside is fairly unprepossessing: it is low rise, slightly scruffy and looks more like an unloved neo-classical market hall than one of the main transport terminals in the city. However, when you walk through the foyer and waiting room you enter the glorious Main Concourse, with its gorgeous soft Cotswold gold stonework, vast windows, ticket offices and central information booth, topped by its brass clock. To escape the hullaballoo of the commuters, climb the stairs at either end of the hall and look over the scene. It is like peering down on an L.S. Lowry painting, as the workers scurry to their destinations, intent only on getting there as quickly and as painlessly as possible. The ceiling with its turquoise paint and celestial scene is a thing of wonder, especially if you can spot the square left untouched by the restorers to show how filthy the whole place was before they did it up.

The station was famously refurbished in the 1970s, with the involvement of Jackie Kennedy Onassis, eventually bringing the interior back to its current spectacular condition. A plaque on the wall of the Main Concourse celebrates the role she played. Interestingly, at the time of writing, the Wikipedia page for Grand Central Terminal did not acknowledge the role of the former Democratic president's wife, only trumpeting that of the current Republican president.

South of Grand Central, between 42nd Street and Houston, the height of the city drops as the older, more residential buildings dominate. Many small and interesting backstreets around the hip Greenwich and East Villages contain the classic New York tenement buildings beloved by film and TV directors. Trendy shops sell expensive designer clothes and furniture to the rich and famous, whilst the traditional locally owned bars and cafés teeter on the brink of extinction, awaiting replacement by the inevitable coffee-shop chain.

The Financial District occupies the southernmost point of Manhattan Island and is as detached and impersonal to your average tourist as is its London equivalent. Things go on in towering offices, perpetrated by anonymous blue-suited experts, which only touch the individuals in the streets below when they cause ripples in the global economy that impact house prices, interest rates, investor confidence or government debt.

We stayed in another anonymous corporate hotel on Canal Street – not below it so we weren't in Tribeca – just along from the unexpectedly juxtaposed areas of Chinatown and Little Italy. It is impossible to see where one starts and the other ends and they interlock like the fingers of two mismatched gloves. Eating in a proper Italian restaurant in Little Italy involves being surreptitiously checked out, and approved with a barely perceptible nod, by a pair of *The Sopranos*-style gentlemen in black shirts, sitting at an outside table.

Just behind our hotel was the finest New York dive bar I've ever encountered, with the stroppiest bartender in Christendom. Nancy Whiskey Pub is long and narrow, with very little standing space and a shuffleboard table right in the way as you enter. As ever, we grabbed two barstools and two beers and settled in for the night. It was Friday and the after-work crowd were in, with many really going for it, which made for a lively atmosphere and much fun and frolics. The bartender didn't keep tabs going, and seemed to randomly add up our drinks total. It came to an acceptable number so we paid it and left, only figuring afterwards that we'd got at least one round for free.

Sitting next to Áine Two at the bar was a rather large gentleman who was quietly sipping a beer. He had very short hair and his muscles created an almost landscaped canvas onto which his tattoos had been inked. It was like his arms had been sculpted by Capability Brown.

"Excuse me, sir," he began. I love being called "sir", even if it does mean that I'm old enough to be his father. "Is that a Manchester accent I can hear?"

I nearly responded by saying that people have died for less than accusing a Scouser of being from Manchester, but I figured that people may have suffered worse fates at his hand for less than answering back.

It turns out that he was a serving soldier in the United States Army and had been stationed in the Middle East alongside the British Army. He had become friendly with several soldiers from Manchester and thought he had recognised a familiar accent. He was very apologetic when he found out I was from Liverpool, obviously aware that I could have taken great offence to his innocent slip-up. He wouldn't go into details, but did say that it was part of his job to have a good ear for accents, and to be fair he did very well to pinpoint mine to within 40 miles of its origin.

He was intelligent, charming, interesting and friendly, and just goes to show that you should never judge a book by its tattooed and muscular cover. He could drink for America, too.

We went back again on the Saturday night and fell in with a crowd who were setting up a model launch for a famous German car manufacturer. The bartender was giving all of her attention to the big American chap in charge of the show, to the frustration of some of his very drunk German guests. One of them, having failed to catch her distracted eye, banged on the bar. She ignored him, so he did it again and all hell broke loose. He was told in no uncertain terms that banging on bars was unacceptable behaviour in New York, and that he should leave. Man In Charge managed to calm things down and the poor, apologetic German left with his head hung low but his balls just about intact. I know he was drunk and banging on bars isn't very polite, but a decent bartender should know exactly what every punter needs and make sure they get it, even when she is drowning in the eyes of one of them.

Sunday lunch was to be on Áine One, and she arranged to meet us in her favourite Irish pub in Manhattan, O'Lunney's on West 45th Street, just off Times Square (it's pronounced "O'Looney's" in case you're wondering). She insisted that she would come over from her home in New Jersey to meet us, and also insisted that, as she was on home turf, she was buying lunch. We had a lovely time nursing our hangovers and comparing notes on Irish pubs from around the world. The Traditional Irish Breakfast was just what the doctor ordered, even if the bacon was the crispy American streaky type, not your proper Irish rashers.

A wander up 3rd Avenue to the area around the junction with E 34th Street brings many of the old Irish bars into play, and we stopped in a few to test the Guinness for any quality defects. We stumbled across an English pub called Mad Hatter hidden amongst them. It had Fuller's London Pride on a proper, real ale handle, which we ignored in favour of a local brew. Sitting at the bar I began to notice the light blue décor, including a New York City FC shirt in a frame behind the bar. A quick question to the bartender confirmed that we were in New York City's very own Manchester City pub.

The Premier League is becoming more and more popular in America, no more so than in New York, so it shouldn't be a surprise that a Man City pub exists. Jamie Carragher, Liverpool FC's former central defender, owns a bar in Midtown that bears his name and displays items from his collection of memorabilia. According to some friends whose recent visit to New York coincided with a Liverpool match, Carragher's Pub & Restaurant was packed to the rafters with happy drinkers at 8 am. Entirely by accident we came across another Liverpool FC-themed bar on John Street in the Financial District, a stone's throw from Wall Street. Called The Irish American Pub, its entrance leads you down a short flight of stairs over which is displayed a version of the famous "This is Anfield" sign that hangs in a similar position in the players' tunnel. Inside, there were a few interesting bits and pieces on the walls, and even a Scouse accent or two to be heard. Barstools were secured, and two happy-hour beers along with a plate of very happy-hour chicken wings. The bartender was wearing a hoodie with a stylized version of the Liverpool club crest on the back, but she wasn't from Liverpool; she was from Tipperary in Ireland. It turns out that the bar is owned by Jamie Carragher's business partner in the Midtown venture, and it has a second room next door that was worth a look at. I wandered around a corner and entered a shrine to Liverpool FC. There were flags, scarves, shirts, banners and pictures hanging from every part of the walls and ceilings, many from Liverpool FC fan clubs from all over America.

New York City, of course, has many connections with Liverpool, its mirror-image port on the other side of the Atlantic. The *Titanic*, although never in either port, was a Liverpool-registered vessel owned by a Liverpool company, and was on its maiden voyage to New York when it hit the guilty iceberg. Its owners, the Ismay family, and its captain, Edward J. Smith, lived on the same terraced road, facing the River Mersey in well-to-do Waterloo. They were just south of Great Crosby and no more than a mile from where the *Carpathia*'s Captain Rostron lived. Frederick Law Olmsted, the man who designed Central Park, took inspiration from Birkenhead Park on the Wirral, whilst on a visit to the area.

The *Wavertree*, another Liverpool-registered vessel, is in permanent dock in New York's South Street Seaport. The word "skyscraper" originated in Liverpool, and was used to describe the highest sail on the tallest mast on a ship. Throughout both World Wars, ships steamed in convoy from New York, across the Atlantic to Liverpool, carrying vital supplies for the war effort, at an astonishing cost in sailors' lives. The Beatles – and the whole Merseybeat movement – began because Liverpool sailors brought records back from New York of all the latest American rock and roll musicians, giving young Scousers a head start over their equivalents in Manchester, London and elsewhere when it came to the next big thing. John Lennon lived and was murdered in the Upper West Side of New York, where a tastefully designed memorial to him and his legacy sits in Central Park, not far from his apartment block. Liverpool's world-famous Liver Building is designed to look like the base of a New York skyscraper. Indeed, walking around certain parts of either city centre gives you the impression you could be in the other one, at least until you look up. If you can see the sky you're probably in Liverpool.

Fuelled by alcohol, aided and abetted by Dramamine, and much to Áine Two's shock, I volunteered to take a tourist boat ride around Manhattan Island. The experience exposed us to the appallingly cavalier attitude one particular New York tourist business has to its paying customers. I won't name the company publicly, but its namesake appears in yellow on the London Tube map and goes around in a circle.

Áine Two booked the tickets online for a 3 pm sailing, and got the hotel to print off the blurb that said we had to be at the ticket office half an hour before departure time to pick them up. We turned up in the appointed place at around 2:15 to find two long queues in front of four serving windows, two of which were shut. The queues were moving very slowly, with people turning away and leaving without boarding the boat. Just as we reached the head of the line, a young lad opened up a third window and called us forward. Áine Two presented him with our voucher to prove that she had booked and paid specifically for the 3 pm sailing, only to be told that it was full and that we could either have tickets for the 7 pm sailing that night, or another one the next day. Drawing herself up to her full 5 ft 3 in of irate Irishness, she informed the poor unsuspecting fellow that she had booked the tickets for this specific sailing, wasn't available for any alternative times and that he would either have to refund us in cash or give us tickets that very moment. He blustered a little, and tried to explain that he couldn't give us a refund, as we had booked through an agent. This was untrue and reduced his options by one. He glanced behind us at the still lengthy queue and, faced with the prospect of further Celtic stubbornness, took the right decision. He checked with his supervisor before issuing us with two tickets for the 3 pm sailing. The German family behind us in the queue must have witnessed the whole thing because, funnily enough, the 3 pm sailing had enough room for them too.

Once you get through the unutterably shite ticketing system, the ferry journey itself is brilliant. It takes you from Pier 83 on the Hudson River, south past Downtown and all the really tall buildings, and out to the Statue of Liberty and Ellis Island, the processing point for all 19th and early-20th century immigrants into New York. The boat then turns around the southern tip of Manhattan Island and heads north up the East River. It passes under the iconic Brooklyn Bridge and sails up the eastern shoreline, before turning into the Harlem River and around the northern channel back into the Hudson. The commentary is excellent, and much fun is to be had dodging a soaking from the waves coming over the prow as the boat turns against various currents. The tour guide insisted on everyone upstairs sitting down so that all could have a fair view, and called people out by their distinguishing features to embarrass them into complying. The "big lady in the orange jacket" received several entertaining tellings-off.

After our waterborne adventures we wandered south and joined the High Line at the junction of W 34th Street and 11th Avenue. The High Line is a disused overhead railway that used to serve the docks and warehouses that lined the Chelsea shoreline of the Hudson River. It has been brilliantly converted into a linear park, with a boardwalk, seating and landscaped greenery, and runs for 1.45 miles north to south, from W 34th Street to Gansevoort St, just south of Little West 12th Street.

The High Line runs parallel with the river and affords glimpses of it in the gaps between the old warehouses and modern apartment and office blocks. Amusingly, walkers can peer into the living rooms of multi-million dollar apartments, just to see how the Manhattan metropolitan elite live.

Unfortunately, the High Line has become a victim of its own success, and the walk degenerated into a frustrating slalom through groups of tourists who seem to think that stopping en masse on a narrow elevated walkway is a bright thing to do.

Much of the Lower East Side of New York was made up of tenement blocks during the immigration boom times of the 19th and early 20th centuries. Families landed in the port, often after dreadful journeys across the Atlantic, with nowhere to go and only a vague idea of the geography of the city. Many simply walked the streets, often for days, until they heard an accent or a word that they recognised, spoken by someone who they could ask for help or for directions to the centre of their own community. The tenement blocks were typically four-storey townhouses that had been divided into 16 flats, four on each floor. Large families, often with several children and with grandparents in tow, were crammed into these small apartments, sharing beds at night that doubled as seats during the day. Sanitation was primitive and the streets were crammed with people and horses, the latter contributing to the lack of hygiene and the spread of disease. Cholera, TB and scarlet fever outbreaks were impossible to avoid, and killed thousands of the young, elderly and infirm. Work was available for those who were prepared to put in the effort, and the rewards enabled newcomers to participate in the great American Dream. Whilst this lifestyle is almost impossible to imagine for Westerners today, it fuelled industry in the North and allowed it to advance at a greater and more prosperous pace than the South's uncompensated slave workforce.

As sanitation and rent laws became more stringent, many landlords could no longer afford to maintain their properties and simply shut up shop, evicting their last tenants in the process. The superb Tenement Museum on Orchard Street in the Lower East Side owns a tenement building that was closed in just such a way, and sat empty and untouched for over 50 years before it was opened to the public.

Each apartment tells the story of a family from one of the many nationalities that make up New York's population, and is occupied by an actor playing the role of one of the original immigrants who lived there. The children on our tour were enthralled by the Jewish Armenian teenager, who explained patiently to them in her broken English how she and her family lived in such a small place. The real life story of our young lady ended well, with her living until she was in her eighties in a large townhouse in the Upper East Side.

New York reflects the fortunes of the country in which it exists. It was made great by immigrants, many of whom had the courage to sacrifice what little they had at home to move somewhere where risk and opportunity were uncomfortable bedfellows. Others were slaves who didn't have a choice but to come to America and make of it what they could. Many immigrants failed, but many succeeded and their legacy can be seen in the city's street names, and in the surnames of the current residents.

Every single person in America who is not 100% Native American is an immigrant or is descended in part or in full from an immigrant, be they slave or free person. The fortunes of the self-styled greatest country on Earth were built by people who arrived from all over the world, taking untold risks to create meagre opportunities.

President Trump has a German surname, a Scottish mother, a Czech ex-wife, and a Slovenian First Lady.

The America of today is the rowdy, randy and rambunctious bastard love child of four long-defunct European empires. The Spanish, French, Dutch and British invaded it, colonised it, lost it and have been beholden to it for over 300 years.

America is a wonderful country. The landscape is glorious and makes a road trip, particularly through the long straight flat bits out west that contrast so starkly with the UK, unmatched anywhere in the world. The history is fascinating, partly because it is so recent and partly because it reflects the good, the bad and the ugly aspects of Great Britain. The food is simple, inexpensive and delicious, especially in New Mexico where my eyes were opened to the glories of jalapeño chillies. The beer is not always brilliant, but is worlds away from the weak and feeble yellow horse piss that we were forced to drink there in the time "before craft".

Most of all America is full of generous, kind, friendly and sincere people. Some have unfortunate views, but that doesn't make them bad people, and as long as you don't get to talking politics, religion or guns with them, we can all get along just fine.

EPILOGUE

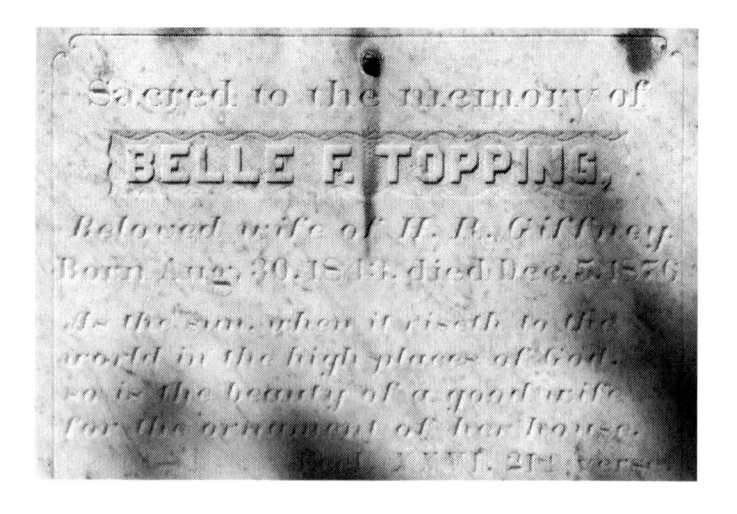

> Sacred to the memory of
> **BELLE F. TOPPING,**
> Beloved wife of H. R. Giffney.
> Born Aug. 30, 1843, died Dec. 5, 1876
> As the sun when it riseth to the
> world in the high places of God,
> so is the beauty of a good wife
> for the ornament of her house.

In the Lafayette Cemetery in the Garden District of New Orleans is a headstone for Belle F. Topping, who died in New Orleans on December 5th 1876. Belle was wife of Harry R. Giffney, and one of the New York Toppings who originated in Bedfordshire, England. She has no known relationship with the Toppings of Wavertree, Liverpool.

Printed in Great Britain
by Amazon